RESISTING CULTURAL NARRATIVE ENTRAPMENT IN AUTOETHNOGRAPHY

Resisting Cultural Narrative Entrapment in Autoethnography delves into the nexus of cultural narratives and takes the reader on a journey through the intricate landscape of identity and cultural critique. Each chapter, enriched with dialogues with 'Ash,' our imaginary interlocutor, presents a profound exploration rooted in the philosophical fabric.

This book amplifies the discourse on ontological and epistemological reflections often overlooked in narrative autoethnography. Central to its narrative is the concept of cultural narrative entrapment, meticulously dissected to unveil its philosophical underpinnings. It focuses on probing inquiries, from the essence of resistance to cultural narrative entrapment to its pivotal role in shaping autoethnographic scholarship. Through meticulous textual 'archaeology' chapters unfold, excavating layers of literature to redefine cultural identity and narrative constructs, offering a meta-autoethnographic lens. The discourse evolves, addressing critiques and paradoxes, while inviting readers to engage with the complexities of perception, representation, and the paradoxes of emplotment. Culminating with an illuminating appendix summarising the author's extensive body of work, this book serves as a beacon for scholars and practitioners navigating the nuanced terrain of philosophical autoethnography.

This book transcends the boundaries of traditional scholarship, offering a compelling narrative that challenges conventions and ignites intellectual curiosity. It is an indispensable companion for those seeking to unravel the profound intersections of culture, identity, and philosophical inquiry.

Alec Grant, PhD, is an independent scholar and former Visiting Professor at the University of Bolton. He was the recipient of the International Conference of Autoethnography Inaugural Lifetime Contribution Award in 2020.

RESISTING CULTURAL NARRATIVE ENTRAPMENT IN AUTOETHNOGRAPHY

Alec Grant, PhD

Routledge
Taylor & Francis Group

LONDON AND NEW YORK

Designed cover image: from the original painting, *Stay in the Frame*, by Alec Grant

First published 2025
by Routledge
4 Park Square, Milton Park, Abingdon, Oxon OX14 4RN

and by Routledge
605 Third Avenue, New York, NY 10158

Routledge is an imprint of the Taylor & Francis Group, an informa business

© 2025 Alec Grant

British Library Cataloguing-in-Publication Data
A catalogue record for this book is available from the British Library

ISBN: 9781032851457 (hbk)
ISBN: 9781032855400 (pbk)
ISBN: 9781003518594 (ebk)

DOI: 10.4324/9781003518594

Typeset in Galliard
by codeMantra

I dedicate this book to my esteemed autoethnographic friends and colleagues: Marcin Kafar, Trude Klevan, Gayle Letherby, Lizzie Lloyd-Parkes, Andrew Sparkes, Phiona Stanley, and Susan Young.

CONTENTS

ABOUT THE AUTHOR

Alec Grant, PhD, is the recipient of the International Conference of Autoethnography Inaugural Lifetime Contribution Award in 2020 (https://youtu.be/VXqCw-Tyq0E?si=MVguL5vczyorS9Mj) and is widely published in journals such as *Qualitative Inquiry*, *The Qualitative Report (TQR)*, and the *Journal of Autoethnography*. His Routledge co-edited and co-authored books include *International Perspectives on Autoethnographic Research and Practice* (2018), *An Autoethnography of Becoming a Qualitative Researcher: A Dialogic View of Academic Development* (2022), *Writing Philosophical Autoethnography* (2024), *Meaningful Journeys: Autoethnographies of Quest and Identity Transformation* (2024), and *Autoethnographies in Psychology and Mental Health: New Voices* (2025). He was affiliated with the University of Bolton as a Visiting Professor until May 2024, before reverting to his previous unaffiliated title of Independent Scholar. He was awarded a second PhD (by Publication) in May 2024.

ACKNOWLEDGEMENTS

I'm grateful for all the help given to me by the critical readers of the book while it was in progress: Marcin, Trude, Gayle, Lizzie, Phiona, and Susan.

I also want to thank the following people for their support and inspiration along the way: Tony Adams, Art Bochner, David Carless, Kitrina Douglas, Carolyn Ellis, Mark Freeman, Graham Lever, Andrew Herrmann, and Nigel Short.

And hats off to the good folks at Routledge: Shraddha Saikia, Hannah Shakespeare, Georgia Thompson, and Adam Woods, and their proofreading and production colleagues.

Finally, much love to my dear family: Mary, Oakley, and Mabel Grant; Amy, Mark, Charlotte, and James Selley; Anna, Graeme, and Bruce Corris.

PERMISSIONS

I would like to thank:

Taylor & Francis Group LLC (Books) US for permission to reproduce in Chapter 2:

the quote beginning 'Culture as the "space of the familiar" – when we feel ourselves to be in culture,' in Alec Grant, 'The Philosophical Autoethnographer,' pp. 16–17, in *Writing Philosophical Autoethnography*, ed. Alec Grant (New York and London: Routledge, 2024);

the quote beginning 'Some … are able to straighten themselves despite being in a crooked room' in Renata Ferdinand, 'Which Way is Up? A Philosophical Autoethnography of Trying to Stand in a "Crooked Room",' pp. 82–83, in *Writing Philosophical Autoethnography*, ed. Alec Grant (New York and London: Routledge, 2024);

the quote beginning '…autoethnographers intentionally highlight the relationship of their experiences…,' in Stacy Holman Jones, Tony E. Adams, and Carolyn Ellis, 'Introduction: Coming to know autoethnography as more than a method,' p. 23, in *Handbook of Autoethnography*, ed. Stacy Holman Jones, Tony E. Adams, and Carolyn Ellis (Walnut Creek, CA: Left Coast Press, Inc., 2013);

and in Chapter 3:

the quote beginning 'A premise held by many philosophers (and many autoethnographers) is that autonomy entails a capacity for self-constitution…,' in Alec Grant, 'The Philosophical Autoethnographer,' p. 11;

the quote beginning 'Galen Strawson … in particular has through the years consistently argued against…,' in Alec Grant, 'The Philosophical Autoethnographer,' p. 14;

and in Chapter 5:

the poem and translation of 'Fowk's ideas bide in waardrobes…,' in Alec Grant, and Susan Young, 'A Scot an' a Sassenach scrieve aboot leid: A three pairt Scotoethnography (A Scot and an English person write about language: A Scotoethnography in three parts,' pp. 100–101, in *Meaningful journeys: Autoethnographies of quest and identity transformation*, eds. Alec Grant and Elizabeth Lloyd-Parkes (London and New York: Routledge, 2024).

Informa UK Limited for permission to reproduce in Chapter 2:

the quote beginning 'an indispensable component of doing "genuine" autoethnography…,' in Marcin Kafar, 'Traveling with Carolyn Ellis and Art Bochner, or how I became harmonized with the autoethnographic life: An autoformative story,' p. 59, in *Advances in autoethnography and narrative inquiry: Reflections on the legacy of Carolyn Ellis and Arthur Bochner*, ed. Tony E. Adams, Robin M. Boylorn, Lisa. M. Tillmann (New York and London: Routledge, 2021).

John Wiley & Sons Limited for permission to reproduce in Chapter 2:

the quote beginning 'A significant strand on my road to recovery was eventually being allocated a CPN who worked within a recovery value system…,' Alec Grant, Helen Leigh-Phippard, and Nigel P. Short, 'Re-storying narrative identity: a dialogical study of mental health recovery and survival Re-storying narrative identity,' in *Journal of Psychiatric and Mental Health Nursing*, 22: 282, https://doi.org/10.1111/jpm.12188

The University of California Press for permission to reproduce in Chapter 5:

the poem and translation of 'Fowk's ideas bide in waardrobes…,' in Alec Grant, and Susan Young, 'A Scot an' a Sassenach scrieve aboot leid: A three pairt Scotoethnography (A Scot and an English person Write about Language: A Scotoethnography in Three Parts),' *Journal of Autoethnography*, 5, no. 1 (Winter, 2024), 39–55: 42–43, https://doi.org/10.1525/joae.2024.5.1.39

FOREWORD

By Professor Mark Freeman

On the very first page of the Preface of Alec Grant's fascinating, provocative, and occasionally maddening book, we learn that he decided to write the book alongside 'Ash,' his 'imaginary interlocutor,' motivated apparently 'by a need to better engage with [his] own cultural assumptions.' Ash will therefore serve as a kind of foil and will often call Alec out for his arrogance and sense of superiority, especially in regard to those members of the autoethnography community he finds to be sorely lacking in the kind of critical 'autoethnographicity' he deems central to the endeavour of carrying out high-level, sophisticated autoethnography. From the get-go, we know from Alec himself that although he is 'regarded by many as a kind, caring, and generous man,' he 'can also be irascible and verbally combative … get annoyed by lots of things in the world,' including autoethnography and its various communities, especially those members of these communities who insist on heaping praise on palpably inferior work. 'Well, gee,' I found myself saying shortly after beginning reading. 'Who *is* this guy, and how does he get off slamming all these people? And how come, if he gets so annoyed, he wants to be part of the enterprise? Why not just cut bait and go it alone, maybe as an "autophilosopher"?'

Alec is also well aware that some people find some of his antics, particularly his use of naughty swear words, positively offensive. 'Well, fuck them!', he seems to be saying; 'those words have more meanings than the undeniably crude ones they've come to be associated with, and I'm not going to kowtow to all the pc bullshit that's out there suffocating self-expression in the name of silly bourgeois conventions and niceties.' (I wasn't sure whether to use some of these naughty words, but didn't want Alec to think that I was just another member of the pc police. Fuck no!) It's high time all of this politeness and prissiness, so often found (in Alec's views) in autoethnographies themselves, is called out for what it is. It's time for radical honesty and Nietzschean vitality, for the plainspeak of this irascible, combative Scot to finally have its day. At least Ash will be there throughout to voice the anger and indignation that some readers are bound to feel. At least he's there to show that, through it all, Alec knows who he is and is perfectly fine with it, thank you. But is it so? Is Alec who he says he is? What about Ash?

It would be easy enough to say, 'Alec is who he says he is, and Ash, as his imaginary interlocutor, is a composite figure comprising Alec's insights into his own darker, more contentious regions, his fantasies of what others think of him, and, not least, his somewhat weak conversation partner, readily overwhelmed by the bold audacity of his creator.' I think it may be too easy, though. After all, aren't Alec and Ash *both* creations, issuing from the narrative imagination? Maybe *neither* are who they seem to be! Now from a strict narrative identity standpoint, it could be argued that we are who we tell ourselves (and others) we are. That is to say, it could be narrative 'all the way down.' We could be walking stories. And if this is so, there is no reason to even ask the question of whether Alec is who he says is, for we could only take him at his word. But this is too easy as well. For it is patently the case that people can be utterly deceived about the stories they tell themselves and thus utterly deceived about who they are. This doesn't invalidate such stories; they remain constitutive, in part, whatever their truth value. Has Alec spoken the truth? Has Ash?

It's hard not to wonder. And the reason it's hard not to wonder is that the central premise of the book all but insists upon it. Consider the title: *Resisting Cultural Narrative Entrapment in Autoethnography* – and, presumably, in one's *life*. Consider as well that Alec confesses to have gotten a bit trapped himself at times. Now maybe, after having caught himself in the entrapped act enough times, he has finally shed the various guises and disguises so readily available and, unlike lots of other autoethnographers out there, is able to tell just tell the kind of 'warts and all' (as he puts it) story that ought to be told. In this respect, he underscores 'the importance of getting the represented other' depicted in the narrative 'as close to the day-to-day "I" as possible, in the interest of coherence, integrity, and honesty.' Well, hmmm ... It's not that I disagree with this broad aim; again, it's that it's hard not to wonder, given how salient the problem of narrative entrapment appears to be (according to Alec), he could have managed let it all go.

Then again, what could it possibly mean to let it all go? Is the goal here a 'true' story, a more authentic, experience-near story than the flimsy, inauthentic one that's (too) often told? Is the goal *no* story, in some sort of just-the-unvarnished-facts way? Alec does raise this possibility if only to dismiss it: 'Is the idea of a post-resistance culture-free space plausible or ridiculous? I find this, for me non-trivial, thought experiment interesting: if available and attainable, what would absolute and ultimate resistance to cultural narrative entrapment feel and be like?' What indeed? 'I can't really imagine anything other than that it would amount to an absence of everything.' Quite right. So, it must be some variant of the former – which is to say, some variant of the entrapment thesis that moves in the direction of something less entrapped and thus more in keeping with one's own (dare I say) true self and true story.

Even in this latter, more plausible case, there are bound to be some entrapments still at work. In this context, I was immediately brought back to a book I had tried to make sense of some years ago,[1] Philip Roth's *The Facts*, subtitled *A Novelist's Autobiography*.[2] Roth begins the book with a seemingly heartfelt letter to one of his fictional creations, Nathan Zuckerman. Exhausted with having had to disguise his life in the form of fiction, Roth has decided to undertake the arduous task of 'rendering experience untransformed,'[3] leading to the 'bare bones, the structure of a life without the fiction,' the *facts*. 'If this manuscript conveys anything,' he adds, 'it's my exhaustion with masks, disguises, fiction and lies[4] … I needed clarification, as much as I could get—demythologizing to induce depathologizing.'[5] It was at this juncture that I asked: 'Is it possible to live one's life *without* fictions and myths? And if so, what might such a life look like?'[6] Following Alec, it would indeed be 'the absence of everything' – or something close to it. Galen Strawson,[7] well known for his anti-narrativity diatribe, would disagree; he, among others, he asserts, is not only living his life without fictions and myths but without *narrative* altogether. Or so he says. Hard to imagine him really believing this line of thought when it came time to put together his dossier for tenure or promotion. That he might turn to narrative less than some other people is plausible. People vary. But the idea that he has managed to wholly shed his narrative skin is, well, silly.[8]

But let us return to Roth. He knows that shedding the role of fiction writer will be virtually impossible. He would have to 'resist the impulse to dramatize untruthfully the insufficiently dramatic, to complicate the essentially simple, to charge with implication what implied very little – the temptation to abandon the facts when those facts were not so compelling as others I might imagine.'[9] Then there's the philosophical problem, already alluded to, of assuming that the facts can somehow speak for themselves. 'I recognize that I'm using the word "facts" here, in this letter, in its idealized form and in a much more simpleminded way than it's meant in the title. Obviously the facts aren't just coming at you but are incorporated by an imagination that is formed by your previous experience.' What's more, 'memories of the past are not memories of the facts but memories of your imaginings of the facts.'[10] Finally, there is the reality of narrative itself. In writing an autobiography – or an autoethnography,

> You search your past with certain questions on your mind—indeed you search out your past to discover which events have led you to asking those specific questions. It isn't that subordinate your ideas to the force of the facts in autobiography but that you construct a sequence of stories to bind up the facts with a persuasive *hypothesis* that unravels your history's meaning.[11]

There are some problems with Roth's rendition of things: the focus on 'events,' the recourse to the language of 'hypothesis,' and the idea that history's meaning can somehow be 'unraveled,' among others. But the main point of this brief excursion still stands: there is no getting to the unvarnished facts, no recovery of pristine memories untouched by the imagination, and, with all due respect to Strawson and company, no getting around narrative – unless, perhaps, one has become a yogi or some other wholly in-the-moment style human. I assume that Alec knows all this, which is precisely why 'absolute and ultimate resistance to cultural narrative entrapment' can only 'amount to an absence of everything.'

Let us assume, then, that some measure of narrative is bound to remain in the autoethnographic picture, no matter how successful one is in resisting its potentially entrapping features. In view of this putative fact, our next challenge is to get clearer what Alec means by 'entrapment.' I suppose it could be argued – in fact, it *has* been argued[12] – that, to a greater or lesser extent, *all* narratives entrap. Plausible though this idea is on some level, it really doesn't help matters in the present case. That's because there is no question but that Alec wants to differentiate narrative entrapment from … something else, that is, something that is somehow *less* entrapped, less beholden to cliché and worn out convention and gooey niceties and pieties. About this, it's hard to disagree. (Score one for Alec!)

But what about Roth? Did he succeed in his effort to tell it like it was, unadorned with all the froufrou finery of fiction? Well, according to Zuckerman, his imaginary interlocutor, the answer is an all too clear *No*. One problem is that he's had to be a bit too discreet. 'In the fiction,' Zuckerman writes, 'you can be so much more truthful about worrying all the time about causing direct pain. You try to pass off here as frankness what looks to me like the dance of the seven veils – what's on the page is like a code for something missing.'[13] Alec seems to have fared better in his own efforts by 'letting it fly' more than Roth has. He's still (somewhat) discreet; when he lays into some members of the autoethnographic community, he stops short (thankfully) of naming names or discussing specific stories. But it seems to me that he's being pretty frank throughout most of the book.

The second problem Zuckerman has identified is that Roth has not given enough attention to himself as he ought to have. 'Your gift is not to personalize your experience,' Zuckerman tells him, 'but to personify it, to embody it in the representation of a person who is *not* yourself.' Indeed, he continues, 'My guess is that you've written metamorphoses of yourself so many times, you no longer have any idea what *you* are or ever were. By now what you are is a walking text.'[14] How has Alec fared in this context? To what extent have I really gotten to know him in these pages? I'm not sure. I definitely know more about him – or at least some of his leading predilections – than I did beforehand, but because so much of the story he tells is about his own outsider status, his disaffection with certain strands of autoethnography, and, perhaps most centrally, his all-out effort to break through the stultifying cage of cultural narrative entrapment, there's much about Alec (I have to assume) that I/we *don't* know – including the specific nature of the traps he's apparently fallen into. His book isn't an autobiography, I realise. It's not an autoethnography either. It's a kind of a meta-autoenthnography, actually. So, I/we really shouldn't expect to learn a whole lot about Alec the person from this sort of endeavour.

Nevertheless, I do have to ask – and this brings us to Zuckerman's third problem with Roth's account, 'How close is the narration to the truth? Is the author hiding his or her motives, presenting his or her actions and thoughts to lay bare the essential nature of conditions or trying to hide something, telling in order *not* to tell? ... Is this really "you" or is this what you want to look like to your readers?'[15] Given the nature of Alec's book, I doubt whether he has engaged in some sort of self-embellishment in order to present himself in a favourable light to his readers! I could be wrong about this. It could be that Alec *wants* to present himself as the outsider iconoclast, perhaps to consolidate his own unique identity and status. Through it all, though, I'm not sure that he has done a lot of 'hiding' in this book. On the contrary, he seems to have a good deal of the laying-bare that Zuckerman had wished for from his creator-friend Roth.

Are we done? I don't think so. So let us continue for a little while longer, homing in on the idea of resisting cultural narrative entrapment. For starters: Why use the language of 'entrapped'? Why not 'enmeshed' or 'immersed' or 'hermeneutically enfolded' (or something else akin to these)? Given the ostensible inevitability and even (one could argue) necessity of narrative, why frame the situation as a trap rather than just a constitutive condition of being a person, at least in modern Western culture? Again, there's no question but that narrative *can* be, and often is, a trap. But must it be? Can't it also at times be a vehicle for *liberating* oneself from entrapment? Isn't this what narratively oriented modes of therapy seek to do? Or is it the case that we are destined and doomed, ultimately, to replace one trap with another?

What about the idea of 'resistance'? '(A)t the level of hopefully advancing *social justice* a little, I write in resistance to cultural narrative entrapment. This is because such entrapment can force people into stories they don't want to be part of, often experienced as narrative violence, or an assault on narrative identity.' Alec even goes on to refer to 'the social justice agenda of philosophical autoethnography.' Let me hasten to note (lest I be seen as some antisocial justice warrior) that I am basically on board with this idea. But I must also confess to having a somewhat cynical thought here (one that Alec might actually appreciate, though time will tell): Isn't the idea of 'advancing social justice' in the service of diminishing oppression of one form or another a rather conventional move these days? One might also ask once more: What exactly is the purpose, or *telos*, of the resistance being called for? Authenticity? True individuality? Untrammeled freedom? And then there's Ash, poor guy, stuck as he is in his soft truisms. Yes; Alec admits to have employed some hyperbole in crafting his own imaginary interlocutor. But it's not clear how much. 'In short,' Alec says to Ash at one point, 'at its worst, I'm talking about stuff that's high on personal and vicarious – for performers, audiences, and organisers – therapy, and low in social science and cultural engagement, contributing little to social justice.' Low in social science?! Oh no! Contributing little to social justice?! God forbid!

Yes, I'm getting a bit cynical. I apologise, Alec. Or maybe I don't need to? Might you not want some of these sarcastic rejoinders? You can't want me to just heap praise upon you! After all, 'Unconditional praise drowns out any possibility of critical dialogue' and would therefore lead us into some of the very traps you're trying to get us all out of.

Moving on: 'I contend that critical autoethnographicity constitutes a continual alertness to the seductive power of cultural narrative entrapment. In contrast, cultural acceptance for non-culturally critical autoethnographers amounts, at worst in my view, to passively slotting cultural experiences into stock discursive categories without thinking too much about them, and without worrying that these categories might be problematic or that aspects of culture might be problematic.' I concur with this basic idea, though I find myself more inclined towards being pluralistic about these matters. (My own belief is that not everyone has to be a critical/philosophical autoethnographer.) More important, in any case, is that I ask: Has Alec practiced continual alertness to the seductive power of cultural narrative entrapment in this book? The answer is radiantly clear to me: Yes and I'm not so sure/Yes: by all indications he has done well, especially via Ash, to catch himself in the act of his own aggressive shtick. He's very clever about this, actually. Just when I was ready to say 'Come on, Alec!' for this or that reason, Ash did it for me.

At the same time, much of what he's doing in this book is thoroughly in keeping with some of the traditional lore of critical sociology and psychology and may thus not be quite so 'free' and unfettered as Alec suggests. What Alec calls 'queering culture,' for instance, involves 'taking an oppositional, activist stand in word and deed to what is considered culturally normal and natural' by highlighting the processes by which these very categories and judgements are constituted and produced. As he continues,

> An important act of resistance to cultural narrative entrapment, 'queering' therefore directly maps onto autoethnographicity in constituting a kind of 'noticing', or an attitude or sensibility, and a refusal of inscription within cultural narratives, if such inscription is experienced as a compromising and integrity-violating mismatch between personal identity and cultural environment.

This idea and ideal seems to me to be a variant of critical liberal humanism, and worthy though it is, it would be illusory to suppose that it represents a wholesale refusal or rejection of prevailing cultural narratives, especially in disciplines like sociology, humanistic psychology, and certain areas of philosophy. So yes indeed, Alec acknowledges, 'even when we think we're resisting freely, we are restricted in the alternative cultural material we mobilise in the service of resistance.' How could it be otherwise?

Consider as well some of Alec's comments about the importance of hospitality to and care for different and distant others: 'Heightened consciousness of the lives of people in different parts of the world entails for the cosmopolitan a developing empathic appreciation of what would otherwise, from a national culture-centric position, possibly seem strange and alien.' Sounds good to me too. Given how Alec and I and most others in the autoethnographic community have been academically reared, how could it not?

I could go on, but no need. Much of what Alec is calling for, here and elsewhere, is, not surprisingly, familiar. To be clear, none of what is being said is meant to imply that Alec is an unwitting dupe or hypocritical carrier of the status quo or some such thing. Nor does it mean that he's hopelessly and irrevocably entrapped. MacIntyre speaks cogently to this very issue: 'I inherit from the past of my family, my city, my tribe, my nation, a variety of debts, inheritances, rightful expectations and obligations. These constitute the given of my life, my moral starting point. This is in part what gives my life its own moral particularity.'[16] And so, he continues,

> The story of my life is always embedded in those communities from which I derive my identity. I am born with a past; and to cut myself off from that past, in the individualist mode, is to deform my present relationships. The possession of an historical identity and the possession of a social identity coincide ... What I am, therefore, is in key part what I inherit, a specific past that is present to some degree in my present. I find myself part of a history and that is generally to say, whether I like it or not, whether I recognise it or not, one of the bearers of a tradition.'[17]

Tradition – narrative tradition, in particular – can and does bring some traps too. MacIntyre might have said more about these, if only to show that he's not the traditionalist 'conservative' he is sometimes deemed to be. Following MacIntyre in broad outline, I repeat: none of what I have said about Alec's liberal humanism or cosmopolitanism (or whatever) should be taken to mean that he's been swept up, unwittingly, by some ideological tide. Rather, it simply means that he is ... *human*, living in the world with language, with widely circulated ideas and ideals, and, in this case, with dreams of redemption and a kind of perfection, concerning the further realisation of both his own and his autoethnographic colleagues' authenticity and *élan vital*.

I don't mean to sound too charitable in framing things this way. Alec levels some serious criticisms in this book, and I don't want to dilute them; it's simply not my place, and it's for other readers to decide their worth. But in the end, I'm finding myself seeing Alec as a kind of gadfly, hyperbolic in his own right, here to prod, poke, and provoke, and, in so doing, maybe help the Ashes of the world to let it fly a bit more and become more of what they might be, as autoethnographers and as persons. If, Alec, I'm making you sound too wise and teacherly, I apologise; I know you don't like tight neckties! But isn't it true that you're seeking something more, something more *real*, for you and for them, so that the wider world becomes that much more interesting, just, and inhabitable? Meanwhile, you might try to cut some of your autoethnographic brothers and sisters a little slack. They may not be where you are in the tenacity of their resistance to cultural narrative entrapment or the ferocity of their life-affirming zeal, but aren't they too, committed as they are to the autoethnographic project, after many of the same basic goods as you?

Mark Freeman, PhD
Distinguished Professor of Ethics and Society in the
Department of Psychology
College of the Holy Cross
Worcester, Massachusetts, USA

PREFACE

My decision to write the chapters in this book alongside 'Ash,' my imaginary interlocutor, was in large part motivated by a need to better engage with my own cultural assumptions, or 'paradigm boundedness,' as a 'straight ... white British guy of a certain vintage.'[18] This worked out well as the project progressed. I found myself defending, reflecting on, and frequently feeling uneasy about what I'd written. The Ash-Alec exchange also gave me the opportunity to bring my writing closer to both who I am and what I feel about the autoethnography worlds I inhabit. By disposition, although regarded by many as a kind, caring, and generous man, I can also be irascible and verbally combative. I get annoyed by lots of things in the world, and this sometimes includes autoethnography and autoethnography communities. There are in my view differences between what autoethnography should be about and what many who claim the autoethnography tag *are* about, often with support from autoethnography and related communities.

* * *

Those who know me well enough will testify to the fact that I frequently live up to the working-class Scot stereotype of swearing a lot, 'fuck' and 'cunt' being my all-time favourite words. (Qualifier: I fully acknowledge and abhor the fact that the 'cunt' word is often used in a misogynistic way, including, as Deborah Cameron critically discusses, in the contexts of sexual violence, 'locker room banter,' and greeting card culture.[19] However, as I argue in Chapter 5 (more on the fuck word there too), it has a long and varied history and was and is legitimately used in other meaning contexts).

* * *

I often feel a bit fraudulent about the fact that my autoethnographic writing to date hasn't been entirely honest in sufficiently representing these aspects of my 'off-duty' personhood as they relate to my problems with the autoethnography world. Hopefully this book will go some way towards repairing the disconnect.

* * *

I sometimes wonder what other high-profile autoethnographers are like when they're off-duty? Even when their texts give the impression of full disclosure, the jointly and individually written work and conference presentations of some (not all) well-known autoethnography couples and individuals often seem to me to be too squeaky clean, tidied up, sanitised. My musings here go beyond the worthy and much-needed calls for greater honesty in autoethnography from situated perspectives of either personal troubles[20] or from the 'writing stories' that combine the academic with the domestic.[21] In either case, the interests of displaying professional respectability can still be served. In an imaginative need to get 'behind,' or perhaps in front of, these concerns, I find myself wondering how other autoethnographic grandees behave when, sometimes like me, they're wandering aimlessly about their homes in their underwear, feeling pissed off with themselves, with each other, and with things autoethnographic.

* * *

We're all caught up in categories, aren't we?[22] These enable and constrain us, shaping our front-stage presentations of who we claim to be and are expected to be. This form of cultural narrative entrapment understandably exerts a pressure to keep us, enthusiastically or otherwise, togged out in our representational Sunday Best. Linked to this, it seems to me, there's a paradox to be found in autoethnographies written by people who seem to be saying lots about themselves while, to my mind, revealing next to nothing. Apropos social scientific work, Gayle Letherby writes, 'those who protect themselves from scrutiny could well be labelled self-satisfied and arrogant in presuming their presence and relations with others to be unproblematic.'[23] Quite right, and I think this can also point to *cultural narrative entrapment within an academic persona*,[24] even when this persona is purportedly authoethnographic.

* * *

Accepting that we always inevitably need to/hold some things back, the messiness left out of the displayed act is what really interests me – or would if I could see more of it. Although this may sound like an appeal to voyeurism, I regard it as a call for greater honesty – to bring more of who we actually are into the autoethnographic frame. I for one would welcome such 'warts and all' autoethnographic displays and role modelling. The sociologist David Morgan reminds us that when we write about ourselves, we're effectively othering ourselves to the extent that the characters we portray are different from who we are day-to-day.[25] I think the ethical implication emerging from this for autoethnographers is the importance of getting the represented other as close to the day-to-day 'I' as possible, in the interest of coherence, integrity, and honesty.

* * *

The approach I've taken throughout this book has been critically dialogic on several levels: I talk with myself as *other*; with culture and the cultural *other* – whether interior alter ego or anticipated reader/defender of conventional culture; with and to my own autoethnographic stories, thus my past and current personhood; and I dialogue with what I regard as conventional autoethnographic assumptions, discourses, and social worlds.[26]

* * *

From his first critical reading of the book-in-progress, Marcin Kafar emailed me to say that in his opinion:

> All these positions result from your outsider status, your movement on the margins of cultures and communities. The essence of this attitude is the search for difference in order to resist the usual conceptualizations, questioning what is taken for granted.[27]

I agree with Marcin but need to add to his comment. Thinking to some extent with the philosophers Homi Bhabha and François Jullien,[28] and moreso with another autoethnographic colleague-friend, Chris Poulos,[29] I always experience myself to be in the 'in-between' of cultural locations.[30] Often feeling trapped in the cultural interstices of my own stories, I find myself wanting to break free to move on. As Jullien asserts, 'what is most amenable to characterization is also what is most arbitrary.'[31] Since there is no determinate identity in the liminal in between, the identity characterisation of myself represented across my work amounts to a paradox in being simultaneously rhetorically necessary and inappropriate.

* * *

Constantly gravitating towards transformation,[32] I never worry too much about violating cultural boundaries. Martin Heidegger wrote that a boundary 'is not that at which something stops but ... is that from which something *begins its presencing.*'[33] With that idea in mind, it personally seems important to me to regard 'cultural narrative engagement' as a simultaneous process of visiting, untrapping (as far as this is possible), and moving on/transforming.[34] My tendencies towards cultural hybridity and cultural dissent play important roles for me here in challenging cultural traditions, when I regard these traditions, or aspects of them, as habits having long exceeded their range of convenience for me.[35]

* * *

I experience a few paradoxical 'yes, but, and' issues with this, what might be regarded as 'iconoclastic presencing.' I value autoethnography but loathe what often passes for it and need to say so. I find myself lingering in and on the margins of autoethnography culture, but often want to leave autoethnography completely behind me, and need to publicly declare this. I like what I've written critically in this book (and elsewhere) about autoethnography culture, but fear the consequences, and/but don't really care about what ensues from those consequences. I'm worried that I've gone too far in the chapters that follow but need to get them out there in the world, and – perhaps defensively and self-protectively – I don't have of an expectation that my words will make much of a difference. I like many of the people in the autoethnographic community, love a few even, but need to risk upsetting them, and I've had more than a few disturbed nights over anticipated disapproval and rejection from a club to which I've never felt I truly belonged.

All these 'yes, but, ands' constitute more or less subtle forms of narrative entrapment, perhaps?[36]

* * *

The need to write this book emerged from my belief that culture is insufficiently scrutinised in autoethnography,[37] an argument I developed in my recently completed second PhD (by Publication) where my critical focus was on 'cultural narrative entrapment.'[38] The book is a modified and greatly extended version of my doctoral thesis. From an understanding of 'culture' in both 'ordinary' and oppressive senses, which I've more fully defined, discussed, and contextualised in its chapters, my take on cultural narrative entrapment is:

> the state of being actually or potentially stuck in oppressive, toxic, and life-limiting stories – willingly, unwillingly, or by default because of personal and life circumstances.

* * *

I mostly critically address the 'ethno' or culture element of autoethnography throughout the book, although this necessarily implicates the 'auto' element as it relates to cultural narrative identity. I do so autoethnographically and meta-autoethnographically when I signpost my published work with reference to selected philosophical, social science, and other relevant perspectives. More specifically, my narrative focuses on the *how* and *why* of *Resisting Cultural Narrative Entrapment in Autoethnography*. How does (can, should) one resist? And why is it important to do so? I respond to the first question mostly in the often irreverent and increasingly mutually antagonistic Ash-Alec italicised exchange dialogue running through, and topping and tailing, all the chapters. Drawing from and extending my doctoral thesis, the answer to the second question is explicitly developed in the more formal academic writing sandwiched between the two parts of the Ash-Alec conversation in each chapter.

* * *

It seems to me that emerging from the question of how autoethnographers resist cultural narrative entrapment is a related one: What are the challenges and limits of such resistance? In addressing this question, the origins and meanings of 'entrapment' and 'resistance' interest me. The Standard English noun 'entrapment' dates from the late 16th century.[39] It has overtones of criminality in referring to the act of being ensnared, or caught in a trap, because of trickery. In the context of my sustained standpoint position throughout this book, trickery can in turn imply various permutations of naivety, wilful blindness, unscrutinised trust, and ignorance on the part of the person tricked. Two questions arise for me: how does entrapment relate to resistance? and how is entrapment resisted? I think the smart trick here is in making a serious effort to shift from trickee to trickster – from being ensnared by culture to being *in* but not *of* culture through maintaining a resistant, constantly sceptical distance.

* * *

What does 'resistance' entail? The concept, also dating from the late medieval/early modern period,[40] has militaristic overtones in referring to the need to *oppose* or *make a stand against*. In definitional terms, the *Oxford English Dictionary* tells us that 'resisting' can mean: '**1.** the action of resisting,' or '**2.** the ability not to be affected by something undesirable,' or '**3.** the impeding or stopping effect that one material thing has on another.' While subjective agency is implicated across all three meanings, the first seems tautological and non-explanatory, with the second implying that it's not necessary to fully understand that which is resisted against, and the third suggesting the need for some kind of combative blocking.

* * *

While meanings **2** and **3** capture my own resistance agenda, meaning **2** troubles me. What are the possibly unseen pitfalls of resisting something you don't get on with or don't like, if that something is a culture or an aspect of culture within which you feel caught up? To effectively resist cultural narrative entrapment, I like to think that I need to know as much of the details as are necessary for me about the actual cultural story I'm up against, who its protagonists are, and whether they really belong in that story. But what if I get the wrong end of the cultural identity stick, so to speak, given that my best efforts in this regard are never likely to be sufficient or rigorous enough? And worse, what if I construct false cultural others by projecting defensive stereotypes onto them? To paraphrase the philosopher Simon Blackburn,[41] what if I inappropriately impose on my imagined other(s) by squeezing them into whichever bespoke prejudice I've tailored for them?

***

To a large degree, this seems inevitable in autoethnographic inquiry, and in life more generally. Phiona Stanley rightly reminds us that we humans 'don't see things as they are, (but) as we are.'[42] Problems ensue when such projection exceeds ordinary and forgivable human error through being motivated by stereotyping and wilful prejudice,[43] which might of course go unrecognised or be defensively denied. Entrapped in our cognitive biases, such *othering* may enable us to feel safe, morally superior, and relatively more powerful, but may also be ontologically, epistemologically, and ethically unsupportable. The obvious relational ethical problems at play here encompass personal violations of moral responsibility and self-care. Ideally, as an autoethnographer and educated human, I should generally strive to relate well to myself and others since the other is always me. I'm not always good at this, and perhaps it's the case that I'm avoiding healthy social psychological growth through my failure to strive.

***

I'm troubled by another issue. Even if resistance to cultural narrative entrapment is valid for me in terms of my accurate identification of narratives which truly merit resisting against and have fewer ethical challenges, can the act of resistance sometimes be more imagined than real? Might it simply amount to the substitution of one, more appealing, form of entrapment for another? Is the idea of a post-resistance culture-free space plausible or ridiculous? I find this, for me non-trivial, thought experiment interesting: if available and attainable, what would absolute and ultimate resistance to cultural narrative entrapment feel and be like? I can't really imagine anything other than that it would amount to an absence of everything. A nothing. A kind of pre-cultural identity

Big Bang state, minus cultural identities and everything else. This wouldn't be much fun – the long evenings wouldn't exactly whizz by. There wouldn't be any long evenings.

* * *

So, I conclude, at least for now, that resistance to cultural narrative entrapment doesn't and shouldn't imply wishing for, or trying to engineer, its total absence. While biologically alive, we're all of us humans inescapably culturally entrapped. The idea of some forms of entrapment working out better than others implies for me their existence on a moral hierarchy. If this idea is plausible, can this also be true for some forms of resistance? From the perspectives of interculturality,[44] and intercultural competence,[45] is, for example, the ability to gain knowledge of, and shift between, geographical or linguistic cultures in a sophisticated way tantamount to a superior form of resistance to cultural narrative entrapment? In terms of the dictionary meaning **2** above, could it also function as a kind of salve in making one's 'home base' culture feel more bearable because of its permanent relegation to a subordinate position? Or can this scenario be alternatively conceived of as a temporary act of consumer thrill-seeking? Can the base culture be analogous to a much loved and reassuringly familiar family home to safely get back to after the exotic tourism experience that regularly punctuates many lives?[46]

* * *

And does meeting and being changed by the difference of the other, insofar as such difference can be apprehended, really constitute morally good resistance?[47] The problem for me is that – as with bats[48] so with humans – comprehensively accessing the phenomenological or subjective 'what is it like to be' of the cultural *other* must always be something of a failed project. There are times when people, including my own close friends and family, feel to me like Blackburn's 'incomprehensible aliens,' when I clearly and palpably experience the 'massive dissociation between … minds, each of which has locked on to different versions of the world.'[49] I'm pretty sure I'm by no means on my own here. While it's less distressing to pretend otherwise, the idea of us all talking about the same thing in human encounters often seems a socially convenient fiction – and I didn't really need Wittgenstein to come to increasingly realise that for myself over the years.

* * *

But this truism is countered by scholarship that presents intercultural meeting events as fluid and dynamic, and reflexively mediated rather than fixed and static,[50] with people always adjusting in the presence of others in the code switch from individualised to social.[51] While I don't think that this can seriously be contested, isn't it also often the case that when two people meet each other, an essentialism of cultural identity in and between both parties is not only mutually presupposed but reified? Humans are self- and other-stereotyping animals, and what often prevails are disengaged monologues for two. Rather than thoughtful, mutually attentive dialogue,[52] I wait for your culturally othered mouth to stop moving so I can start moving mine.

***

And what about the issue of meeting difference in one's own self as *the other*, resulting in letting go of one's previously held cultural allegiances?[53] Does this constitute a morally good form of resistance from the perspective of interculturality? It has been argued that all interactions are intercultural.[54] Yes indeed, and this must surely apply to our personal interactions with our various other interlocutor selves. However, we can remain blithely and defensively unaware of or resistant to meeting them, all the while experiencing the 'wholeness and continuity' (and safety) of our dominant cultural narrative identities.[55]

***

Moreover, I think of the reflectivity and reflexivity hype, much of which I've joined in with and promoted in my own autoethnographic work over the years. I've developed increasing levels of scepticism to this throughout my three decades in qualitative inquiry and autoethnography. That said, it seems to me to be worthwhile to question the extent to which we really and seriously engage with and are changed by encounters with our – always necessary, and necessarily challenging – interior interlocutors. Whether these critical voices hang out on the most accessible level of consciousnesses or in the dark intrapsychic recesses, I believe that we need to access, closely attend to, respect, and pay more attention to them – if only to get a better purchase on our individual identities rather than necessarily change them. This issue directly links to addressing the 'how' of resisting cultural narrative entrapment. Never a straightforward task, for me the difficulties of doing this go hand in hand with its necessity.

***

The question 'how do I resist cultural narrative entrapment?' is inseparable from 'why do I need to?' My approach to the issue of *why* I think we should resist is hopefully straightforward. I believe that people don't sufficiently know about, recognise, or acknowledge the oppressive nature of the cultures they engage with, and/or that they're constrained by their discursive impoverishment, and/ or that they don't take those cultures sufficiently seriously – sometimes regarding them as neutral or relatively unimportant backdrops to their lives, or simply non-existent in the sense that 'only foreigners have cultures.'

* * *

I think that we-autoethnographers *ought* to get more serious about the cultures we speak to, or that speak us, via the discourses available to us, and that we should continually strive to increase on those discourses. Even if we believe ourselves to be optimally discursively sophisticated, we're inevitably stymied by our cultural discursive blind spots. In related terms, we often don't recognise when our cultural narrative identities are under assault, compromised, violated, taken hostage, or shanghaied by outside cultural forces.

* * *

And sometimes we assault, kidnap, or solo press-gang ourselves. Perhaps a more serious issue at play here is when we mistake our identity act for its essence, when our investments in our constructed identities are made at the expense of our integrity and awareness of the absurd and unruly aspects of our lives. Forgetting that our acts are really only that – *just acts* – can turn us into caricatures, or parodies, of who are as autoethnographers when writing or performing. In this regard, it may be wise for us to, in Clifford Geertz's terms, think backward about who we are more often: 'first you write and then you figure out what you are writing about.'[56] Confusing act with identity essence can invite pomposity to the party. And bad faith. Hats off to Sartre for this last point.[57]

* * *

It seems to me that bad faith can endure because letting go of a longstanding act can result in serious loss of face, notwithstanding the possibility that at least some acts have degenerated into tired old habits. I trained as a psychotherapist many years ago but grew out of it when I began to *feel*, as well as realise, the organisational and practice contradictions and problems within the trade. I'm pretty sure that some of the people I still know in the psychotherapy game are switched to automatic pilot, so to speak, in their never-ending project of voicing superlatives about it, and about their place in it, and about how much it still means to them.

* * *

I've recently gotten more of a handle on this issue through better understanding the difference between 'selfhood' and 'personhood.' In *Losing Ourselves: Learning to Live Without a Self*,[58] Jay Garfield argues – from Buddhist philosophy and the early modern philosophy of David Hume – that the 'self' is a social construct and convention that can neither be had (as in 'I have a self') or serve to exhaustively define (as in 'I am a self'). As a shorthand way of describing a constant state of experiential flux, 'the self' can never be convincingly unified, either synchronically or diachronically.

* * *

This is not to say that people don't exist, but that as 'persons' they are inscribed far more loosely within the constantly shifting and changing flow of life. In this regard, argues Garfield, *believing* in oneself as 'a self,' as opposed to *describing* oneself as such for the pragmatic purposes of social convention, amounts to a psychologically hard-wired illusion. Although such a belief in selfhood may have social as well as longstanding evolutionary advantages, its downside in my view is that people who strongly cling on to the idea that they are enduring *selves*, separate from nature and somehow immune from its vicissitudes, may be at greater risk of suffering when their 'self' acts are threatened or undermined.

* * *

In related terms, the cultural narrative identities which have defined the social and cultural world of modern societies for so long – distinctive traditional identities of gender, sexuality, race, class, and nationality – are clearly in rapid decline. While we can never completely escape the categories with live by,[59] new forms of cultural narrative identification and fragmentation impact the modern person, further undermining the idea of unified selfhood.[60] Presupposing the reasonableness, relevance, and appropriateness of the 'choice' concept, we're all potentially tempted by a smorgasbord of burgeoning cultural narrative identity permutations which weren't on offer until relatively recently. The loss of traditional identities is surely, for many, existentially discombobulating. In the face of this, it's tempting for some of us oldies to dig our pre/boomer heels in and scoff at such things as gendered pronoun choices.

* * *

In more positive terms, the search for a preferred cultural narrative identity in our fragmented postmodern times might be thought about in terms of a 'quest,' or extended secular pilgrimage.[61] However, given the hyper-intersectionality and the inescapable social category conferment that either tempts or is imposed on us as we move through the series of cultural situations that is life,[62] the risk always seems to me to be that we might choose unwisely, or myopically in failing to sufficiently consider long-term consequences.

* * *

But, many will argue, 'some cultural narratives, and the corresponding identity positions that go with them, are helpful, healthy, or simply benign.' Of course they are. We willingly bring them into being all the time in our ordinary cultures, or – to borrow from Adrian Holliday – the 'small culture formations on the go' that constitute our day-to-day lives.[63] However, accepting the liberal-humanist idea of *choices made by unified individuals* as flawed but important for autoethnographic representation, careful and thoughtful informed choice is, or should be, still always implicated. Equally implicated to my mind is the healthy scepticism towards cultural narrative entrapment afforded by critical autoethnographicity, which I argue for throughout this book.

***

I hope that readers will find it useful.

Alec Grant,
April-September, 2024

Notes

1 See Chapter 5, 'Fact and Fiction', from my own *Rewriting the Self: History, Memory, Narrative* (London: Routledge, 1993).
2 Philip Roth, *The Facts: A Novelist's Autobiography* (New York: Farrar, Straus and Giroux, 1988).
3 Philip Roth, *The Facts: A Novelist's Autobiography* (New York: Farrar, Straus and Giroux, 1988), 5.
4 Philip Roth, *The Facts: A Novelist's Autobiography* (New York: Farrar, Straus and Giroux, 1988), 6.
5 Philip Roth, *The Facts: A Novelist's Autobiography* (New York: Farrar, Straus and Giroux, 1988), 7.
6 Freeman, 'Fact and Fiction', from my own *Rewriting the Self: History, Memory, Narrative* (London: Routledge, 1993), 115.
7 Galen Strawson, 'Against Narrativity,' *Ratio* 17, no. 4 (2004): 428–452.
8 For a slightly more scholarly argument, see Mark Freeman, 'Narrative as a mode of understanding: Method, theory, praxis,' in *The Handbook of Narrative Analysis*, eds. A. De Fina and A. Georgakopolou (London: Wiley Blackwell, 2015), 21–37.
9 Philip Roth, *The Facts: A Novelist's Autobiography* (New York: Farrar, Straus and Giroux, 1988), 7.
10 Philip Roth, *The Facts: A Novelist's Autobiography* (New York: Farrar, Straus and Giroux, 1988), 8.
11 Philip Roth, *The Facts: A Novelist's Autobiography* (New York: Farrar, Straus and Giroux, 1988), 9.
12 See Crispin Sartwell, *End of Story: Toward the Annihilation of Language and History* (Albany, NY: SUNY, 2000).
13 Philip Roth, *The Facts: A Novelist's Autobiography* (New York: Farrar, Straus and Giroux, 1988), 162.
14 Philip Roth, *The Facts: A Novelist's Autobiography* (New York: Farrar, Straus and Giroux, 1988), 162.

15 Philip Roth, *The Facts: A Novelist's Autobiography* (New York: Farrar, Straus and Giroux, 1988), 164.
16 Alasdair MacIntyre, *After Virtue: A Study in Moral Theory* (Notre Dame: Indiana University Press), 205.
17 Alasdair MacIntyre, *After Virtue: A Study in Moral Theory* (Notre Dame: Indiana University Press), 205–206.
18 Phiona Stanley, review of my Routledge proposal for this book, April 1, 2024.
19 Deborah Cameron, *Language, Sexism and Misogyny* (London and New York: Routledge), 130, 139.
20 Gayle Letherby, 'Thirty Years and Counting: An-other Auto/biographical Story,' *Auto/Biography Review* 3, no. 1 (August 2022): 13–31, https://doi.org/10.56740/abrev.v3i1.7.
21 Laurel Richardson, 'Getting Personal: Writing Stories,' *Qualitative Studies in Education* 14, no. 1 (2001): 33–38, https://doi.org/10.1080/09518390010007647.
22 Ásta, *Categories We Live By: The Construction of Sex, Gender, Race, and Other Social Categories* (New York: Oxford University Press, 2018).
23 Gayle Letherby, 'Thirty Years and Counting: An-other Auto/biographical Story,' *Auto/Biography Review* 3, no. 1 (August 2022): 14, https://doi.org/10.56740/abrev.v3i1.7.
24 Thanks to Lizzie Lloyd-Parkes for helping me think through and clarify this.
25 David Morgan, 'Sociological Imaginations and Imagining Sociologies: Bodies, Auto/Biographies and Other Mysteries,' *Sociology*, 32, no. 4 (1998): 647–663, https://doi.org/10.1177/0038038598032004002.
26 Thanks are due to Marcin Kafar for clarifying this point as central to my book.
27 Marcin Kafar, Email message, May 24, 2024.
28 Homi K. Bhabha, *The Location of Culture* (London and New York: Routledge Classics, 2004), 2; François Jullien, 'Between Is Not Being,' *Theory, Culture & Society* 40, no. 4–5 (December 2022): 239–249, https://doi.org/10.1177/02632764221111324.
29 Christopher N. Poulos, 'A Liminal Awakening,' in *Writing Philosophical Autoethnography*, ed. Alec Grant (New York and London: Routledge), 150–166.
30 Arne De Boever, *François Jullien's Unexceptional Thought: A Critical Introduction* (London and New York: Rowman & Littlefield, 2020), 23–24.
31 François Jullien, 'Between Is Not Being,' *Theory, Culture & Society* 40, no. 4–5 (December 2022): 242, https://doi.org/10.1177/02632764221111324.
32 Thanks are due to Marcin Kafar for recognising that my words in this paragraph point to my constant 'gravitating towards transformation.' (Marcin Kafar, email to me, June 29, 2024).
33 Martin Heidegger, *Poetry, Language, Thought* (New York: Harper Perennial Modern Thought, 2013), 152.
34 Alec Grant, 'In Search of My Narrative Character: A Philosophical Autoethnography,' in *Writing Philosophical Autoethnography*, ed. Alec Grant (New York and London: Routledge), 123–131.
35 Homi K. Bhabha, *The Location of Culture* (London and New York: Routledge Classics, 2004), 3.
36 Graham Lever, email to author, August 7, 2024.
37 Alec Grant, 'The Philosophical Autoethnographer,' in *Writing Philosophical Autoethnography*, ed. Alec Grant (New York and London: Routledge, 2024), 1–22.
38 Alec Grant, 'Developing Philosophical Autoethnography: Resisting Cultural Narrative Entrapment' (PhD thesis, University of Bolton, 2024).
39 Entrapment | Search Online Etymology Dictionary (Etymonline.Com).
40 Resistance | Search Online Etymology Dictionary (Etymonline.Com).
41 Simon Blackburn, *Truth: A Guide for the Perplexed* (London: Allen Lane, 2005), 199.

42 Phiona Stanley, *A Critical Auto/Ethnography of Learning Spanish: Intercultural Competence on the Gringo Trail?* (Abingdon and New York: Routledge, 2017), 38, my brackets.

43 Adrian Holliday, *Understanding Intercultural Communication: Negotiating a Grammar of Culture*. 2nd edn. (London and New York: Routledge, 2019).

44 Lisal Paulsen Galal, 'Interculturality in Ethnographic Practice: Noisy Silences,' in *Researching Identity and Interculturality*, eds. Fred Dervin and Karen Risager (Abingdon and New York: Routledge, 2015), 151–168.

45 Adrian Holliday, *Understanding Intercultural Communication: Negotiating a Grammar of Culture*. 2nd edn. (London and New York: Routledge, 2019), 8–30; Phiona Stanley, *A Critical Auto/Ethnography of Learning Spanish: Intercultural Competence on the Gringo Trail?* (London and New York: Routledge, 2017), 18–35.

46 Alec Grant and Elizabeth Lloyd-Parkes, 'Meaningful Journeys, Identity Transformation, and Autoethnographic Selfhood,' in *Meaningful Journeys: Autoethnographies of Quest and Identity Transformation*, eds. Alec Grant and Elizabeth Lloyd-Parkes (London and New York: Routledge, 2024), 1–16.

47 Lisal Paulsen Galal, 'Interculturality in Ethnographic Practice: Noisy Silences,' in *Researching Identity and Interculturality*, eds. Fred Dervin and Karen Risager (Abingdon and New York: Routledge, 2015), 151–156.

48 Thomas Nagel, 'What Is It Like to Be a Bat,' *The Philosophical Review* 83, no. 4 (1974): 435–450, https://doi.org/10.2307/2183914.

49 Simon Blackburn, *Truth: A Guide for the Perplexed* (London: Allen Lane, 2005), 205.

50 Adrian Holliday, *Understanding Intercultural Communication: Negotiating a Grammar of Culture*. 2nd edn. (London and New York: Routledge, 2019).

51 Marilynn B. Brewer and Wendi Gardner, 'Who Is this "We"? Levels of Collective Identity and Self Representations,' *Journal of Personality and Social Psychology* 71, no. 1 (1996): 83–93, https://doi.org/10.1093/oso/9780199269464.003.0006.

52 Elizabeth Minnich, *The Evil of Banality: On the Life and Death Importance of Thinking* (London: Rowman & Littlefield, 2017).

53 Sara Ahmed, *Queer Phenomenology: Orientations, Objects, Others* (Durham, NNC: Duke University Press, 2006).

54 Karen Risager and Fred Dervin, 'Introduction,' in *Researching Identity and Interculturality*, eds. Fred Dervin and Karen Risager (Abingdon and New York: Routledge, 2015), 4; Adrian Holliday, *Understanding Intercultural Communication: Negotiating a Grammar of Culture*. 2nd edn. (London and New York: Routledge, 2019), x.

55 Katherine P. Ewing, 'The Illusion of Wholeness: Culture, Self, and the Experience of Inconsistency,' *Ethos* 18, no. 3 (1990): 251–278, http://www.jstor.org/stable/640337?origin=JSTOR-pdf.

56 Clifford Geertz, *The Interpretation of Cultures*. 2000 Edition (New York: Basic Books, 1973), v.

57 Jean-Paul Sartre, *Being and Nothingness* (London and New York: Routledge, 2003 [1943]).

58 Jay L. Garfield, *Losing Ourselves: Learning to Live Without a Self* (Princeton and Oxford: Princeton University Press, 2022).

59 Ásta, *Categories We Live By: The Construction of Sex, Gender, Race, and Other Social Categories* (New York: Oxford University Press, 2018).

60 Homi K. Bhaba, 'Culture's In-Between,' in *Questions of Cultural Identity*, eds. Stuart Hall and Paul du Gay (London: SAGE Publications, 1996), 53–60; Alec Grant and Elizabeth Lloyd-Parkes, 'Meaningful Journeys, Identity Transformation, and Autoethnographic Selfhood,' in *Meaningful Journeys: Autoethnographies of Quest and Identity Transformation*, eds. Alec Grant and Elizabeth Lloyd-Parkes (London and New York: Routledge, 2024), 8–10.

61 Alec Grant and Elizabeth Lloyd-Parkes, 'Meaningful Journeys, Identity Transformation, and Autoethnographic Selfhood,' in *Meaningful Journeys: Autoethnographies of Quest and Identity Transformation*, eds. Alec Grant and Elizabeth Lloyd-Parkes (London and New York: Routledge, 2024), 1–16.
62 Ásta, *Categories We Live By: The Construction of Sex, Gender, Race, and Other Social Categories* (New York: Oxford University Press, 2018).
63 Adrian Holliday, *Understanding Intercultural Communication: Negotiating a Grammar of Culture*. 2nd edn. (London and New York: Routledge, 2019), 14–15.

1
RESISTING CULTURAL NARRATIVE ENTRAPMENT

Setting the Scene

Ash: Why do you need to write another book about autoethnography? And how many books on autoethnography are needed, tell me!? That's all been done to death! And, while we're about it, why did you do, and why do you need, another PhD!!??

Alec: Get out of my head, Ash ... no, wait, stay.

Ash: Is it to do with your 'mad craze' for collecting things ... like your fiddles, books, bodhrans, paintings, whistles, running shoes?

Alec: You're obviously in league with wives one and two. I forgive you for that. I'm a pain to live with.

Ash: You're a bit 'excessive' though, from what I know of you and have heard about you. I'm guessing you always have been!! Why can't you just try to be like 'everyone else'???!!!!!

Alec: There's a fair amount of judgemental stereotyping, inferential leaping, confirmation bias, category conferment, and intended cultural narrative entrapment in what you've just said, Ash. Moreover, 'normal' implies its opposite and us autoethnographers should be concerned about binaries that pathologise, should we not (such a hypocrite am I)? But you're right about one thing: I never seem able to do moderate. I think that's in large part to do with having had an increasingly serious problem with alcohol for a large part of my life (sober for fifteen years now, hooray!).[1] We're too much people, as we used to say at the AA meetings.[2] Perhaps my conversation with you throughout the book can help me de-extreme myself a wee bit, although I think I might be a bit

DOI: 10.4324/9781003518594-1

too long in the tooth now (I know I am). And do you really have to do all these exasperation marks and inappropriate perverted commas?

Ash: (Cheeky sod!) Okay, points taken, you are who you are, I guess (and we're never going to be buddies). But who am I supposed to actually be, given that you've had the cheek to write me into your book, rather than choosing a real person – a bit strange, no? And why do you need me?

Alec: Because you live in my imagination, you are a real person in lots of ways, Ash. You're a composite of quite a few of the people using the autoethnography tag, who are likely to have problems with my position, or not really get it at all. I specifically mean some of the people I know personally within those autoethnographic communities I connect with and others I've come across at conferences and other live and online events, and from doing reviews of journal article submissions, and from past conversations I've either participated in or overheard. A single flesh and blood person, or a group of them, couldn't have fulfilled all those roles, and even if they could I'd have all those relational ethical problems to deal with, wouldn't I? It's simpler this way. Consider me an ethical bypass surgery team of one (ha ha). Regarding your last question, I need **you** in order to get **me** a bit more out of my own culturally narratively entrapped arse, or at least to feel more comfortably constipated.

Ash: Okay then … not too sure about your choice of language here, and you're starting to sound more than a bit superior, but let's get going…

***

Introducing Cultural Narrative Entrapment

Resistance to cultural narrative entrapment has increasingly been my sustained and philosophically informed critical cultural standpoint position since I started writing autoethnography in the mid-1990s. This position has three components:

- At the *philosophical* level, I try to reflexively engage with who I want myself to *be* (ontology), and with what I *know* about myself in relation to the world, culture, and the world more broadly (epistemology), and how the world – subsuming the humans within it – works (metaphysics). I do this in terms of my enduring dispositional tendency to often react against centripetal forces pulling me into conformist identities – what I *should* be doing according to tacit or unspoken, normative cultural rules.
- At the *sociological* level, this tendency is played out in my scholarly work, in celebrating, justifying, and reflexively representing outsider as opposed to mainstream culturally conformist choices and ways of living.

- Finally, at the level of hopefully advancing *social justice* a little, I write in resistance to cultural narrative entrapment. This is because such entrapment can force people into stories they don't want to be part of, often experienced as narrative violence, or an assault on narrative identity.

The idea of crafting this book grew out of my second PhD thesis (by Published Works), the title of which was *Developing Philosophical Autoethnography: Resisting Cultural Narrative* entrapment. As I mentioned in my preface, except for a few alterations, a little contraction, and a lot of expansion (including adding the Alec-Ash dialogue, which wasn't in my PhD thesis), this is the more developed book emerging from my doctoral study.[3] The idea for the topic and focus of the doctorate emerged before this in the summer of 2023, when my edited volume *Writing Philosophical Autoethnography* was nearing its publication date.[4] My doctoral study aimed to respond to a problem, described and discussed in Chapter 1 of the volume, which I've seen displayed across narrative autoethnographic work,[5] and in the autoethnographic community activity I'm familiar with more generally, for many years. Identifying as a critical philosophical autoethnographer – an autoethnographer who troubles conventional culture- and self-related assumptions and practices from a philosophical perspective, my standpoint position is that this problem can be expressed in 'broad-' and 'narrow-lens' terms. From a broad-lens focus on the narrative autoethnographic literature in general, I argue that as a body of work it is insufficiently philosophical. By this I mean that while philosophical ideas and references are of course often routinely used in published narrative autoethnographic work (and at conferences and other presentation venues), the two issues of ontology (being) and epistemology (knowing), fundamental to cultural narrative identity, are often left inadequately scrutinised in such work.[6]

Through the narrower lens, two concepts related to this more general problem come into critical focus: *narrative entrapment* and *cultural entrapment*. I coined the former one in my autoethnographic writing and thinking years back,[7] gradually coming to see its fusion with cultural entrapment. Together, these concepts directly relate to the fundamental importance of honouring all three of the auto-ethno-graphy elements, which in an earlier text I described as crucial to an adequate understanding of the 'fundamental concept'[8] of autoethnography in any single piece of work purporting to be autoethnographic. This is supported in the more recent assertion by Andrew Herrmann and Tony Adams, that 'work classified as "autoethnography" must demonstrate a care for, and commitment to, the auto, the ethno, and the graphy – for us ... a rigid, prescriptive, and non-negotiable expectation.'[9]

Narrative entrapment and cultural entrapment are two sides of the same conceptual coin in that narrative autoethnographic work always has a cultural basis to it. Like all other people, we-autoethnographers are to varying degrees trapped in the stories we tell ourselves about ourselves, others, the world, and our cultural locations. As I've already suggested and will argue in the chapters

4 Resisting Cultural Narrative Entrapment in Autoethnography

that follow, and as will be apparent in the appendix to the book, unless this is reflexively appreciated, grappled with, and written about and against, such entrapment can be oppressive and silencing.

As a long-standing, sometimes reluctant,[10] member of club autoethnography, many of my fellow members often seem to me to be too comfortably and unreflexively stuck in the stories they tell and write. In Arthur Frank's terms, they tend to 'finalise' and 'monologise' themselves in a single self-in-relation-to-culture story.[11] At this point, I should stress that I don't claim privileged immunity or transcendence from such tendencies. However, as a seasoned autoethnographer with an academic background that includes philosophy, I do claim the right to write critically about this phenomenon, and I think that my doing so will benefit the autoethnogaphic communities.

Now for some conceptual clarification: because of the fusion of narrative with cultural entrapment, I used the concept 'cultural narrative entrapment' throughout my doctoral study and do so again in this book. Building on the brief definition given in my preface, I define this concept as:

> The insufficiently reflexive autoethnographic display of stuckness, complacency, or indifference in accepting – potentially or actually – life-limiting auto/biographical storied constructions of the cultural narrative identity of oneself and others as ontologically, epistemologically, and metaphysically adequate, whether these constructions are individually or socially assumed, or externally conferred or imposed.

Linking directly to my inquiry focus, and inquiry questions stated below, the authors of such work inevitably write from an explicit or implicit cultural standpoint position. I propose that they do so within a continuum ranging from uncritical acceptance of the cultures they represent to their partial or wholesale critical rejection. There can of course be 'shades of grey' positions of qualified cultural acceptance within this continuum.

Posing my own culturally critical standpoint position on this issue in stark terms for analytic purposes,

> I regard narrative autoethnographic work displaying uncritical acceptance of oppressive aspects of/culture as simultaneously displaying cultural narrative entrapment. In contrast, I regard narrative autoethnographies displaying critical resistance to oppressive aspects of/culture as simultaneously displaying resistance to cultural narrative entrapment.

I include my autoethnographic work discussed throughout this book in this latter category. Such resistance is by no means an easy task, and I should stress that I continue to regard my work as uneven in sufficiently achieving this. The centripetal pullback into entrapment is unforgiving and relentless.

I engaged with and answered the following four questions in my doctorate and do so again in this text. Readers might want to keep these questions in mind and return to them as they work their way through the chapters that follow (I'll be writing reminders along the way):

- What constitutes resistance to cultural narrative entrapment in philosophical autoethnography?
- Why it is important to resist cultural narrative entrapment in autoethnography?
- What philosophical and related conceptual, theoretical, and social scientific issues emerge from the ways I address resistance to cultural narrative entrapment across my autoethnographic scholarship over the last decade?
- What implications arise from these issues for the development of philosophical autoethnography?

Some readers may of course take issue with these questions and with the premises that govern them. However, engaging with and answering them in the chapters that follow will I believe help others in remedying an *incompleteness* in the autoethnographic literature, if there is agreement with me that it neglects these questions.[12] Moreover, raising the importance of the *cultural narrative entrapment* concept for the autoethnographic communities will hopefully advance the social justice agenda of philosophical autoethnography. To repeat myself, and as I argue later in the book and show in its appendix, such entrapment can be oppressive, damaging, and life-limiting.

In terms of my methodological standpoint, my approach and my book cohere to constitute a critical philosophical, dialogic, meta-autoethnography: critical because I trouble culture rather than taking it for granted; philosophical because I interrogate the meaning and conceptual basis of cultural narrative identity; dialogic in the ways I've stated in the preface; finally, meta-autoethnographic to the extent that the narrative throughout the book refers and adds layers of analysis to my selected autoethnographic work which I wrote, or co-wrote, over the last decade, described in its appendix.

Because of my need to bring me and my writing closer together, I didn't want to conceal the extent of my feelings and beliefs about resisting cultural narrative entrapment and related issues by solely writing in the voice of 'Alec the philosophical autoethnographer.'[13] The parallel conversation running through the book fulfilling this need is my separate, 'interior' autoethnography – the Ash-Alec exchange. This is informal, and irreverent, and is based on many years of skin in the autoethnographic game and, as I said in the preface, my 'off-duty' dispositional style. I anticipate that readers will either hate, love, or feel indifferent towards this exchange, depending on who they are; how seriously or otherwise they take autoethnography; how much experience they've had of autoethnography in terms of doing it and being involved in it; their relational politics and attitudes towards dialogical power; and where they are in the autoethnographic community (more properly, communities) pecking order.

I believe from my own experience (which some will no doubt take issue with) that there are quite a few Ash-types in our autoethnography communities; I personally know some of them. I've deliberately employed hyperbole in the Ash-composite character construction to produce a necessary caricature. Had I made our conversational relationship more equal in terms of knowledge and power, I wouldn't have been able to do this, and my beef with composite Ash would have disappeared. As Trude Klevan says apropos the Alec-Ash dialogue, 'making characters a bit one-dimensional and caricatured can for sure be a useful way of making a point (or many points) visible.'[14] Whatever the response to it, the dialogue might hopefully encourage readers to join in and make it a trialogue in negative (anti) or positive (pro) terms. To pull on a concept from Arthur Frank, the last thing I want is for readers to be left out of an *unfinalisable* story.[15]

In more formal social and moral philosophical terms, in addition to the need to seek clarity by hinting at the possibility of Socratic dialogue, without perhaps ever wanting to achieve this, the textual presence of Ash represents my need to engage with role taking of the composite other. Discussed by George Herbert Mead in *Mind Self and Society*,[16] role taking is a useful strategy for putting oneself in the shoes of others, and reflexively developing appropriate responses. Mead argues that role taking helps in exercising control over one's response, as well as improving cooperation in social interactional exchanges. I demonstrate in the book that I'm more controlling than cooperative, but hats off to Mead anyway. At a more fundamental and personally appealing level, the Russian philosopher Vladimir Bibler is reported as holding the position that 'thinking is substantiated by thinking itself…,' when initiated as '…a self-dialogue, a dialogue of thinking with thinking.'[17]

Critically thinking with, and about, my thinking, and reflecting on my identity and standpoint position in relation to what my imaginary, often understandably antagonistic *other* might think, and think of me, is more than simply useful. It makes sense in the context of my positive and, for some, less desirable, dispositional tendencies. I regard my constant guilt, self-doubt, and pride in myself and my achievements simultaneously as creativity-inducing gifts and existential burdens. Dialoguing with Ash helps me clarify and defend my standpoint positions as well as putting my misanthropy and lack of charity on display.

In terms of personal reflexivity, internal dialoguing is advocated from another Mead-aligned perspective by Carolyn Ellis, who argues that it helps develop compassion for views that are not your own.[18] Even if I don't develop sufficient compassion through taking the role of my imagined other – I'm never ever likely to – some degree of acceptance, or perhaps resignation, and an oppositional tolerance laced with humour, sarcasm, and controlled animosity seem to me to be reasonable aspirations, me being me.

This points to a downside of the Ash-Alec dialogue for some, but hopefully not all, readers: we subject each other to stereotyping rancour and sarcasm, in a kind of sado-masochistic mutuality of accusation, negative projection and counter projection, and confirmation bias. That said, I frequently consciously try to write my part of the exchange reason-ably and civilly – I would say that, wouldn't I? For readers of a more liberal-humanistic, power-sensitive, and inclusive disposition, it will no doubt become quickly apparent that this doesn't make things any better. Indeed, some will quite rightly argue, what I've produced is more one-sided egologue than dialogue, with Ash function-ing as a convenient foil used to peddle Alec's agenda. Alec, not Ash, comes out on top as more learned and erudite. And Alec, not Ash, decided on this dialogue-as-method in the first place, However, the conversational exchange represents a rehearsal of the rebuttal and rejoinder arguments I use against Ash-composite disaggregated, flesh and blood antagonists – usually, for the sake of social decorum, minus the sarcasm and expletives. It's much easier to let rip with an imagined interlocutor **(and readers should note that the bracketed text throughout the exchange signals verbally unexpressed, covert thinking on the part of either Ash or Alec**).

All that said, I hope I'll always remain a reflexive work-in-progress, even if I contradict myself by asserting that the idea of increasing self-awareness and moral worth through reflexivity is a chimera. Always ultimately – beyond its use as a convenient slogan – a failed project, I believe that reflexivity promises much more to autoethnographers than it can ultimately deliver, whatever 'it' is. In philosophical terms, *equivocation* rules often in autoethnographic writ-ing, in that authors deploy the 'reflexivity' word in different, often inconsistent ways, in and between texts. In moral terms, as I've suggested in the pref-ace, how autoethnographers actually live, and behave individually and socially among themselves, is often more telling than what they say and write about this in the name of something called 'reflexivity.' And as I argue later in the book, there seems to me to be a big difference between standard autoethnog-raphy and autoethnographicity-informed autoethnography around the signifi-cance of 'reflexivity' for life and work, if 'reflexivity' is accepted as a loose but sometimes useful concept of indeterminate meaning. For me, dialoguing with myself over how I make sense of the world is possibly the best I can do to clarify my understanding and usage. In this regard, I've long argued for and tried to role model what I coined years back as 'the reflexivity koan,'[19] the key and central question in this being: *What do you think about the way you think?*

After its opening Alec-Ash exchange, the formal section of Chapter 2 is the first of a two-part, scene-setting, selective discussion of background and context literature, within which I critically explore the philosophical, concep-tual, and related social scientific basis of *culture and cultural identity*, I do likewise with *narrative and narrative identity* in the second part in Chapter 3. Following this, in Chapter 4, my formal focus shifts to the nub of the book:

I subject my autoethnographic work from the last ten years to philosophical and related social scientific interrogation. In the last chapter (Chapter 5), I respond – point by point – to an extensive autocritique of the arguments and standpoint positions I've raised throughout.

The appendix at the end of the book will enable readers to get to know more about my work in summary form, cited and discussed in preceding chapters. Perhaps, after reading the appendix, they might also want to follow up on the full versions of some of the texts.

* * *

Ash: (What a superior sod!) Okay, a few things ... first, being stuck in 'oppressive,' 'life-limiting' stories. Who's to judge that a cultural story for any person is like that? Are you God? If so, hallebl**dylujah!

Alec: Fair comment. Okay, can I qualify what I said at this point? Sure – I'm prone to value judgements about cultural narrative entrapment. There are those who are perfectly happy with their lot, so amen to that. Some of these people have always worshipped at the Church of Low Expectations, but of course wouldn't agree at all that this is what they're doing. I think that being happy with one's lot relates to natural potential, curiosity, and education. Some people don't seem to have the ability to be anything other than what they are. Some seem constitutionally incurious. Education, or its lack thereof, can breed low expectations, which feeds back, reifying this lack and its consequences (more about all of this, next chapter). But there are others who are really not happy, sometimes without being or allowing themselves to be aware of this, who, given the right opportunities and circumstances, might palpably begin to realise and feel that they've been drifting along in a life-limiting way, through entrapment in stories imposed on them by others, by institutions, by organisations, and by life. I was one of those people, and I've written a fair bit about this.[20]

Ash: Hmmm! Beware solipsism, Alec! If people feel and tell themselves that they're happy, they're happy, so why should they bother resisting?

Alec: (Typical liberal-humanist reaction!) I can see how my need to get out of cultural bubbles and using my own experiences and work to justify this risks accusations of solipsism, Ash, but there's an implicit normative judgement in what you've just said. This is that I should leave people alone in their own bubbles (and, perhaps, be content to stay in mine?). The trouble with this view is that people are often unhappy in the face of others repeatedly telling them that they should be content with their lot. The title of Jeanette Winterson's great book, *Why Be Happy When You Could Be Normal*, springs to mind here.[21] Winterson's adoptive mother spoke these words to her, exemplifying a common tendency for 'normality' and 'happiness' to be imposed on people – one of the worst and cruellest examples of being pulled back into cultural line.

Ash: Okay, I get some of this ... but it seems linked to your rather pompous celebration of yourself as an 'outsider.' What makes you one of those? And are you implying you're outside everything? God stuff again!

Alec: Nobody can escape cultural narrative entrapment, Ash. Like everyone else, my cultural and narrative identities are always intersectionally and categorically situated at any one point in place and time of resistance to a cultural story which I feel is entrapping me. So, in that sense, my outsider status is both relative and reactive, and I'm no doubt flawed regarding aspects of my own privilege and power that regularly escape me. Phiona Stanley wisely reminds us that: 'We must problematize the "voice" in the ethnographic texts we produce. We must be aware of our own paradigm (and its inherent, non-neutral epistemology, ontology, and axiology).'[22] However, as I'll argue in the next chapter, I need to at least believe that I'm always on duty – continually alert to the potential for the cultures I'm inscribed within to **feel** entrapping.

Ash: Bit of a smartarse answer, Alec, and **believing** doesn't equate to actually **doing**, but I'll let that go. What I won't let go of is that you make far too much of all this philosophical and theoretical stuff! Let's get back down to earth! Autoethnography's primarily about storytelling, isn't it!? And anyone can tell a story.

Alec: I'm surprised and a bit exasperated by your comment here, Ash (you fucking dingbat!), given that you identify as an autoethnographer. Autoethnography's much more than just storytelling, although of course that's an important component. I've put quite a bit of effort in recent years into trying to educate people out of this lazy view,[23] and esteemed colleagues across the pond are currently trying to do likewise.[24] With a bit of luck, you might change your mind about this by the end of our book.

Ash: We'll see. You say it's not just about telling stories,[25] but it really is, isn't it? Too much theory can get in the way of a good story in my view. And do autoethnographers really need philosophy? While we're at it, stop being so rank-pulling patronising!

Alec: (Oh dear, autoethnography's just about the craic!) Again, I agree with you, Ash – at least to some extent. Theory-heavy work can drown out the significance and impact of autoethnographic stories. That said, if autoethnography is **just** about telling stories, writers can miss cultural issues altogether, or they can simply allude to them uncritically and unreflexively, as if culture was simply a neutral, uninteresting backdrop. In related terms, I believe that autoethnographic writers should strive to develop a working relationship with the philosophy that meets their writing and life needs.[26] If they don't have a sufficiently good philosophical handle on culture, cultural identity, and the concept of cultural narrative entrapment, they're in a relatively poor position to do anything about the latter when it impacts on them. Regarding your last point, I apologise, Ash. I always know I should express things more sensitively, but this would seriously get in the way of my 'Caledonian Antisyzygy' tendencies – how, as an often-irascible Scot, I combine the morally good and bad of my identity simultaneously in my work.[27] If only I'd been born with a tact gene! Too late now, I think – I'm too far gone (I bloody well know I'm too far gone).

Ash: Hmm ... another thing ... perhaps your standards and expectations are too unrealistically high! Do you always live up to them yourself?

Alec: Perhaps they are, and no, I don't. My standards and expectations are representative of ideal typical me rather than me as I am, but, thinking with Weber, the 'ideal type' is a great heuristic concept for helping us critically think about cultural issues. If I might suggest, you should, ideally, get yourself familiar with it, Ash! (you won't)[28] While we're on the topic of ideals, let's broaden things out a bit by looking at an important aspect of the autoethnographic community – specifically how some members and groups seem uncritically entrapped in their own autoethnographic practice cultures which, in my opinion, leaves a lot to be desired. That's me being tactful here, Ash. I really mean that what I'm about to describe grates on me to the extent that I want to scratch the soles of my feet until they bleed. Qualifier: I'm not talking about **all** people and **all** autoethnographic communities, just the ones I engage with regularly.

Ash: Go on.

Alec: Okay. There are people who claim the autoethnography tag in what they write/perform without bothering to find out much, if anything, about the approach, or its history, or its context in the social and human sciences. There are also those who write/perform 'evocative autoethnography' in slack, lazy ways,[29] who neither respect nor do justice to the seriousness of this methodological strand.[30] You can see them – they range from autoethnography neophytes to the more experienced and established – at conferences, churning out either sob stories,[31] or sentimental stories, or facile art modality pieces, or solipsistic, self-celebratory texts of little or no social or cultural significance, often in 'work' that seems to have been knocked up the night before.[32] In short, at its worst, I'm talking about stuff that's high on personal and vicarious – for performers, audiences, and organisers – therapy, and low in social science and cultural engagement, contributing little, if anything, to social justice.

In either case of ignorant or lazy performances – they sometimes overlap, of course), the necessary preparation and craft of serious engagement with autoethnography is sidestepped.[33] This is because of the complacent belief that writing culture- and analysis-free life stories and presenting those at conferences and smaller venues (they also sometimes creep into journal articles),[34] sometimes with sweet family pics, constitutes doing autoethnography. Now, I'm not saying these stories aren't important for their writers – I'm sure they're very meaningful, simply that I believe they're out of place in autoethnography performance and writing spaces. What I find particularly irritating and astonishing about these examples is that they often elicit enthusiastic reactions, sometimes of evangelical proportions, among audiences, and conference and local autoethnography interest group organisers, as opposed to mass embarrassment. Unconditional praise drowns out any possibility of critical dialogue.[35] So, **Poundshop autoethnography**:[36] The fun hobby requiring minimal effort. All win prizes!

I'm by no means on my own in taking a critical public stand against work which is either wrongly claimed by authors as autoethnographic or of too low a standard to be taken seriously. Andrew Herrman posted the following in a recent International Association of Autoethnography and Narrative Inquiry Facebook strand:

> As one of the JoAE[37] editors, I find too many people using the term Autoethnography in inappropriate ways … Writing a life chronology is not Autoethnography. Moreover, many people writing Autoethnography can't write well enough to satisfy the graphy of autobiography AND/OR the graphy of ethnography. We see so many submissions with these issues.
>
> *(10th February, 2024)*[38]

Ash: Woah!!!! That's all far too provocative and intemperate! Why raise this? It's just your deeply unpleasant opinion, and you're going to seriously upset people!!!! Also, Alec, in addition to being Professor Bl**dy High and Mighty, Virtuous and Superior, aren't you doing a fair bit of unwarranted and offensive labelling and stereotyping, to support your presupposed exalted, squeaky-clean position? Don't you do irony at all? You're projecting your prejudices onto loads of others!!

Alec: I fully acknowledge that it's provocative and intemperate, Ash. Like I said earlier, I find it difficult to be tactful. In any case I have a problem with the temperate-intemperate couplet. In my view, some things just need to be called out. Here's a serious theoretical but fairly obvious point now for this book: one 'how you do it' strategy for resisting cultural narrative entrapment is writing about those aspects of the culture or cultures you're inscribed with in that you find objectionable, offensive, and difficult to go along with. In related terms, this is also a great way to write yourself into a preferred identity.[39] That's exactly what I'm doing.

Ash: But you're a senior member of the autoethnographic world and, moreover, a professor![40] Should you not act in a more dignified and restrained way?!

Alec: What exactly is your idea of 'dignified and restrained'? Do you mean always engaging in nicespeak and happytalk? Thinking metaphorically, there's more than the over-controlled 'suit and tie' way of being a professor, Ash. And, by the way, I always look like I'm in fancy dress when I wear a suit, and that I'm being strangled on the rare occasions when I'm expected to wear a tie. In any case – talk about the pot calling the kettle black! – aren't you doing offensively expressed labelling and stereotyping yourself without acknowledging this, given that your position is premised on support for the people, groups, and the cultural-taken-for-granted I'm criticising? I know I'm breaking cultural decorum rules,[41] but I also know it to be the case that I'm giving voice to what a lot of well-seasoned people in the autoethnographic communities really believe but might be reluctant to publicly express.

This situation exists in large part in my view because of two types of cultural entrapment: first, an ethic of unconditional kindness emanating from the top down,[42] and second, the idea that professors and other grandees must always be restrained and polite. In terms of intercultural communication, the people in the first type are, I believe, driven by insufficiently scrutinised humanistic ideology and related values.[43] In moral terms, this is well intentioned, motivated as it is by the need for inclusivity and heartfelt human decency. However, I think it also functions in the interests of keeping silent that which needs speaking out about. I'm a miserable hypocritical sinner in this regard in allowing myself to be pulled into complicity with dodgy autoethnographic group norms, from conference and local interest group membership to book projects. I'm not an unkind man, and when people are nice and welcoming, and when projects are going smoothly, I find it difficult to be too critical. That's the social psychology of any form of organised human life for you – a centripetal pull into group cultural narrative entrapment is exerted, coming from everywhere and nowhere at the same time! It happens at a virtual level too: how many times do you see critical, including oppositional, debate on Facebook autoethnographic sites?

Ash: You'll never make Distinguished Professor Emeritus.

Alec: Tell me something I don't already know, Ash! I'm quite happy to end up as Extinguished University Professor Demeritritus. It's always great to be in my club for one. In any case, all the 'Distinguished' types will join me in extinguishing sooner or later, and by that time – like them – I'll be too dead to care. Can we move on to the next chapter now?

Ash: Hmmm! Okay. If we must!

Notes

1 Alec Grant, A. 'Drinking to Relax: An Autoethnography of a Highland Family Viewed through a New Materialist Lens,' in *Auto/Biography Yearbook 2017*, ed. Andrew Sparkes (Nottingham: Russell Press, 2018), 33–46. (6) (PDF) Paper for British Sociological Association Yearbook 2017, Drinking to Relax. (researchgate.net).
2 Alcoholics Anonymous.
3 My doctorate was formally a PhD by Publication (Retrospective). The thesis, or 'Critical Commentary,' was an exegesis – a critical analysis of 11 of my autoethnographic and theoretically autoethnography-related texts published between 2015 and 2024. These are all described and summarised in the appendix to this book. The chapters from my doctoral thesis, although greatly expanded, form the basis of this book.
4 Alec Grant, ed., *Writing Philosophical Autoethnography* (New York and London: Routledge, 2024).
5 I use the descriptor 'narrative autoethnography' to mean written, lived-experientially and auto/biographically based work of the kind found in journal articles, book chapters, and books. I distinguish this from arts-based autoethnographic modality work – for example, documentary film and animation – and have discussed this distinction in: Alec Grant, 'The Philosophical Autoethnographer,' in *Writing Philosophical Autoethnography*, ed. Alec Grant (New York and London: Routledge, 2024), 1–22.
6 Alec Grant, 'The Philosophical Autoethnographer,' in *Writing Philosophical Autoethnography*, ed. Alec Grant (New York and London: Routledge, 2024), 1–22.
7 Alec Grant, 'Living my Narrative: Storying Dishonesty and Deception in Mental Health Nursing,' *Nursing Philosophy* 17, no. 3 (2016): 194–201, https://doi.org/10.1111/nup.12127; Alec Grant, Helen Leigh-Phippard, and Nigel P. Short, 'Re-storying Narrative Identity: A Dialogical Study of Mental Health Recovery and Survival,' *Journal of Psychiatric and Mental Health Nursing* 22, no. 4 (2015): 278–286, https://doi.org/10.1111/jpm.12188.
8 Alec Grant, 'The Philosophical Autoethnographer,' in *Writing Philosophical Autoethnography*, ed. Alec Grant (New York and London: Routledge, 2024), 4.
9 Andrew Herrmann, and Tony E. Adams, *Assessing Autoethnography: Notes on Analysis, Evaluation, and Craft* (London and New York: Routledge, 2025).
10 My reluctance to be fully part of the club stems from the simple fact that – for the sake of integrity, given my standpoint position – I don't want to be culturally entrapped in it.
11 Arthur W. Frank, *Letting Stories Breathe: A Socio-Narratology* (Chicago: University of Chicago Press, 2010).
12 Lynn P. Nygaard and Kristin Solli, *Strategies for Writing a Thesis by Publication in the Social Sciences and Humanities* (London and New York: Routledge, 2021).

13 Alec Grant, 'The Philosophical Autoethnographer,' in *Writing Philosophical Autoethnography*, ed. Alec Grant (New York and London: Routledge, 2024), 1–22.

14 Trude Klevan, Email message to author, June 27, 2024.

15 Arthur W. Frank, *Letting Stories Breathe: A Socio-Narratology* (Chicago: University of Chicago Press, 2010).

16 George Herbert Mead, *Mind, Self, & Society from the Standpoint of a Social Behaviourist* (Edited and with an Introduction by Charles W. Morris) (London: The University of Chicago Press, Ltd. 1967 [1934]).

17 Vladimir Bibler, 'Arche,' in Vladimir Bibler (1918–2000), *Filosofia: An Encyclopedia of Russian Thought*, eds. Alyssa DeBlasio, and Mikhail Epstein, Filosofia: An Encyclopedia of Russian Thought (dickinson.edu).

18 Carolyn Ellis expressed this view online, at the 2024 International Symposium on Autoethnography and Narrative (IAANI) 'Ethics and Autoethnography' session, on the 1st of March, 2024.

19 Alec Grant, 'Writing Teaching and Survival in Mental Health: A Discordant Quintet for One,' in *Contemporary British Autoethnography*, eds. Nigel P. Short, Lydia Turner, and Alec Grant (Rotterdam: Sense Publishers, 2013), 38.

20 Alec Grant, A. 'Drinking to Relax: An Autoethnography of a Highland Family Viewed through a New Materialist Lens,' in *Auto/Biography Yearbook 2017*, ed. Andrew Sparkes (Nottingham: Russell Press, 2018), 33–46.

21 Jeanette Winterson, *Why Be Happy When You Could Be Normal* (London: Vintage, 2012).

22 Phiona Stanley, 'Autoethnography and Ethnography in English Language Teaching,' in *Second Handbook of English Language Teaching*, ed. Xuesong Gao (New York: Springer International Handbooks of Education), 1085, https://doi.org/10.1007/978-3-030–02899-2_55

23 Alec Grant, 'Dare to be a Wolf: Embracing Autoethnography in Nurse Educational Research,' *Nurse Education Today* 82 (2019): 88–92, https://doi.org/10.1016/j.nedt.2019.07.006; Alec Grant, 'Crafting and Recognising Good Enough Autoethnographies: A Practical Guide and Checklist,' *Mental Health and Social Inclusion* 27, no. 3 (2023): 196–209, https://doi.org/10.1108/mhsi-01-2023-0009; Alec Grant, 'In Praise of subjectivity: My Involvement with Autoethnography, and Why I Think You Should be Interested,' *Social Work and Social SCIENCES Review* 23, no. 3 (2023): 66–79, https://doi.org/10.1921/swssr.v23i3.2151

24 Andrew Herrmann and Tony Adams, *Assessing Autoethnography: Notes on Analysis, Evaluation, and Craft* (New York and London: Routledge, 2025).

25 Alec Grant, 'Crafting and Recognising Good Enough Autoethnographies: A Practical Guide and Checklist,' *Mental Health and Social Inclusion* 27, no. 3 (2023): 196–209, https://doi.org/10.1108/mhsi-01-2023-0009

26 Alec Grant, 'The Philosophical Autoethnographer,' in *Writing Philosophical Autoethnography*, ed. Alec Grant (New York and London: Routledge, 2024), 1–22.

27 Alec Grant, and Susan Young, 'A Scot an' a Sassenach Scrieve Aboot Leid: A Three Pairt Scotoethnography (A Scot and an English Person Write about Language: A Scotoethnography in Three Parts),' *Journal of Autoethnography* 5, no. 1 (2024): 39–55, https://doi.org/10.1525/joae.2024.5.1.39

28 Richard Swedberg, 'How to Use Max Weber's Ideal Type in Sociological Analysis,' *Journal of Classical Sociology* 18, no. 3 (2018): 181–196, https://doi.org/10.1177/1468795X17743643

29 Alec Grant, 'The Philosophical Autoethnographer,' in *Writing Philosophical Autoethnography*, ed. Alec Grant (New York and London: Routledge, 2024), 3.

30 Arthur P. Bochner, and Carolyn Ellis, *Evocative Autoethnography: Writing Lives and Telling Stories* (New York and London: Routledge, 2016).

31 Lifetime Contribution Award: Alec Grant (youtube.com).

32 Alec Grant, 'The Philosophical Autoethnographer,' in *Writing Philosophical Autoethnography*, ed. Alec Grant (New York and London: Routledge, 2024), 5.

33 Alec Grant, 'Crafting and Recognising Good Enough Autoethnographies: A Practical Guide and Checklist,' *Mental Health and Social Inclusion* 27, no. 3 (2023): 196–209, https://doi.org/10.1108/mhsi-01-2023-0009

34 Alec Grant, 'Crafting and Recognising Good Enough Autoethnographies: A Practical Guide and Checklist,' *Mental Health and Social Inclusion* 27, no. 3 (2023): 196–209, https://doi.org/10.1108/mhsi-01-2023-0009

35 Alec Grant, 'The Philosophical Autoethnographer,' in *Writing Philosophical Autoethnography*, ed. Alec Grant (New York and London: Routledge, 2024), 4.

36 Or 'dollar shop' in the USA, and international equivalents.

37 Journal of Autoethnography. Journal of Autoethnography | University of California Press (ucpress.edu).

38 International Association of Autoethnography and Narrative Inquiry (iaani.org).

39 Alec Grant, and Laetitia Zeeman, 'Whose Story Is It? An Autoethnography Concerning Narrative Identity,' *The Qualitative Report (TQR)* 17, no. 72 (2012): 1–12, http://doi.org/10.46743/2160-3715/2012.1735; Alec Grant, A. 'Drinking to Relax: An Autoethnography of a Highland Family Viewed through a New Materialist Lens,' in *Auto/Biography Yearbook 2017*, ed. Andrew Sparkes (Nottingham: Russell Press, 2018), 39.

40 At the time of writing this chapter, I was a visiting professor at the University of Bolton. At the beginning of May, 2024, I reverted back to my previous title of 'Independent Scholar.'

41 Adrian Holliday, *Understanding Intercultural Communication: Negotiating a Grammar of Culture*. 2nd edn. (London and New York: Routledge, 2019), 8–30.

42 I'm with many academics who believe that unconditional 'kindness' – in the sense of being too lenient and accepting of bar-lowering academic work – isn't only confined to autoethnography conferences. The neoliberalisation of universities across the world in our current times must inevitably result in more people being given prizes undeservedly.

43 Adrian Holliday, *Understanding Intercultural Communication: Negotiating a Grammar of Culture*. 2nd edn. (London and New York: Routledge, 2019), 24–25.

2

CULTURE AND CULTURAL IDENTITY

Alec: It's great that you're still with me, Ash?

Ash: Where do you imagine I'd be?

Alec: I've heard from you and your pals several times over the years that you start to disengage when autoethnography goes off-story into theory terrain – you said as much in the last chapter – and we're about to explore the philosophical and social scientific basis of culture and culture identity, with, I anticipate, a bit of dramatic literature and modern history thrown in for good measure. Strong in my mind right now is the memory of someone close to you who told me she'd rather play Candy Crush than read the theoretical and 'heavy' parts of my own and other autoethnography pieces?

Ash: God, you're insufferable!

Alec: That I am – for many people, Ash, but everything I've just said is objectively true. Anyway, let's crack on and see what you make of this....

***

Introduction

I approach this two-part background and context discussion – extended from the original in my doctoral thesis – in a selective and purposeful way. From the metaphorical position of the discussion constituting a textual 'archaeology,' I dig down in each part to define, explore, and interrogate the concepts central to my doctoral topic and research questions. Here, in Part 1, I discuss *culture*

DOI: 10.4324/9781003518594-2

and cultural identity, and, as in Part 2, I provide a developing answer to my first two doctoral inquiry questions:

- what constitutes resistance to cultural narrative entrapment in philosophical autoethnography?
- why is it important to resist cultural narrative entrapment in autoethnography?

I approach culture and cultural identity from the related perspectives of narrative autoethnography, philosophical discussion and argumentation, and social science. This gives me a purchase on autoethnographic cultural identity, which I discuss in the context of the continuum from uncritical acceptance to critical resistance I discussed in Chapter 1.

Autoethnography

A trawl through the ways in which autoethnographers relate to culture concept reveals commonly accepted views. These are well expressed by Stacy Holman Jones and her colleagues:

> ...autoethnographers intentionally *highlight* the relationship of their experiences, and stories to culture and cultural practices, with many authors choosing to launch a critique of this relationship in their work. If an author experiences an epiphany, reflects on the nuances of that experience, writes to show how the aspects of experience illuminate more general cultural phenomena and/or to show how the experience works to diminish, silence, or deny certain people and stories, then the author writes autoethnographically.[1]

Quite so, and notwithstanding the work of critique launchers, autoethnographers highlighting their lived-through experiences and narratives in relation to aspects of culture makes it likely that some will accept, endorse, and reify cultural narratives. This is implied in the phrase 'aspects of experience illuminate ... cultural phenomena,' since cultural lighting up can never be too far away from cultural celebration. The assumption that the decision to either celebrate or object to cultural narratives is made through choice rather than compulsion further suggests the likelihood of insufficiently scrutinised acceptance of, or complacency about, or possibly passive resignation to, the hegemony of cultural narratives among some claiming the 'autoethnographer' tag.

Moreover, although the centripetal pull of culture seems to be resisted by many autoethnographers in their claim to 'speak truth back to (cultural narrative) power,' as the popular autoethnographic slogan goes, there's a key distinction to be made between this and *resisting cultural narrative entrapment*.

If, for example, speaking truth to power proceeds from a liberal-humanist political philosophical cultural standpoint where freedom of choice over cultural positioning is assumed,[2] this can signal the legitimacy and status of *the* overarching, dominant cultural story represented. Those who buy into this story may believe themselves free to choose to either accept or reject their cultural positioning. In contrast, a critical cultural standpoint demands that autoethnographers display a greater degree of critical cultural consciousness regarding their relationship with culture, to the extent that the concepts of 'freedom,' 'choice,' and 'culture' itself, all need to be interrogated.

If, as was argued in Chapter 1, there's no escape from cultural narrative entrapment, it's important now to explore the issues of freedom and choice over cultural positioning. To recapitulate, the implicit continuum at play in what follows is between acceptance and resistance (and, by implication, between movement and inertia).

Culture as Ordinary

The philosopher and sociologist Raymond Williams argues in favour of the positive aspects of culture. According to Williams, culture is created through the performance of everyday human life in the service of sustaining and developing community purpose and meaning.[3] Williams contends that 'Culture is ordinary ... Every human society has its own shape, its own purposes, its own meanings ... The making of a society is the finding of common meanings and directions....'[4] Williams's phrase 'Every human society' can be understood in macro and micro senses. In macro terms, Williams refers to institutional life broadly, including centres of arts and learning, and from a micro perspective to the mundane particulars of ordinary life, 'with its emphases of neighbourhood, mutual obligation, and common betterment.'[5]

In relation to both macro and micro meanings, Williams's position is that culture is active and purposeful at individual and collective levels. In short, culture amounts to the varieties of ordinary life that people constantly bring into being. If we all co-create culture in this sense, then, notwithstanding constant cultural flux, change and development, and individual and collective resistance, clearly our relative choices and freedoms are constrained. For our day-to-day individual and collective lives to work and be reasonably coherent, although we can play about with and change the words, melody, and rhythm to some extent, we need to be singing from roughly the same cultural hymn sheet.

The psychologist Jerome Bruner complements Williams's position on culture and its implications for freedom and choice in arguing that culture is 'lifemaking' at the mundane, locally produced level.[6] In Bruner's sense, culture and storying culture are one and the same thing: 'Through cultural shaping ... we *become* the autobiographical narratives by which we "tell about" our lives.'[7] Anthony Giddens similarly supports this positive, agentic, and productive understanding of local, reflexively held culture.[8] His sociological standpoint is that people's knowledge about culture and skills in its performance are directly and dialogically 'geared to the flow of their day-to-day conduct.'[9] This theme, with similar implications for notions of choice and freedom, is also explored in *Learning to Labour*, Paul Willis's ethnography of working-class teenage schoolboys.[10] From the situated context of 1970s English Industrial Midlands working-class life, Willis argues the importance for the boys, and for their parents, of regarding culture – at school and in later working life – in the positive terms of local practical knowledge. This is directly oppositional to the kinds of formal, theoretical knowledge enshrined in academic paradigms, disparaged by this cultural group.

When understood as a local phenomenon, *doing*, *knowing about*, and *talking* culture necessitate purposeful rejection of the extensive and sophisticated, reflexively held wider and deeper cultural knowledge that only sustained engagement with education can provide. Moreover, thinking with Pierre Bourdieu,[11] the career and status-enhancing social capital that accompanies an education-centred cultural route is, by implication, also rejected. In sympathetically critiquing Willis's work, Giddens robustly presses this point home:[12] Willis's culturally resistive 'lads' had practical knowledge of their interlocking proximal, or local, cultures, and of how to negotiate those cultures to their advantage. However, this did not extend to sophisticated knowledge of the broader distal cultures within which these local cultures were embedded. In Giddens's words, the lads rejected this choice and the freedoms it promised, having 'at most an imprecise awareness of aspects of the wider society that influence the contexts of their own activity.'[13] This inevitably presaged a future of unskilled, unrewarding labour and regret – a point starkly expressed by Willis himself: '...as the shopfloor becomes a prison, education is seen retrospectively, and hopelessly, as the only escape.'[14]

Having analogous relevance to my doctoral thesis, an interesting issue emerges here: Giddens and Willis argue that schoolboys bound to better job prospects through being conformists to the school system might display a different form of cultural unsophistication, thus cultural narrative entrapment, *precisely because of their lack of critical cultural consciousness*. This relates to the concepts of 'discursive poverty' and 'discursive sophistication' which I'll pick up on in Chapter 3. For the moment it seems sufficient for me to assert that, despite relatively better educational preparation, a lack of criticality over aspects of culture conventionally accepted as hegemonic puts school conformists and their adult equivalents at a disadvantage. This directly relates to constraints around choice and freedom of cultural positioning that accompany the possession of a restricted discursive repertoire.

Critical Autoethnographicity

The idea of understanding culture and cultural identity in terms of people performing culture – bringing culture into being – positively and unselfconsciously in the flow of their daily lives cannot really be seriously argued against. I accept the obvious relevance and importance of such an understanding at the levels of progressive sociological and ethnographic work, and commonsense folk psychology. However, from my standpoint position and inquiry questions, and as a critical autoethnographic scholar, I have problems with this mundane take on culture. All humans simultaneously re-create and reify culture through its unending performance. The important question for me is the extent to which autoethnographers do this with adequate levels of critical reflexivity.

A moral requirement of critical autoethnography must be to rigorously interrogate the philosophical bases of cultural narrative identity, rather than taking this for granted.[15] The most promising concept for resisting cultural narrative identity in autoethnography is, I believe, captured in the term coined by my Polish autoethnographer colleague, Marcin Kafar: 'autoethnographicity.'[16]

Although the two concepts partially overlap in meaning, Kafar places autoethnographicity at a conceptual and moral remove from autoethnography. He defines autoethnographicity from a humanistic standpoint as

> ...an indispensable component of doing 'genuine' autoethnography ... autoethnographicity is not the same as 'autoethnography.' We are prone to see autoethnography as exclusively tied up with research practices ... whereas autoethnographicity refers to *common ideas, values and beliefs of humanistic origin,* available only to a few of us, *skilfully used to tell us about the inner and outer life of people.*[17]

When applying Kafar's autoethnographicity concept to resisting cultural narrative entrapment in my own autoethnographic writing, I need to shift its meaning in a critical direction, moving it from the domain of human relations to that of cultural critique. While agreeing that, in both its humanistic and critical readings, autoethnographicity sensibilities are available to the few rather than the many, I revise Kafar's original meaning, defining *Critical Autoethnographicity* as

> The commitment to live one's life autoethnographically, while being critically and robustly curious about, and reflexively open and responsive to the negative impact of cultural narratives on lived-through experience. This must be matched by a commitment to story resistance to cultural narrative entrapment in autoethnographic work.

I contend that critical autoethnographicity constitutes a continual alertness to the seductive power of cultural narrative entrapment. In contrast, cultural acceptance for non-culturally critical autoethnographers amounts, at worst in my view, to passively slotting cultural experiences into stock discursive categories without thinking too much about them and without worrying that these categories might be problematic or that aspects of culture might be problematic.

In this regard, based on my experience as a major contributor to the discipline, I have robustly critiqued a current trend I see in some of the autoethnographic literature and at conferences. This is of people claiming narrative autoethnography as their methodological orientation who often seem to take culture for granted in their writing, and therefore not in need of critical scrutiny,[18] beyond – as illustrated in the Holman Jones et al. quote above – illuminating aspects of culture in their work. This clearly fits with the uncritical acceptance of culture continuum position I raised in Chapter 1. A question naturally arises for me about whether such writers regard culture as benign, neutral backdrops to their lives or problematic. In the absence of seeing clarification of this in their work, I cannot answer this question.

My problem with such storied displays of culture and cultural identity is that I believe they are symptomatic of critical autoethnographicity deficiency. To put this more elaborately, what seems to me to be implicitly displayed are tacit assumptions of individual choice and freedom over cultural positioning. Combined with insufficient levels of reflexive critical scrutiny directed towards the negative aspects of culture overlapping with, and informing, cultural identity, this amounts to uncritical acceptance.

Cultures have Agency

What's gradually emerged for me through my autoethnographic work and doctoral study is the belief that *cultures have agency*. By this I mean that as socio-material forces they can exert a coercive centripetal pull-on people to conform, to toe the line. This makes notions of choice and freedom irrelevant – at least up to the point where individual and collective resistance might push back, or negative culture unexpectedly shifts in an atypical, positive direction. Writing from her lived-through experience as an inpatient in supposed 'mental health recovery' in our 2015 article, co-written with myself and Nigel Short, Helen Leigh-Phippard describes this last point well:

> A significant strand on my road to recovery was eventually being allocated a CPN who worked within a recovery value system and who seemed to want to patiently listen to me and help me to explore my own recovery path. Through dialogue with this CPN, whom I eventually came to trust, I found therapeutic value in beginning to understand what my experiences meant and what was happening to me. This contrasted with years of being simply given a diagnosis and told I should accept treatment provided on the

basis of mental health professionals knowing what was best for me and having any questioning by me of either diagnosis or treatment being regarded as further signs of illness. All of this contributed to me feeling *helped* as opposed to simply *managed*....[19]

As an autoethnographer sympathetic to the need for critical scholarship to destabilise cultural politics in the advancement of social justice,[20] my own interest in, and concerns about, culture consistently focuses on such negative aspects. Agentic culture understood in a negative sense is best represented for me by the critical scholar Sara Ahmed, in her description of it often constituting the entrapping 'space of the familiar.'[21] This understanding of culture is at the heart of my recent philosophical autoethnographic work[22] and the work of my autoethnographic colleague, Renata Ferdinand. Using the metaphor of the 'crooked room,' Ferdinand starkly describes the oppressive aspects of her own – gendered and racist – experiences of culture and how she is sometimes pulled into cultural line, again without much of a sense of either choice or freedom:

> Some ... are able to straighten themselves despite being in a crooked room; others unconsciously tilt themselves to align with the crooked surroundings. You would think I was a contortionist in the ways that I have bent myself into unimaginable and unnatural positions. I have had to navigate a world that has plagued Black women; Saphire, Mammy, Jezebel ... at various times I have both played into the role of a stereotype and actively resisted it.[23]

Agentic Cultures Need Queering

In understanding the performance of cultural identity in such a negative sense, in ways sympathetic to Ferdinand's description, I have argued based on my own lived-through experience and Ahmed's work that colluding with oppressive agentic culture can constitute *a bad habit*. This can override, cancel out, any feelings of freedom and choice over cultural positioning:

> Culture as the 'space of the familiar' – when we feel ourselves to be *in* culture – invites the critical philosophical autoethnographer to exercise the *queering gaze*. If we imagine culture as 'the skin of the social', then culture acquires a functional snug fit through how bodies, and by extension stories, inhabit and shape it ... Equally, bodies and stories acquire coherence through being inhabited and shaped by culture. Self thus flows through culture and culture flows through self, where 'culture', understood in this sense, is co-constructed and reified through habit and repetition ... By implication, some cultural habits are bad, and beg to be broken. Ahmed ... speaks to the benefits of profitably capitalizing on times of cultural

disorientation. Such 'queer moments' occur when you don't feel at home in the familiar.[24]

'Queering culture' can be understood as taking an oppositional, activist stand in word and deed to what is considered culturally normal and natural by 'bring(ing) to light the processes by which the normal and natural is produced.'[25] An important act of resistance to cultural narrative entrapment, 'queering' therefore directly maps onto autoethnographicity in constituting a kind of 'noticing,' or an attitude or sensibility, and a refusal of inscription within cultural narratives if such inscription is experienced as a compromising and integrity-violating mismatch between personal identity and cultural environment. Along with others, in highlighting and resisting their oppressive aspects, I have argued in recent years that health and mental health cultures need to be subjected to queering for them to change for the better.[26]

Research Questions One and Two

What provisional answers can be inferred for the first two of my research questions from Part 1 of my background and context discussion?

> *What constitutes resistance to cultural narrative entrapment in philosophical autoethnography?*
>
> Resistance to cultural narrative entrapment is evidenced by writing that displays critical rather than acceptance sensibilities towards represented culture or aspects of culture. It is conditioned by autoethnographicity-mediated continual alertness and opposition to the seductive power of cultures that might otherwise be regarded as 'ordinary,' timeless, non-contingent, or benign.
>
> *Why is it important to resist cultural narrative entrapment in autoethnography?*
>
> Far from being harmless, cultures can be experienced by many as harmful and oppressive. When this happens, it is important therefore to resist their power through the exercise of cultural queering, to pre-empt the often life-limiting centripetal pull towards cultural acceptance.

Conclusion

Having purposefully and selectively explored the literature on culture and cultural identity, I will end Part 1 with some clarification to my answers above. The qualified positive position of 'culture as ordinary' taken by Bruner, Giddens, Williams, and Willis displays both the benefits of conformity to local cultural life and its life-limiting consequences. From this position cultural narrative entrapment sneaks in through the back door, problematising the notions of 'freedom' and 'choice.' It is clearly not in the interests of cultural members to stand out in oppositional resistance to local values and mores, unless they set their sights on shifting their cultural locations to broaden their range of cultural resources and simultaneously accrue social capital. Many do not get to realise this until it is too late.

Resistance to accepting culture entails the accrual of cultural resources, and social and intellectual capital. Storying resistance to culture, by being alert in a cultural queering sense to the lived-through experience of being centripetally pulled back into line by oppressive cultural entrapment via reflexive critical autoethnographicity, thus emerges as vitally important in advancing critical philosophical autoethnography.

Conversely, cultural narrative entrapment is in large part defined by and entails cultural acceptance. Even if this is done willingly, the capacity for individual and collective lives to develop is restricted. This raises the question of how all this links to narrative and narrative identity, the focus of Chapter 3.

***

Ash: I really don't care what you say above, Professor Cleverspeak. I and a lot of other people, whom you seem to disparagingly categorise as bog-standard autoethnographers, still believe we have freedom of choice over cultural positioning. As do most people in the world, I might add.

Alec: Is that so, Ash? Let me run something past you. I recently sent a very close friend of mine – a Buddhist scholar, not an autoethnographer – a copy of the volume I recently co-edited with my colleague Elizabeth Lloyd-Parkes: *Meaningful Journeys: Autoethnographies of Quest and Identity Transformation.*[27] After he read the introductory chapter, he said the following in an email to me (I've his approval to share):

> *Your introduction has certainly caused me to think about the places I have been and what I got out of getting there and being there ... I've always seen myself as a somewhat independent traveller, making my own meaning out of the experience, even when on study tours of Israel and India, or pilgrimage in Nepal. It's always been my experience, my own interpretation, my own memory....*

Do you see any problems in what my friend said?

Ash: No, not at all. He's saying what I and a lot of others believe: cultural positioning is individual and underpinned by choice and freedom.

Alec: I agree of course that we have some degree of freedom about how to make sense of and interpret our experiences, but that 'freedom' is culturally shaped. Take my friend's comments about exclusive owner-ship of his memory. When we look back at our lives, we pull on other people's memories, not just our own. We also draw on popular culture material such as books and films, and on intergenerationally transmit-ted material of things, ideas, and concepts happening long before our birth. I'll be talking a lot about this in the next chapter, by the way.

Ash: I can't wait!!!!

Alec: Now now, Ash! Your defensive sarcasm does you no favours. Notice also how my friend uses the word 'my' a lot: my experience,' 'my inter-pretation,' 'my own meaning.' As well as using shared memory from which to construct meaning out of experiences, we all draw from the range of cultural discourses that go to make up our identities. Ris-ager and Dervin describe this well, arguing that our cultural identities constantly intersect with our interculturality, and we code switch as a function of the relational and material encounters we happen to be in.[28] We do so by deploying whichever of the myriad cultural identities happens to be available to us and is situationally dominant at any one time.[29] Interestingly for our conversation, this universal phenomenon usually escapes our notice – unless, of course, we're actively exercising our autoethnographicity sensibilities to queer the encounter.

In directly related terms, according to the cultural anthropologist Katherine Ewing, people across all cultures display context-dependent, rapidly shifting, multiple, and inconsistent self-representations. Ewing argues that although people experience themselves as whole, their dis-played selves at any one point in time can be quickly displaced by differ-ent 'selves,' as a function of the shifting definitions of the situations they find themselves in. It seems that we remain unaware of such shifts, and of the inconsistencies we display between different self-presentations, experiencing ourselves all the while as whole and continuous.[30]

So, in summary, Ash, it looks like we're not as free as we might like to think. Neither do we have unlimited scope for choice. Moreover, it seems unlikely that we're not in exclusive charge of our memories, experiences, or the interpretation of either of these. And, so the argu-ment goes, we switch codes and presented selves rapidly in response to context and situation, without tending to notice any of this.

Ash: But lived-through experience just doesn't feel like that at all! We should respect it and take it at face value.

Alec: I agree with you. We should. How would any of us get by regard-ing storying ourselves individually and collectively without doing this? But, ultimately, even the idea of 'storying ourselves' is problematic, to the extent that we tend to imagine that these stories are ours, and ours alone. This is a convenient fiction which doesn't make onto-epistemological sense.

Ash: Here you bl**dy well go again, Alec, with your ontology and epistemology!

Alec: Don't you think being and knowing are important for we-autoethnographers, given that we claim to be in the business of writing about our being and knowing? Just sayin'!

Ash: I can write about my being and knowing simply and straightforwardly, and evocatively I might add, despite your disparaging comments about this in the last chapter, without obscuring everything with philosophy, social science, and cultural studies stuff.

Alec: Well, personally, I don't think you can seriously do without these areas as an autoethnographer, or without the use of literature and poetry. They all intertwine. Let me ask you a question: somewhere along your life course, did you learn enough of the rules of grammar to be able to write reasonably coherently – rules that hold your writing together?

Ash: (What's he bl**dy getting at now!?) Yes, of course I did! So what?

Alec: So, there's also a grammar of culture that holds cultural positioning together. This is exactly what the linguistics and intercultural education scholar Adrian Holliday argues.[31] Let me summarise his model for you, as I understand it.[32] He describes our culture positioning as originating in the social and political structures we're born into. These give us cultural resources such as language and ideology, locating us politically in terms of the grand narratives of nationhood and history that shape and inform who we are, irrespective of how much and in what ways we take issue with them. At the level of personal trajectory, these grand narratives feed into our experiences of family and ancestry, our peer relationships, and even our choice of work and work relationships.

Underpinning all of this according to Holliday are what he calls 'underlying universal cultural processes.' These processes govern our 'small cultural' transactions (or small stories) where, like the positions expressed by Williams, Bruner, Giddens, and Willis that I discussed earlier, we make culture or bring culture into being through constructing its rules and meanings. This helps us in imagining ourselves and our intra- and intercultural others more effectively.

Lastly, according to Holliday's model, we have the 'particular cultural products' of our home culture. Thinking with Williams, these include the macro cultural institutional artefacts of art, literature, the media, and other cultural practices. Also included in the 'particular cultural products' category are statements about culture, which include cultural discourses, ideology and prejudice, and the cultural acts that constitute the outward performance of self and intra- and intercultural other.

Holliday writes that his model is more guiding metaphor than accurate map of interculturality, and that its stages should be imagined in circular rather than linear terms. Regarding his latter point, although particular social and political structures feed into personal trajectories, in turn governed by underlying universal – so transcultural – processes resulting in particular cultural products, there exists a kind of homeostatic 'pulling back into line' or centripetal force emanating from our particular social and political structures. As I understand Holliday, and if his argument is accepted – I find it compelling, this force tends to undermine resistance to cultural narrative entrapment. Thinking with Risager and Dervin, and Ewing again, even when we think we're resisting freely, we're restricted in the alternative cultural material we can mobilise in the service of resistance. This material is likely to have at least some of its roots in the shared cultural resources, and global positioning and politics, of the particular social and political structures that have come to shape who we are. The notions of 'choice' and 'freedom' over cultural positioning should therefore be thought about in constrained or limited, rather than absolute, terms.

Ash: You've made everything far too complicated for autoethnography in this chapter!

Alec: (Oh God!) Really?!

Ash: Yes!

Alec: How so?

Ash: Look, autoethnographers don't need to know all that stuff to do autoethnography! Simple as that! In any case, despite what you say, people are much more in charge of what they believe in and take from culture. I think that most ordinary people have enough of a sense of morality and common sense to do this, and to not cave in to cultural pulling and shaping.

Alec: Well, let's explore that a wee bit. What about the phenomenon of cultural trickery?

Ash: What do you mean?

Alec: Being ensnared in cultures you otherwise wouldn't sign up to, heart and soul, if you regarded them with a greater degree of suspicion.

Ash: You're paranoid! You want me to go around being suspicious of cultures, presumably like you!

Alec: Have you by any chance read Hannah Arendt's book, *Eichmann in Jerusalem: A Report on the Banality of Evil*?[33]

Ash: No (he's going seriously off-piste).

Alec: You seriously should (but you won't). It's the book of trial of Nazi leader, Adolf Eichmann, which Arendt was present at and covered for *The New Yorker* magazine in 1961. It's a fascinating read, not least because it shows how an ordinary person – Eichmann – can be suckered into believing in and doing unspeakably horrible things through a gradually increasing allegiance to culture. So successfully socialised into the Nazi regime was Eichmann that he couldn't countenance a point of view outside of his narrow cultural discourse. This is a good example of discursive poverty – again, more about this in the next chapter.

Arendt wrote that as she listened to Eichmann speak at the trial, it became obvious to her that he demonstrated both an inability to think and an inability to think empathically from the point of view of another person.[34] The ideas of thinking, and thinking about how other people might think, are important to hold in mind here, Ash. Arendt shows Eichmann to have been an unimaginative bureaucrat with zero empathy, who couldn't reflect outside of the Nazi box. Moreover, as Arendt also flagged up, he seemed only able to account for himself in self-serving clichés. In doing so, he failed to display any ability to operate beyond the narrow confines of facilitating and managing the mass deportation of millions of Jewish people to Nazi ghettoes and extermination camps, while seeing nothing wrong in any of this. In his estimation, he was simply doing his job and doing it well and faithfully, thank you very much. Hanged a year later, in 1962, Arendt writes that his 'horrible gift for consoling himself with clichés did not leave him in the hour of his death.'[35]

Ash: Okay, but come on? People like him are surely atypical, aren't they? He was far from ordinary. He and all these other Nazis were obviously just beasts.

Alec: Well, that's certainly the impression people had and have of him, then and now, and that was the presupposition of the legal people tasked with prosecuting him. However, although attracting a lot of flak for publicly expressing this at the time, as you'll realise if you read her book, Arendt argues that despite their best efforts, people could see he was much more clown than monster. As are many people, he was narrow-minded, rule-following, one-dimensional. Outside of his Nazi work environment, he comes across as boring and ineffectual. If he hadn't become caught up in Nazi culture and rewarded with the high rank of Lieutenant Colonel, it seems to me that he might have made an effective non-military bureaucrat in a different time and place, precisely because of his unquestioning adherence to rules and procedures.

Ash: You're implying that this could have happened to anyone at any time – that there are lots of Eichmanns around? Get real!

Alec: I'm saying that given the right time and place, lots of people, while harmless in other circumstances, could be easily recruited into cultures of evil. I'm not only talking about the Eichmanns of the world. In the historical study **Ordinary Men...**,[36] for example, Christopher Browning writes of 'middle-aged family men of working- and lower-middle-class background ... too old to be of use to the German army ... drafted instead into the Order Police ... facing the task of shooting some 1,500 Jews in the Polish village of Józefów in the summer of 1942.'[37]

Browning argues throughout his book that these men were often average, run-of-the-mill types. Some of them – like Eichmann – might have been lacking in imagination, including empathic imagination, but not all were. Some were reluctant executioners, asking to be excused of the task before the slaughter began. According to Browning, this amounted to only a dozen out of almost 500 men, with, he estimates, 10–20 percent evading the shooting or asking to be released from the firing squads after the executions began.[38] So, approximately 400 fulfilled the task. Some of those, again like Eichmann, might have been culture- and nation-centric without either reflexively recognising this or being particularly nationalistic, at least to start with. Others were like you and me. How many people fitting this broad picture do you know, Ash? I know loads – just about everyone.

Ash: How can you say that? Most people wouldn't be instrumental in genocide.

Alec: History doesn't support what you've just said. It's not just people like Eichmann – one-dimensional in their experience of the world – who get pulled into vile cultural stories such as the Shoah.[39] Ordinary, non-extreme, more rounded people are also susceptible, and the pressure to socially conform is always strong: Browning describes 'the basic identification of men in uniform with their comrades and the strong urge not to separate themselves from the group by stepping out.'[40]

Elizabeth Minnich, Hannah Arendt's teaching assistant, describes the kind of systematic horrific harm-doing that Eichmann and less extreme others perpetrated as 'Extensive Evil.'[41] This phrase suggests that such harm-doing can be widespread, raising questions about the psychological states that are required on the part of perpetrators for this to happen. In the introduction to Eichmann in Jerusalem..., Amos Elon describes Arendt's view of the extremes of this kind of banal thinking in striking terms, asserting that she came to regard the 'faceless bureaucratic' culture that entrapped Eichmann required him to have 'a kind of brainlessness, and an "inner void" of 'moral and intellectual shallowness.'[42] However, if you think of a continuum, Ash, from a pole of Extensive Evil to an opposite, place-of-saints pole of Extensive Good, Minnich supports Arendt in asserting that, contra popular opinion, the people on the Extensive Evil end are not the psychopaths and monsters of the world. Echoing Browning's study, they can be ordinary, ranging from shy and retiring next door neighbours to ambitious colleagues, and often banal in their thinking and behaviour.

Why do people allow themselves to be caught up in such cultures? Minnich argues in her book that people who perpetrate Extensive Evil are incentivised to buy into cultural value systems – as all of us buy, and are bought, into cultural value systems to greater or lesser extents – not just by national loyalty and the social conformity pressures Browning mentions, although these play a part, but by such things as better jobs, pay rises, and better housing. In the face of this, ordinary goodness goes out the window, even for people at the edges of cultures of Extensive Evil. In Elon's words, 'Conventional goodness became a mere temptation which most Germans were fast learning to resist.'[43] Isn't there a sense that we're most of us complicit in entrapment in morally egregious cultures, Ash?

Ash: No! I strongly disagree. More intelligent and thoughtful people wouldn't fall prey to such things!

Alec: Well, it's interesting that you say this. The Glaswegian Jewish Marxist writer, C.P. Taylor wrote a marvellous play in the early 1980s, called Good.[44] Set in 1930s Germany, it centres around Halder, a liberal Professor of German literature. Through a combination of moral cowardice and low-level corruption, he becomes socialised into the Nazi war machine and gets involved in the Auschwitz death project. A bit like Eichmann, he continues to convince himself that he's a good man who's behaving honourably. He does this despite his becoming a Nazi Schutzstaffel officer, his complicity with, and self-justification of, anti-intellectual book burning in the name of the regime, and the betrayal of Maurice, his Jewish psychiatrist long-term and closest friend.

Ash: Yes, but fiction isn't real life. Intellectuals in general have stronger moral convictions.

Alec: We clearly come from different planets, Ash, so can I take the opportunity at this point to welcome you most fucking warmly to ours and to its modern history. Established and rising intellectuals were implicated in the support and development of Nazism from the get-go – philosophers and sociologists, scientists and physicians, theologians and spiritual leaders, and a range of others, some like Halder. Go onto Wikipedia and type in 'List of Nazi ideologues' if you doubt me!

See what comes up. Think of Martin Heidegger and the argument, based on textual evidence, for the appearance of anti-Semitism in his philosophy.[45] Think also of the disparagement of books our times, their banning from libraries in parts of the US, because of shit-stupid hard right Trumpy attitudes. And think of the fact that you're not exactly an enthusiastic bibliophile yourself. People like you are always banging on about the importance of 'lived experience' over theory, thus books. Join the dots, Ash, and win a major prize.

Ash: (What a b*st*rd!) I don't like your superior tone, and the fact that you've got a bl**dy answer for everything!

Alec: (Idiot!) I'm just responding to your questions, and I read and think a lot. So should you as a self-styled autoethnographer. I couldn't very well answer through the medium of mime or dance – but maybe you'd prefer that? Less taxing? Good time to move on now, to look at narrative and narrative identity? Before we do, do you fancy a wee game of Candy Crush?

Ash: You're a complete a***hole!

Notes

1 Stacy Holman Jones, Tony E. Adams, and Carolyn Ellis, 'Introduction: Coming to know Autoethnography as More than a Method,' in *Handbook of Autoethnography*, eds. Stacy Holman Jones, Tony E. Adams, and Carolyn Ellis (Walnut Creek, CA: Left Coast Press, Inc., 2013), 23.
2 Alec Grant, 'Troubling "Lived Experience": A Poststructural Critique of Mental Health Nursing Qualitative Research Assumptions,' *Journal of Psychiatric and Mental Health Nursing* 21 (2014): 544–549, https://doi.org/10.1111/jpm.12113; Alec Grant, 'Storying the World: A Posthumanist Critique of Phenomenological-Humanist Representational Practices in Mental Health Nurse Qualitative Inquiry,' *Nursing Philosophy* 17 (2016): 290–297, https://doi.org/10.1111/nup.12135
3 Raymond Williams, 'Culture is Ordinary,' in *Resources of Hope: Culture, Democracy, Socialism*, ed. Robin Gable (London and New York: Verso, 1989 [1958]), 3–18.
4 Raymond Williams, 'Culture is Ordinary,' in *Resources of Hope: Culture, Democracy, Socialism*, ed. Robin Gable (London and New York: Verso, 1989 [1958]), 4.
5 Raymond Williams, 'Culture is Ordinary,' in *Resources of Hope: Culture, Democracy, Socialism*, ed. Robin Gable (London and New York: Verso, 1989 [1958]), 8.
6 Jerome Bruner, 'Life as Narrative,' *Social Research* 71, no. 3 (Fall 2004): 691–710, http://doi.org/10.1353/sor.2004.0045
7 Jerome Bruner, 'Life as Narrative,' *Social Research* 71, no. 3 (Fall 2004): 694, http://doi.org/10.1353/sor.2004.0045
8 Anthony Giddens, *The Constitution of Society: Outline of the Theory of Structuration* (Cambridge: Polity Press, 1984).
9 Anthony Giddens, *The Constitution of Society: Outline of the Theory of Structuration* (Cambridge: Polity Press, 1984), 281.
10 Paul Willis, *Learning to Labour: How Working-class Kids get Working-class Jobs* (Aldershot, Hants: Gower Publishing 1988 [1977]).

11 Pierre Bourdieu, 'The Forms of Capital,' in *Handbook of Theory and Research for the Sociology of Education*, ed. John G. Richardson (London: Bloomsbury, 1986), 241–258.

12 Anthony Giddens, *The Constitution of Society: Outline of the Theory of Structuration* (Cambridge: Polity Press, 1984), 290–291.

13 Anthony Giddens, *The Constitution of Society: Outline of the Theory of Structuration* (Cambridge: Polity Press, 1984), 292.

14 Paul Willis, *Learning to Labour: How Working-class Kids get Working-class Jobs* (Aldershot, Hants: Gower Publishing 1988 [1977]), 107.

15 Alec Grant, 'The Philosophical Autoethnographer,' in *Writing Philosophical Autoethnography*, ed. Alec Grant (New York and London: Routledge, 2024), 1–22; Alec Grant, 'In Search of My Narrative Character: A Philosophical Autoethnography,' in *Writing Philosophical Autoethnography*, ed. Alec Grant (New York and London: Routledge, 2024), 114–132.

16 Marcin Kafar, 'Traveling with Carolyn Ellis and Art Bochner, or How I became Harmonized with the Autoethnographic Life: An Autoformative story,' in *Advances in Autoethnography and Narrative Inquiry: Reflections on the Legacy of Carolyn Ellis and Arthur Bochner*, eds. Tony E. Adams, Robin M. Boylorn, Lisa. M. Tillmann (New York and London: Routledge, 2021), 48–63; Alec Grant and Elizabeth Lloyd-Parkes, 'Meaningful Journeys, Identity Transformation, and Autoethnographic Selfhood,' in *Meaningful Journeys: Autoethnographies of Quest and Identity Transformation*, eds. Alec Grant and Elizabeth Lloyd-Parkes (London and New York: Routledge, 2024), 1–16; Marcin Kafar and Justyna Ratkowska-Pasikowska, 'Conversational Autoethnography on Experiencing Loss and Grief,' in *Autoethnographies in Psychology and Mental Health: New Voices*, eds. Alec Grant and Jerome Carson (London and New York: Routledge, In Press), 152–170.

17 Marcin Kafar, 'Traveling with Carolyn Ellis and Art Bochner, or How I became Harmonized with the Autoethnographic Life: An Autoformative story,' in *Advances in Autoethnography and Narrative Inquiry: Reflections on the Legacy of Carolyn Ellis and Arthur Bochner*, eds. Tony E. Adams, Robin M. Boylorn, Lisa. M. Tillmann (New York and London: Routledge, 2021), 59.

18 Alec Grant, 'The Philosophical Autoethnographer,' in *Writing Philosophical Autoethnography*, ed. Alec Grant (New York and London: Routledge, 2024), 1–22.

19 Alec Grant, Helen Leigh-Phippard, and Nigel P. Short, 'Re-storying Narrative Identity: A Dialogical Study of Mental Health Recovery and Survival,' *Journal of Psychiatric and Mental Health Nursing* 22, no. 4 (February 2015): 282, https://doi.org/10.1111/jpm.12188

20 Stephen T. Leonard, *Critical Theory in Political Practice* (Princeton, NJ: Princeton University Press, 1990).

21 Sara Ahmed, *Queer Phenomenology: Orientations, Objects, Others* (Durham, North Carolina: Duke University Press, 2006), 34.

22 Alec Grant, 'The Philosophical Autoethnographer,' in *Writing Philosophical Autoethnography*, ed. Alec Grant (New York and London: Routledge, 2024), 1–22; Alec Grant, 'Concluding Thoughts: Selves, Cultures, Limitations, Futures,' in *Writing Philosophical Autoethnography*, ed. Alec Grant (New York and London: Routledge, 2024), 249–269.

23 Renata Ferdinand, 'Which Way Is Up: A Philosophical Autoethnoraphy of Trying to Stand in a "Crooked Room,"' in *Writing Philosophical Autoethnography*, ed. Alec Grant (New York and London: Routledge, 2024), 80–95, quote page 82–83.

24 Alec Grant, 'The Philosophical Autoethnographer,' in *Writing Philosophical Autoethnography*, ed. Alec Grant (New York and London: Routledge, 2024), 16–17.

25 Laetitia Zeeman, Kay Aranda, and Alec Grant, 'Introduction,' in *Queering Health: Critical Challenges to Normative Health and Healthcare*, eds. Laetitia Zeeman, Kay Aranda, and Alec Grant (Ross-on-Wye: PCCS Books, 2014), 9.

26 Laetitia Zeeman, Kay Aranda, and Alec Grant, 'Queer Challenges to Evidence-based Practice,' *Nursing Inquiry* 21, no. 2 (June, 2013): 101–111, https://doi.org/10.1111/nin.12039; Alec Grant, Laetitia Zeeman, and Kay Aranda, 'Queering the Relationship between Evidence-based Mental Health and Psychiatric Diagnosis: Some Implications for International Mental Health Nurse Curricular Development,' *Nurse Education Today* 35, no. 10 (October 2015): e18–e20, https://doi.org/10.1016/j.nedt.2015.07.033; Laetitia Zeeman, Kay Aranda, and Alec Grant, eds. *Queering Health: Critical Challenges to Normative Health and Healthcare* (Ross-on-Wye: PCCS Books, 2014); Alec Grant, 'Breaking the Grip: A Critical Insider Account of Representational Practices in Cognitive Behavioural Psychotherapy and Mental Health Nursing,' in *Queering Health: Critical Challenges to Normative Health and Healthcare*, eds. Laetitia Zeeman, Kay Aranda, and Alec Grant (Ross-on-Wye: PCCS Books, 2014), 116–133; Alec Grant, and Helen Leigh-Phippard, 'Troubling the Normative Mental Health Recovery Project: The Silent Resistance of a Disappearing Doctor,' in *Queering Health: Critical Challenges to Normative Health and Healthcare*, eds. Laetitia Zeeman, Kay Aranda, and Alec Grant (Ross-on-Wye: PCCS Books, 2014), 100–115; Laetitia Zeeman, Kay Aranda, and Alec Grant, 'Queer Challenges to Evidence-based Mental Healthcare,' in *Queering Health: Critical Challenges to Normative Health and Healthcare*, eds. Laetitia Zeeman, Kay Aranda, and Alec Grant (Ross-on-Wye: PCCS Books, 2014), 79–99.

27 Alec Grant and Elizabeth Lloyd-Parkes, 'Meaningful Journeys, Identity Transformation, and Autoethnographic Selfhood,' in *Meaningful Journeys: Autoethnographies of Quest and Identity Transformation*, eds. Alec Grant, and Elizabeth Lloyd-Parkes (London and New York: Routledge, 2024), 1–16.

28 Karen Risager and Fred Dervin, 'Introduction,' in *Researching Identity and Interculturality*, eds. Fred Dervin and Karen Risager (London and New York: Routledge, 2015), 1–25.

29 This links to Nietzschean Drive theory, which I discuss in Chapter 5.

30 Katherine P. Ewing, 'The Illusion of Wholeness: Culture, Self, and the Experience of Inconsistency,' *Ethos* 18, no. 3 (September 1990): 251, https://psycnet.apa.org/doi/10.1525/eth.1990.18.3.02a00020

31 Adrian Holliday, *Understanding Intercultural Communication: Negotiating a Grammar of Culture*. 2nd edn (London and New York: Routledge, 2019).

32 Adrian Holliday, *Understanding Intercultural Communication: Negotiating a Grammar of Culture*. 2nd edn (London and New York: Routledge, 2019), 1–6.

33 Hannah Arendt, *Eichmann in Jerusalem: A Report on the Banality of Evil* (London: Penguin Books, 2006 [1965]).

34 Hannah Arendt, *Eichmann in Jerusalem: A Report on the Banality of Evil* (London: Penguin Books, 2006 [1965]), 49.

35 Hannah Arendt, *Eichmann in Jerusalem: A Report on the Banality of Evil* (London: Penguin Books, 2006 [1965]), 55.

36 Christopher R. Browning, *Ordinary Men: Reserve Police Battalion 101 and the Final Solution in Poland* (London: Penguin Books, 2001).

37 Christopher R. Browning, *Ordinary Men: Reserve Police Battalion 101 and the Final Solution in Poland* (London: Penguin Books, 2001), 1–3.

38 Christopher R. Browning, *Ordinary Men: Reserve Police Battalion 101 and the Final Solution in Poland* (London: Penguin Books, 2001), 71, 74.

39 The Hebrew term for the Holocaust.

40 Christopher R. Browning, *Ordinary Men: Reserve Police Battalion 101 and the Final Solution in Poland* (London: Penguin Books, 2001), 71.

41 Elizabeth Minnich, *The Evil of Banality: On the Life and Death Importance of Thinking* (Lanham, MD: Rowman & Littlefield, 2017).

42 Amos Elon, 'Introduction,' in *Eichmann in Jerusalem: A Report on the Banality of Evil*, ed. Hannah Arendt (London: Penguin Books, 2006 [1965]), vii–xviii.

43 Amos Elon, 'Introduction,' in *Eichmann in Jerusalem: A Report on the Banality of Evil*, ed. Hannah Arendt (London: Penguin Books, 2006 [1965]), xiii.

44 Cecil P. Taylor, *Good* (London: Methuen, 1982).

45 Peter Trawny, *Heidegger and the Myth of a Jewish World Conspiracy* (Chicago: The University of Chicago Press, 2015).

3
NARRATIVE AND NARRATIVE IDENTITY

Ash: I've been thinking about Eichmann. You said at one point that he didn't necessarily have to have a nationalistic cultural identity driving him in a Shoah-complicit direction. Who on earth are you trying to kid?

Alec: I'm pleased you've picked up on this, Ash. I'm sure I couldn't pull the historical wool over your unblinkered sagacious eyes. If you remember, I also qualified what I said by implying that he didn't necessarily have to have this at the start of his increasing cultural entrapment. From reading Arendt's account, I think that his complicit identity gradually developed the more he was socialised into the Nazi cultural story and rewarded for this. This is ironic, given the ideological myth of national cultural identity in the first place – which wouldn't of course have been likely to enter his consciousness.

Ash: What do you mean? In the last chapter, in summarising Holliday's position, didn't you assert that we're all born into structures that 'locate us politically in terms of the grand narratives of nationhood and history that shape and inform who we are.' I get the ideology bit, but why mythical? Nations are nations are nations!

Alec: I did, Ash, that's right. But Holliday intended his model as a kind of metaphorical guide. You're being a bit too literal-realist here. As I went on to say, although we're born into those structures, we can certainly take issue with them as a kind of resistance to meta-cultural narrative entrapment. In the first place, in metaphysical terms, national identity is an 'invented kind' rather than a 'natural kind.' By this I mean that

DOI: 10.4324/9781003518594-3

nature is indifferent to the idea of nationhood; there's nothing built into nature that makes national narrative identity, nationhood, nationalism, and the idea of 'nations' necessary or inevitable. All these concepts are sociocultural constructions – contingent rather than essential. In fact, the political philosopher and historian Benedict Anderson goes so far as to call nations 'imagined communities,' which, he argues, emerged as such with the advent of printing.[1] In Anderson's terms, people in in any one language-field, 'connected through print, formed ... the embryo of the nationally imagined community.'[2]

My own country of birth only gradually became the substantive nation of Scotland in the social, geographical, historical, and administrative imaginaries between the 9th and 11th centuries. During the time of Roman colonisation, my home area – originally the land of my ancestors, the Picts – was called 'Caledonia,' before becoming 'Alba' and, finally, as a collection of increasingly disparate peoples, 'Scotland.'[3] I'm reasonably confident that the glens, mountains and heather didn't give a panpsychic rat's arse about what the space they occupied was called, and neither did the rats for that matter.[4] To pull on the moral philosophy of Alasdair MacIntyre,[5] it's certainly true for me that a major background story I found myself a part of while growing up there was that of British nationhood. This was an Anglicized version; we learned about Scottish battles, and kings and queens at school, but weren't allowed to talk about any of this in our language of Scots.[6] Many of my ancestors joined the military in the service of Scotland extending to 'Great Britain,' my father was in the British Army during the war, and in my teens I followed my brother into the British Royal Air Force.[7] I took my background nationalism for granted, but, at the age of 72, I came to reject the relevance and importance for me of this concept and, in related terms, of 'nation' and 'nationhood.'

Ash: Why? And where does that leave you? If you haven't got a national identity, what have you got, pray tell?

Alec: If I was forced to pigeonhole my narrative identity in political philosophical terms, I'd describe myself as a 'cosmopolitan.'

Ash: (Pretentious sod!) Explain!

Alec: (Ignormamus!) Okay, at a general abstract level, 'cosmopolitanism' refers to a primary allegiance to the worldwide community of human beings.[8] This allegiance is based on the idea of progressing global justice[9] and an assumption that people exist in a shared state of rational interdependency.[10] At a moral philosophical level, this places the person as the fundamental unit of concern irrespective of other affiliations, national or otherwise.[11] So, national geographical boundaries are irrelevant to cosmopolitan thinking. It seems to me that all of this implicates a key moral pedagogic dimension to cosmopolitanism. This is the commitment to civic education for world citizenship, to enable people to see themselves more clearly through intercultural empathy building. Heightened consciousness of the lives of people in different parts of the world entails for the cosmopolitan a developing empathic appreciation of what would otherwise, from a national culture-centric position, possibly seem strange and alien.

Ash: Okay, thanks for the mini-TED talk (boring!), but can't someone be proud of their nation and cosmopolitan at the same time? Your unnecessarily highfalutin argument throws the national baby out with the cultural bathwater.

Alec: Good point, Ash, but please stop knocking how I express things. I'm drawing on a respectable philosophical and historical lines of inquiry that're in the public domain. As always, you should do more reading (but you sodding well wont!).

I'm personally proud of being a Scot. I wear tartan from time to time – purely as a symbolic heritage allegiance gesture given that tartan is part of the invention of Scottish Highland tradition.[12] I also play Scottish music on the fiddle and other instruments, so I'm by no means suggesting the need for a homogeneity of intercultural identity, but that doesn't make me nationalistic. If you can bear it, let's have a look at what I dislike about nationalism, again from a political philosophical perspective, with a wee bit of history and poetic literature thrown in. The Scottish-American philosopher Alasdair MacIntyre views national moral identity through the lens of patriotism, characterised by nationally loyal identity.[13] In MacIntyre's terms, this identity is local and partitioned. Deeply personal national identity thus characterised is learned in a particular place from a particular cultural community. It's bounded by a shared, appreciative construction of a coherent past, present, and aspirational future.

Ash: Okay, here you go again Dr Show-Off (haggis-gobbler)! What on earth is wrong with that?

Alec: What's wrong with it is that it's exempted from impersonal moral scrutiny which would threaten an emotional, as opposed to rational, devotion to one's own nation. From a political philosophical position complementing MacIntyre's, David Miller argues against cosmopolitan identity and corresponding knowledge of the world in favour of 'wilful ignorance,' 'complete indifference,' and, echoing the nationalistic view of the Scottish Enlightenment philosopher David Hume over two centuries before, a 'triumph of sentiment over reasoned argument.'[14]

Such unscrutinised romantic attachment to the local and familiar can get you into deep – sometimes terminal – shit, Ash. Google Wilfred

Owen's great World War I poem, Dulce et Decorum Est, for example – it's easy to find online: Owen issues a warning – to schools, teachers, parents, and adults – not to:

> tell with such high zest
> To children ardent for some desperate glory,
> The old Lie: *Dulce et decorum est*
> *Pro patria mori.*

Owen's warning about 'the old lie,' which translates from the Latin as it is good and fitting to die for one's country, has never been taken very seriously by people in general. Based on what we've been discussing so far, Ash, let me run a hypothetical short story about a boy and his family and community past you:

> Wayne is born into a small-town, English working-class, industrial community, whose inhabitants share a generally high level of national-patriotic identity. Many in the community assume that they live in a geographically-boundaried, real rather than imaginary, nation, having a coherent past, present and anticipated future. The moral status and features of this national and local community-derived shared identity are transgenerational, residually normative, and thus difficult to renounce. Wayne is a bright lad with nascent cosmopolitan tendencies, and some of his more liberal teachers try to encourage him to set his sights on a university education. But he's swayed by the tabloid and social media he's exposed to in his home and town, by some of the more traditional teachers, and by his participation in the local Army cadet force. He's also equally anxious to please his dad who has a military background and values, and who wants him to leave school early to join the Army. Wayne does this, is sent to Afghanistan and dies in 2009, a few days before his 19th birthday when the tank he's in is blown up. His family, and those who knew him in his community, are left simultaneously grieving and proud.[15]

Ash: Your views could alienate loads of autoethnographers, from beginners to seasoned, especially those with a military past, who have a more moderate and normal take on national cultural identity.

Alec: (Yeah, yeah, yawn!) So be it Ash, blessed be the moderate and normal for they shall always inherit more of the bloody same … but let's crack on.

***

Introduction

In this second part of the background and context discussion, I interrogate the conceptual areas of *narrative* and *narrative identity*. This enables me to complete my answers to my first two inquiry questions:

- What constitutes resistance to cultural narrative entrapment in philosophical autoethnography?
- Why is it important to resist cultural narrative entrapment in autoethnography?

Historical and Philosophical Context

To understand the significance of narrative and narrative identity in autoethnography, it is necessary to briefly outline the emergence of both concepts in the historical and philosophical context of narrative inquiry in the social sciences. Narrative inquiry increasingly secured its place there in the last few decades of the 20th century, in the wake of the so-called 'crisis of representation.' This period of academic growth drew attention to the general absence of human stories, emotions, embodied experiences, and artistic issues in social science texts. Storytelling, the positioning of the researcher's perspective within such texts, and the literary and aesthetic status of subjectivist scholarship were all seen to be devalued by mainstream social science representational tendencies.[16] In pushing back against this – still currently lingering – trend from an explicitly philosophical autoethnographic perspective, Art Bochner and Nicholas Riggs argue that stories are critically important in bearing witness to the experience of being human and human suffering.[17]

In this regard, stories, and storytelling in the social sciences, subsuming autoethnography, signal efforts exerted by writers to redeem their humanity. The continued relative absence of such stories from social science research in general is therefore remarkable, given the view that people with storied experiences know best about what it means to live through challenging times.[18] Related to the relative absence of what Tønnessen describes as 'small stories' to combat the bigger stories – or discourses – of positivism, an often-dismissive attitude is directed towards the former by proponents of the latter.

However, this situation has been significantly ameliorated by several landmark 'moments' occurring within the last five decades. These stand out as influential in placing *narrative* as the root metaphor for understanding human social life. From a psychoanalytic perspective, Donald Spence distinguished between 'narrative truth' and 'historical truth.'[19] His argument is that rather than objectively verifiable events (historical truth), the *meanings* given to these events (narrative truth) are key in shaping people's understanding of their lives. In other words, objective historical events are always subjectively and inter-subjectively interpreted and re-storied. In related terms, Theodore

Sarbin and Jerome Bruner promoted narrative psychology as an alternative to positivist psychological research,[20] while equivalent paradigm shifts in communication studies and sociology, spearheaded by Art Bochner and Nicholas Riggs, Carolyn Ellis and Michael Flaherty, and Laurel Richardson, influenced the shape and purpose of a hope-imbued narrative inquiry.[21]

Making the social sciences truly *human* necessitates creatively locating people, meaning, and personal and relational identity centre-stage in social research for the celebration rather than the disparagement of subjectivity. This has emerged as a need to remedy social fragmentation, isolation, and disconnection. Over the last two decades, Gayle Letherby has championed the importance of subjectivity in her narrative sociological research and writing, in the context of feminist scholarship,[22] and in the specific context of what she describes as 'theorised subjectivity.'[23] Letherby uses this term to stress the importance of rigorous and constant critical interrogation of the multifaceted aspects of situated personhood in narrative social research. In her terms, doing so undermines the false binary between 'objective' and 'subjective' positions in making such research *value-explicit* rather than *value-free*.

Methodology and Resisting the Centripetal Pull

The increasingly well-established narrative turn in the social sciences has thus through the years attracted scholars who want 'to imagine, discover, or create … new and better ways of living.'[24] In terms of putting this into methodological practice at trans-disciplinary levels, Catherine Kohler Riessman provides a guide for developing and using narrative methods,[25] while Arthur Frank articulates the need for a change in the status of research narratives.[26] In his terms, more than just central to human meaning, these narratives should be accorded the status of *semi-independent, autonomous agency as social actors*, to the extent that they are dialogic and unfinalised. As open-ended, relatively free-floating entities, stories are always inevitably passed on to readers for further development and meaning creation. To recapitulate, an important negative implication emerging from this as a matter of logic is that some stories exert a centripetal force in pulling people back into, often oppressive, cultural line.

Discourse

Two questions related to this implication – in both its negative and positive senses – need to be asked at this point: 'How do people *live* narrative identity and what are its functions?' Drawing on the work of Mikhail Bakhtin, Daphna Erdinast-Vulcan presents the argument that narrative identity as lived has a dual aspect.[27] For narrative autoethnographers, one side of this is the textual projects they are involved in; on the other side is the more generalised, lived, discourse of identity. From the premise that stories are always social performances, discourses of identity are constituted by the tales people routinely tell about themselves, to themselves and to others. In discourse theoretical terms, these '...form the objects of which they speak.'[28] They become internalised at individual and social phenomenological levels, structuring how people make sense of and live their lives. From my discussion so far, the concepts of 'discursive poverty' and 'discursive sophistication' logically follow and have theoretical relevance. Discursive poverty constitutes a life-limiting inability to adequately interpret and account for lived experiences.[29] The work of Anthony Giddens and Paul Willis especially, discussed in Chapter 2, suggests that this inability can be displayed by people who, although they have accrued social and educational capital, fall back on hegemonic cultural narratives to interpret, and account for, their experiential lives.

The Philosophy of Narrative Identity

All of this points to a need to explore narrative identity in greater depth, beginning with the meaning and philosophical basis of the 'narrative' concept. Whether used in a general sense,[30] or in the more specific methodological senses of narrative inquiry or autoethnography, the term 'narrative' can be simply understood as synonymous with 'story.' I argue that doing or performing narrative refers to storytelling deployed in the service of sustaining a viable human identity:

> A premise held by many philosophers (and many autoethnographers) is that autonomy entails a capacity for self-constitution – 'a capacity, that is, to define or invent or create oneself' ... If this premise is accepted, one way of considering the narrative representation of the self is in terms of either *abstract* or *embodied* storytelling ... the self maintains the illusion of a coherent identity governed by a tacitly assumed central controller. This illusion is sustained by the retrospective and prospective, creative, and continual re-embellishment of stories.[31]

Autoethnographic stories reflect wider cultural discourses in presupposing, entailing, and co-evolving with narrative identities. A deeper question emerges from this: 'How is this played out at a broader metaphysical level?' In teleological terms, summarising and interpreting Paul Ricoeur's work on time and narrative, William Dowling asserts that the seemingly heterogeneous nature of apparently disconnected events and circumstances really co-exist in connected harmony.[32] Such 'concordia discors' (p. 6) implies emplotment as a teleological principle, across a continuum from universal myths to the ordinary life of 'stories waiting to be told.'[33]

In a complementary way, the ubiquity of narrative and its association with the forward movement of human life is captured by Roland Barthes, who argued that that narrative has always been part of what it means to be human.[34] From a related existential perspective, Eisenberg tells us that human identity is an ongoing challenge: that of 'living in the present with the awareness of an uncertain future.'[35] The overarching life narratives shaping people's identities are indeterminate and uncertain. So, to apprehend who we are, how we have become who we are, and in what direction we all seem to be headed, we tend to make meaningful sense of our lives through narrative emplotment.[36] E.M. Forster clarifies this in his text, *Aspects of the Novel*:

> 'The king died, and then the queen died' is a story. 'The king died, and then the queen died of grief' is a plot.[37]

Narrativity and Anti-narrativity

To summarise, as *Homo Narrans*,[38] there seems to be widespread universal, logically underpinned, agreement – accepted within the autoethnographic communities – that being human is a functionally therapeutic and meaning-making, extended narrative condition.[39] However, although at face value this is a compelling argument, it's not without its detractors – most notably, as I argue:

> Galen Strawson … in particular has through the years consistently argued against what he has come to call the 'Psychological Narrativity Thesis' and the 'Ethical Narrativity Thesis' (hereafter PNT and ENT) … Those who subscribe to the PNT (including, at a tacit level, many from the autoethnographic communities) make the *empirical* claim that human beings experience their lives as an extended story. They are likely to support the corresponding – *normative* and *ethical* – ENT claim that a 'richly narrative outlook on one's life is a good thing, essential to living well, to true or full "personhood"'. Strawson numbers himself as one person among others who, based on their lived-through experiences, reject both the PNT and ENT. In Strawson's ethico-political terms, those who are 'nonnarrative' … can have perfectly rich lives in the absence of both experiencing themselves in terms of an unfolding story and believing that they should.[40]

The Narrative Surround and Narrative Inheritance

Although I feel ambivalent about the psychological narrativity thesis, I can accept its utility as a compelling rhetorical position while equally accepting the idea of discontinuous identities. I'm less inclined to over-invest in the idea of human life-as-narrative as an ethical necessity. It's difficult to argue against the empirical truth of us all being born into the stocks of stories we inherit from our parent, parents or guardian(s), later significant others, cultures, and life more broadly. With reference to my research questions and discussion to this point, it seems equally obvious that these stories exert a centripetal pull on us to self-identify with them. Eisenberg describes the socialisation process through which this happens in terms of an environmentally influencing 'surround.'[41] By this concept, he means that each of us is born into a social world that's already in process – a world of pre-existing stories, linguistic and social cultures, rules, networks, and culturally acceptable ways of behaving.

Through the stock of stories made available to us, we are socialised into narrative identities comprised of moral positions and related behaviours, the sophisticated discernment of which must often arguably be deferred until later life.[42] In this regard, Alasdair MacIntyre asks all of us humans living the world to reflect on the stories we find ourselves inscribed within.[43] Trying to pin many of these stories down is difficult, even as a biologically and emotionally mature adult, precisely because of the opaque and often hidden nature of distal forces acting on the formation of moral identity. However, it is arguably morally important that in moving our lives forward we try to remember and make sense of the past as best as we can. Thus, personal narrative, or extended story, is intimately related to memory and time,[44] with the qualifier that there are forces influencing our personal stories which exceed the duration of our lives.[45]

From a philosophical autoethnographic standpoint, there are clear advantages associated with the idea of being born into cultural narratives, and neither trying to resist nor transcend those. Although inevitably always incomplete, and sometimes irreparably fractured,[46] having a reserve of stories can undoubtedly help us. It seems reasonable to accept that the more extensive and sophisticated this reserve is, the more resourceful we will find ourselves in coping with life's vicissitudes.[47] However, whereas *narrative inheritance* may be a blessing and a gift for many,[48] leading as this does not just to a good preparation for life but to inter-generational coherence of stories accepted as true at historical face value, it may be a curse for others. For some individuals, me included, it can trigger their need to resist the pull of cultural narrative entrapment.

Accepting the premise of secrets kept from the outside world and within-family secrets, autoethnographic work on in this area is illuminating in this regard. Christopher Poulos shows how family secrecy can shape communication and relationships within and outside of a family unit.[49] There's a dark side to this: Bud Goodall, for example, starkly describes the psychosocial impact of 'toxic' secrecy, compounded by lies told by close family members.[50] In my own case, my father didn't lie, unless silence counts as a lie, as he failed to pass on family stories to me. This is not surprising – while gregarious with his cronies and other people, he was way beyond taciturn with me. Echoing Stacy Holman Jones's description of how she imagined her parents felt about her,[51] my father seemed to regard me as 'always strange' for not conforming to our hometown's cultural expectations.[52] I barely knew and rarely met his mother, my paternal grandmother, nor my father's brother and half-brother and their children, all of whom lived in the same small town (population 1400). The family stories I got from my mother, an unreliable and paranoid fantasist at the best of times, were usually untrue. Hermetically sealed secrets and lies, as well as omissions, characterised my biological and close extended family relationships. Because of such an impoverished narrative inheritance, like others invested in the therapeutic power of narrative autoethnography to do this job, I eventually had to re-parent myself, redefine what constitutes my 'family,' and repair my narrative identity.[53] As Jeanette Winterson says,

> ...unhappy families are conspiracies of silence. The one who breaks the silence is never forgiven. He or she has to learn to forgive him or herself.[54]

Life-Defeating and Life-Affirming Narrative Identity

A narrative stock characterised, or contaminated, by a poverty of narrative inheritance, unreliable stories, discursive narrowness, or, at worst, mean-spirited, insular, parochial, time-, place- and class-based myopia, may not auger well for success in dealing with shifting life circumstances or may prove a boon. In the face of such circumstances, at least some of us might become aware of hope-imbued choices. Providing we have sufficient dispositional wherewithal, and personal, environmental, and cultural resources, we may work – as I have done – to re-story ourselves in refusing toxic narrative entrapment in family stories and imposed biographies. This facilitates life-affirming distance from our biological and extended families, past relationships, and past identities.[55]

With direct implications for the concepts of cultural acceptance and cultural narrative entrapment, if we do not have such dispositional wherewithal and are deficient in these resources, we may simply, unreflexively and by default, replicate and live out life-denying, life-defeating narratives in the Nietzschean sense of performing self-deceiving identity.[56] I will explain and discuss my standpoint more on this point in Chapter 4. For the moment, a logically emerging implication for me is that, at least for some people, ongoing psychological and related interpersonal problems may well be the result of remaining cathected or stuck in residual and enduring family culture stories. I believe that because such people (I was one of them) are emotionally invested, thus narratively, affectively, and behaviourally entrapped in such stories, they are often destructively repeated in relationships beyond the families of origin. In my own case, for example, I have tended to act towards my partners as if they had the constant potential to be as abusive towards me as my mother was.[57] This points strongly to the importance of the therapeutic and resistance functions of autoethnography in helping process, working through, and letting go through the process of narrative re-storying.[58]

Time and Memory in Cultural Narrative Identity

At this point in the discussion, it seems clear that narrative identity presupposes, co-entails, and supervenes on cultural identity ('supervenes' is a philosophical term referring to the proposition that if narrative identity were removed, there would be no cultural identity remaining). How then is cultural narrative identity constituted by time and memory?

The words from W.H. Auden's poem *In Transit* – the 'places where we have really been' which are remembered as 'unchanging because there we changed' –[59] speak to me of memories of events frozen in past time, against which people may juxtapose and story their changing narrative identities. The premise underpinning this is that past environmental events shape the interiority of the person, provoking identity changes. Across my autoethnographic work in the appendix to this book, changes to my identity are represented by such preservation of the past – of unchanging people, times, and places – in the memories I've written about. In line with, and extending on, Auden, freezing of remembered time is necessary precisely to interpose distance between the past and my developing identity, and to move the latter forward in my writing at each point in time where I do such writing. Regarding my second inquiry question, in resisting cultural entrapment it is arguably important to have pictures of cultural events that remain as clear as possible over shifting time and circumstance. Obviously, the actual places where those events happened have changed with passing years, but I've not had the first-hand lived experience of how and in what ways. However, this issue is irrelevant if a distinction is made between historical and narrative truth.[60]

Because of my memories fading over time, fidelity to narrative truth necessarily requires creatively 'filling in,'[61] to sustain and develop, after Daniel Dennett, my 'centre of narrative gravity.'[62] This term refers to narrative identity constituting the site where stories of the person are made, developed, sustained, and changed. From an operant conditioning perspective, complementing Dennett's thesis, individual memories are built up through 'habit strength.'[63] Habit strength is increased by repeatedly performing mental patterns and routines, which positively reinforce the direction and content of identity and relational construction. Rather than regarding the term 'self-serving' as signalling selfishness, the building of personal memories through habit strength has an adaptive social function: developing and maintaining the coherence of narrative identity.

Hindsight and Character Development in Cultural Narrative Identity

Enhancing such coherence through critically reflexive writing contributes to moral development in providing access to narrative character[64] and the memories upon which this is based. These memories, which have spatial qualities, can be understood as having literal and figurative meanings. They are literal in that they are of places we were in at times in our lives, notwithstanding their 'frozen' status in Auden's sense. They are figurative to the extent that they are 'spatial metaphors of depth,'[65] when an individual life is regarded as a series of rich, detailed memory locations.

From a hindsight perspective, what and how we remember can both add to the clues about the nature of our individual characters and place an ethical demand on us to discern this as well as we are able.[66] However, our memories of people, times, and places are selective, changing as a function of passing years and, to recapitulate, the corresponding need to fill in and elaborate our life stories in our favour. So, in terms of honouring its creative literary demands, the representation of remembered characters as exemplified and defended in my own work legitimately shifts from realist portrayals to lampooned caricatures.[67] Moreover, there is a strong sense in which even the most well-intentioned realist portrayals of humans reflect their status as 'imaginary beings,'[68] because of the impossibility of anyone directly accessing and portraying the subjectivity of another: 'If there is something stranger than a ghost, it is a living person.'[69] This problematises conventionally accepted relational ethical procedures in autoethnography by challenging the widely held epistemic assumption that these should be solely concerned with the accurate representation of 'flesh and blood,' biologically alive or dead, people from a realist perspective.[70]

The Narrative Unconscious in Cultural Narrative Identity

Moreover, forgetting, cultural 'noise,' and unconscious interference all contaminate such accurate representations. In his thesis on the nature of the narrative unconscious, Freeman argues that many of the memories we take to be ours alone are in fact shared or distributed.[71] These shared memories derive from phenomena we encounter in the world, either directly experienced or via mediated representations (for example, through television, films, books, encoded fantasies). It follows that, at both assumed individual and socially shared levels, memory is a farrago of objectively verifiable fact and fiction – again highlighting the difference between historical and narrative truth.

Moreover, according to Freeman, much of the cultural information we possess is held at unconscious levels,[72] and thus not immediately accessible or retrievable. Freeman contends that the narrative unconscious constitutes culturally rooted and latent aspects of our histories, which are not always recognised as part of our life stories. Such sedimented historical layers of 'deep memory' may both precede and happen during our individual lifespans.[73] However, shifts in environments (places encountered in space and time) can bring aspects of the narrative unconscious into consciousness, although '… whether they "rise to the surface" … will depend on what we encounter in our lives….'[74] This adds another dimension to Auden's poetic words, above. In addition to consciously remembering memories frozen in time, the argument is that there are latent, or nascent, unconscious memories lying in wait for environmental triggers to bring them into consciousness.

There is a moral imperative apparent here: exploration of key sites of the narrative unconscious through autoethnographic writing, the act of which produces knowledge not hitherto apprehended, enables us to more coherently and readily discern, or at least creatively imagine, the historical roots of our interior worlds and narrative characters.[75] Freeman argues that in discerning the narrative unconscious – that is, by making the narrative unconscious conscious – we open ourselves to the possibility of exploring new forms of making better sense and meaning of our personal and social life[76] and, as I display in my own writing, to life experienced in institutional environments.[77]

Related to this, John Christman contends that 'People have variable relations to the public language of their surrounding culture.'[78] Linguistic and cultural environments often fail to adequately recognise and support people's individual narratives around cultural memory, and corresponding personal and social definition and identity.[79] Christman argues that the standards of a culture can be externally imposed on the people within it, to varying degrees of acceptance or resistance, a point supported by Willis and Williams.[80] This is made more problematic by the fact that such people often lack the epistemic resources to adequately interpret and account for their own cultural narrative identities.[81] As a result, argues Christman, more or less consciously experienced cultural 'dislocation' can occur. This happens when a person's self-understanding, which makes sense to her or him in terms of one set of cultural values, conflicts with the cultural values of the broader environmental surround they find themselves in.[82]

My Hermetic Solitude

In my early old age, I constantly try to escape from this conflict. From the safety of my Bachelardian internal 'hermetic solitude,'[83] or home as my refuge of the imagination,[84] I write critically in my autoethnographies about those spaces I've had to occupy for much of my life which I've experienced in terms of narrative identity-environment dislocation. In contrast to my felt levels of identity-environment coherence and ordered purposeful life in the house I've lived in for 22 years, I previously found domestic, institutional, and organisational environmental life – from the home shared with my parents in my childhood and adolescence, to school, to the Royal Air Force, the National

Health Service, and later, prior to my retirement, from full-time employment in higher education – as often lacking in coherence and valued purpose; indeed frequently, at worst, violent in various ways, or pointless, boring and full of contradictions.[85] In contrast, signifying the importance of domestic cultural environment, there's a sympathetic affective resonance between my house – particularly my study, libraries over three floors, walls covered in my paintings, and my musical instruments – and my interior psychic life. This makes it easier for me to view my previous periods of acceptance of cultural narrative entrapment with a degree of compassion, especially when aided by resistance writing.

The Gap: Incompleteness in the Autoethnographic Literature

The acceptance-resistance couplet which I'm well sensitised to, and which is displayed across all my autoethnographic work represented in this book and its appendix, points to a significant gap in the autoethnographic literature. To recapitulate, my aim is to advance philosophical autoethnography in promoting the theme of *resisting cultural narrative entrapment*. I endorse such resistance and, I believe, break new conceptual, analytic, and theoretical ground in this endeavour. From this position, and because I see a marked neglect of this across the narrative autoethnography literature, I take it as self-evident that I'm responding appropriately to an 'incompleteness' in this body of literature,[86] and so will not over-labour this point.

Research Questions One and Two

Based on Part 2 of my background and context discussion, I'm now able to complete my answers to my first two research questions:

What constitutes resistance to cultural narrative entrapment in philosophical autoethnography?

Resistance to cultural narrative entrapment is constituted by continual reflexive alertness to the seductive power of culture, through the exercise of critical autoethnographicity. This can be enhanced by discursive sophistication, critical sensitivity to the narrative surround and narrative inheritance, and the corresponding impact of distal forces. These forces may be consciously or unconsciously apprehended, with shifting environments and the exercise of the imagination bringing some unconscious material into consciousness.

Why is it important to resist cultural narrative entrapment in autoethnography?

When assumed to be benign, culture can often be oppressive and life-limiting. It is therefore often important to resist the centripetal pull into cultural entrapment, through the exercise of queering sensibilities. This can contribute to restorying narrative identity in life-affirming ways, to moral character development, and to bringing awareness of distal forces more into consciousness.

Conclusion

Having completed both parts of my background and context discussion and answered my first two research questions, following the Ash-Alec conversation below I move on to Chapter 4: *Silencing*. In it, I rigorously address the critical context of cultural narrative entrapment with direct reference to the texts described and discussed in the appendix to this book. As in previous chapters, my discussion will range across autoethnographic, conceptual, philosophical, social science, and, where appropriate, humanities literature.

***

Ash: Look I've still got a problem with this national cultural narrative identity thing! National identity is more than just a story.

Alec: As an autoethnographer, despite the Strawsons of this world, do you believe that your life is a cradle to grave continual story?

Ash: Of course! Why else would I write autoethnography? Duh!

Alec: Do NOT bloody well Duh me, Ash! I've written an autoethnography explicitly premised on a series of discontinuous identities.[87] Does that make me a phoney in the approach?

Ash: Know your trouble, Alec? You're arrogant! You've an answer for everything!

Alec: Who's the boss of this book, Ash? Me or you? I doubt if you'll even buy a copy when it's published, so make the most of it while you can!

Ash: (A***hole!) You do not tell me what I will and will not buy or read!

Alec: Alright. Now, regarding your view that national cultural identity is more than just a story, do you regard autoethnography as a form of oral history?

Ash: Yes, of course, it can be thought of in this way.

Alec: I agree. So, memory is important here.

Ash: Yes! What's your point?

Alec: Let's have a wee look at what the historian John Tosh has to say about oral history as cultural memory in relation to national identity. Tosh argues that we carry around a sense of the past which is comprised of a selection from our immediate experiences, including experiences of the 'frozen' past – remember Auden from earlier in this chapter? – together with ideas of the nature of the social order in which we live.[88] His position is that on this basis we, and other ordinary people, assimilate and interpret our individual and collective experiences, and that this is both a historical factor and an important element of political culture. Moreover, he argues that there's a difference between the 'official' or general national memory of events and the cultural memory of people with first-hand lived-through experience of them. He asserts, for example, that the black residents of Tottenham, Brixton, and Toxteth don't remember the 1980s riots that happened in these areas in the same terms as the British nation at large. Unlike the latter, the residents lived through these experiences first-hand.[89] This says to me that if writing autoethnography is simultaneously an act of memory, and a contested political and historical act, 'national identity' and its associated implications are likely to constitute a range of contested stories.

Ash: With you so far, but surely there's an objective reality of national identity underneath these stories (another bl**dy lecture coming up!).

Alec: Right, let's explore this point. An individual's cultural identity, because it's grounded in collective and individual memory and history, is always likely to be contested because it's also, by implication, definition, and, with reference to Tosh's example above, political. Thinking with Spence, the **narrative** truth of my frozen in time and interpreted memory of being in the British Royal Air Force in Germany in the early 1970s will jar with the **historical** or objective truth of what happened there, and to me, at the time.[90] But, as an autoethnographor, the narrative truth of my life is always likely to take privilege over its historical truth. It would be impossible for me to represent my past in terms of absolute accuracy. I could only do this from my point of view, which would inevitably jar with accounts from others who were there at the time, in the absence of any bottom line of absolute truth – in nature or by consensus. So, if representing accurate historical truth is ultimately impossible, where, by implication and extrapolation, does this leave national identity which, according to you, is supposedly always alive and kicking underneath narrative truth stories?

Ash: But, you **were** British all along the way. You can't escape your national identity.

Alec: (Please save me!) Despite what my passport says, my sense of national identity then and now has already been contested lots of times along the course of my life. It took me five years to muster the courage to purchase my discharge – buy myself out – of the military, even though I felt a misfit in it.[91] My father and brother took patriotic national identity for granted and had a huge problem with what I'd done, seeing it as yet another smear on the respectability and integrity of the family – a tear in the fabric of our small town family secrecy.[92] You can be bullied out of keeping faith with your narrative identity if the cultural, subsuming social, pullback into line is too strong. The years it took me for me to feel brave enough to get out of the military and eventually get into higher education was in large part, I believe, because of internalised messages from my hometown. It took me ages to stop being the semi-willing victim of other people's biographies of me.

Ash: But surely you still have an identity essence don't you, for God's sake?

Alec: (Oh for fuck's sake!) Look, like you, Ash, I have tendencies, dispositions. But, just like Jay Garfield, 'when I look inside, all I find are psychophysical processes, not some ghostly owner hiding behind the curtains.'[93] Garfield isn't the first to have said this, by the way. He cites the early medieval Indian sage Candrakirti who made the same critique of this idea of the inner self.[94] And in the 1730s the Scottish philosopher David Hume wrote:

> For my part, when I enter most intimately into what I call **myself**, I always stumble on some particular perception or other, of heat or cold, light or shade, love or hatred, pain or pleasure. I never can catch myself at any time without a perception, and never can observe any thing but the perception.[95]

All that said, Ash, if my essence comes out of hiding, or you can track her or him down, please do feel free to make an immediate citizen's arrest. In the meantime, with a nod to Sartre and Heidegger, I'll continue to regard my ongoing cultural identities simply as the possible ways to be during my timeshare of biological life. You unreflexively cling on to imagined essential self and communities. I find it unnecessary to even seriously consider how these, assuming they're real in the first place, can be co-extensive with any essence you imagine I might have. Your assumed cultural identity is off-the-shelf durable, long-lasting, and beige and bland, whereas I regularly shed snakeskins with panache and aplomb on my way through. Let's move on to Chapter 4.

Ash: (Superior sod!) I can barely contain my excitement, you legend in your own mind!

Notes

1 Benedict Anderson, *Imagined Communities: Reflections on the Origin and Spread of Nationalism* (London and New York: Verso, 1983), 37–46.
2 Benedict Anderson, *Imagined Communities: Reflections on the Origin and Spread of Nationalism* (London and New York: Verso, 1983), 44.

3 Michael Lynch, *Scotland: A New History* (London: Pimlico, 1992), 39–50; David Ross, *Scotland: History of a Nation*. NEW EDITION (Broxburn: Lomond Books, Ltd, 2017), 35–50; T.C. (Christopher) Smout, *A History of the Scottish People 1560–1830* (Bungay, Suffolk: Fontana/Collins, 1969), 19–20.
4 Panpsychism is the philosophical position that everything material, however small, has some degree of individual consciousness.
5 Alasdair MacIntyre, *After Virtue: A Study in Moral Theory*. Third Edition (London and New York: Bloomsbury Academic, 2007), 250.
6 Alec Grant and Susan Young, 'A Scot an' a Sassenach Scrieve Aboot Leid: A Three Pairt Scotoethnography (A Scot and an English person write about language: A Scotoethnography in three parts),' *Journal of Autoethnography* 5, no. 1 (January 2024): 29–55, https://doi.org/10.1525/joae.2024.5.1.39; Alec Grant and Susan Young, 'A Scot an' a Sassenach Scrieve Aboot Leid: A Three Pairt Scotoethnography (A Scot and an English Person Write about Language: A Scotoethnography in Three Parts),' in *Meaningful Journeys: Autoethnographies of Quest and Identity Transformation*, eds. Alec Grant and Elizabeth Lloyd-Parkes (London and New York: Routledge, 2024), 96–116.
7 Alec Grant, 'Drinking to Relax: An Autoethnography of a Highland Family Viewed through a New Materialist Lens,' in *Auto/Biography Yearbook 2017*, ed. Andrew Sparkes (Nottingham: Russell Press, 2018), 33–46. (6) (PDF) Paper for British Sociological Association Yearbook 2017, Drinking to Relax. (researchgate.net).
8 Gillian Brock, *Global Justice: A Cosmopolitan Account* (New York: Oxford University Press, 2009); Martha C. Nussbaum, 'Patriotism and Cosmopolitanism,' in *The Global Justice Reader*, ed. Thom Brooks (Oxford: Blackwell Publishing, Ltd., 2008), 306–314; Samuel Scheffler, *Boundaries and Allegiances: Problems of Justice and Responsibility in Liberal Thought* (New York: Oxford University Press, 2001).
9 Gillian Brock, *Global Justice: A Cosmopolitan Account* (New York: Oxford University Press, 2009), 9.
10 Martha C. Nussbaum, 'Patriotism and Cosmopolitanism,' in *The Global Justice Reader*, ed. Thom Brooks (Oxford: Blackwell Publishing, Ltd., 2008), 307.
11 Gillian Brock, 'Cosmopolitanism Versus Noncosmopolitanism: The State of Play,' *The Monist* 94, no. 4 (October 2011): 456, https://doi.org/10.5840/monist201194423.
12 Hugh Trevor-Roper, 'The Invention of Tradition: The Highland Tradition of Scotland,' in *The Invention of Tradition*, eds. Eric Hobsbawm and Terence Ranger (Cambridge: Cambridge University Press, 1983), 15–41.
13 Alasdair MacIntyre, 'Is Patriotism a Virtue?', in *Debates in Contemporary Political Philosophy. An Anthology*, eds. Derek Matravers and Jonathon Pike (London and New York: Routledge in association with the Open University, 2003), 286–300.
14 David Miller, 'In Defence of Nationality,' in *Debates in Contemporary Political Philosophy: An Anthology*, eds. Derek Matravers and Jonathon Pike (London and New York: Routledge in association with the Open University, 2003), 301.
15 Alec Grant, 'How does Nietzschean Self-deceiving Moral Identity in a Modern Context Relate to Lukes' Third Dimension of Power?' (MA Dissertation, Open University, 2020), 39.
16 Stacy Holman Jones, Tony E. Adams, and Carolyn Ellis, 'Introduction: Coming to know autoethnography as more than a method,' in *Handbook of autoethnography*, eds. Stacy Holman Jones, Tony E. Adams, and Carolyn Ellis (Walnut Creek, CA: Left Coast Press, Inc, 2013), 17–47.
17 Arthur P. Bochner, and Nicholas A. Riggs, 'Practicing Narrative Inquiry,' in *The Oxford Handbook of Qualitative Research*, ed. Patricia Leavy (Oxford: Oxford University Press, 2014), 195–222.

18 Siv Tønnessen, 'The Meaningfulness of Challenging the Controlled Drinking Discourse. An Autoethnographic Study,' *Qualitative Social Work* Online First 0 no. 0 (2023). https://doi.org/10.1177/14733250231200499.
19 Donald Spence, *Narrative Truth and Historical Truth: Meaning and Interpretation in Psychoanalysis* (New York: W.W. Norton, 1982).
20 Theodor R. Sarbin (ed.) *Narrative Psychology: The Storied Nature of Human Conduct* (Westport, CT: Praeger Publishers, 1986).
21 Arthur P. Bochner, and Nicholas A. Riggs, 'Practicing Narrative Inquiry,' in *The Oxford Handbook of Qualitative Research*, ed. Patricia Leavy (Oxford: Oxford University Press, 2014), 195–222; Carolyn Ellis, and Michael G. Flaherty, 'An Agenda for the Interpretation of Lived Experience,' in *Investigating Subjectivity: Research on Lived Experience*, eds. Carolyn Ellis and Michael G. Flaherty (Newbury Park, CA: SAGE Publications, Inc, 1992), 1–13; Laurel Richardson, *Fields of Play: Constructing an Academic Life* (New Brunswick, NJ: Rutgers University Press, 1997).
22 Gayle Letherby, *Feminist Research in Theory and Practice* (Buckingham and Philadelphia: Open University Press, 2003).
23 Gayle Letherby, 'Theorised Subjectivity,' in *Objectivity and Subjectivity in Social Research*, eds. Gayle Letherby, John Scott, and Malcolm Williams (London: Sage Publications Ltd, 2012), 79–101.
24 Arthur P. Bochner, and Nicholas A. Riggs, 'Practicing Narrative Inquiry,' in *The Oxford Handbook of Qualitative Research*, ed. Patricia Leavy (Oxford: Oxford University Press, 2014), 198.
25 Catherine K. Reissman, *Narrative Methods for the Human Sciences* (New York: Sage Publications, Inc, 2008).
26 Arthur W. Frank, *Letting Stories Breathe: A Socio-Narratology* (Chicago and London: The University of Chicago Press, 2010).
27 Daphna Erdinast-Vulcan, 'Heterobiography: A Bakhtinian Perspective on Autobiographical Writing,' in *Philosophy and Life Writing*, eds. D.L. LeMahieu and Christopher Cowley (London and New York: Routledge, 2019), 109–110.
28 Michel Foucault, *The Archaeology of Knowledge and the Discourse on Language* (New York: Vintage Books, 2010 [1972]), 49.
29 Miranda Fricker, *Epistemic Injustice: Power and the Ethics of Knowing* (Oxford: Oxford University Press, 2007).
30 Paul Cobley, *Narrative*. 2nd Edition (London and New York: Routledge, 2014).
31 Alec Grant, 'The Philosophical Autoethnographer,' in *Writing Philosophical Autoethnography*, ed. Alec Grant (New York and London: Routledge, 2024), 11.
32 William C. Dowling, *Ricoeur on Time and Narrative: An Introduction to Temps et récit* (Notre Dame, IN: University of Notre Dame Press, 2011).
33 William C. Dowling, *Ricoeur on Time and Narrative: An Introduction to Temps et récit* (Notre Dame, IN: University of Notre Dame Press, 2011), 7.
34 Roland Barthes, *The Semiotic challenge*. Trans. Richard Howard (Berkeley and Los Angeles, CA and London: University of California Press, 1988), 95.
35 Eric M. Eisenberg, 'Building a Mystery: Toward a New Theory of Communication and Identity,' *Journal of Communication* 51, no. 3 (January 2006): 534, https://doi.org/10.1111/j.1460-2466.2001.tb02895.x.
36 William C. Dowling, *Ricoeur on Time and Narrative: An Introduction to Temps et récit* (Notre Dame, IN: University of Notre Dame Press, 2011), 5.
37 E.M. Forster, *Aspects of the Novel*, ed. Oliver Stallybrass (Harmondsworth: Penguin Books Ltd., 1962 [1927]), 87.
38 Walter R. Fisher, *Human Communication as Narration: Toward a Philosophy of Reason, Value, and Action* (Columbia: University of South Carolina Press, 1987).

39 Arthur P. Bochner, and Nicholas A. Riggs, 'Practicing Narrative Inquiry,' in *The Oxford Handbook of Qualitative Research*, ed. Patricia Leavy (Oxford: Oxford University Press, 2014), 195–222; John Christman, 'Telling Our Own Stories: Narrative Selves and Oppressive Circumstance,' in *The Philosophy of Autobiography*, ed. Christopher Cowley (Chicago and London: The University of Chicago Press, 2015), 122–140; Daphna Erdinast-Vulcan, 'Heterobiography: A Bakhtinian Perspective on Autobiographical Writing,' in *Philosophy and Life Writing*, eds. D.L. LeMahieu and Christopher Cowley (London and New York: Routledge, 2019), 109–110.

40 Alec Grant, 'The Philosophical Autoethnographer,' in *Writing Philosophical Autoethnography*, ed. Alec Grant (New York and London: Routledge, 2024), 14.

41 Eric M. Eisenberg, 'Building a Mystery: Toward a New Theory of Communication and Identity,' *Journal of Communication* 51, no. 3 (January 2006): 543, https://doi.org/10.1111/j.1460-2466.2001.tb02895.x.

42 Mark Freeman, *Hindsight: The Promise and Peril of Looking Backward* (Oxford: Oxford University Press, 2010); Alec Grant, 'The Philosophical Autoethnographer,' in *Writing Philosophical Autoethnography*, ed. Alec Grant (New York and London: Routledge, 2024), 14.

43 Alasdair MacIntyre, *After Virtue: A Study in Moral Theory*. Third Edition (London and New York: Bloomsbury Academic, 2007), 250.

44 Mark Freeman, *Hindsight: The Promise and Peril of Looking Backward* (Oxford: Oxford University Press, 2010); Alec Grant, 'The Philosophical Autoethnographer,' in *Writing Philosophical Autoethnography*, ed. Alec Grant (New York and London: Routledge, 2024), 14.

45 Mark Freeman, *Hindsight: The Promise and Peril of Looking Backward* (Oxford: Oxford University Press, 2010).

46 Andrew F. Herrmann, 'The Ghostwriter: Living a Father's Unfinished Narrative,' in *On (Writing) Families: Autoethnographies of Presence and Absence, Love and Loss*, eds. Jonathon Wyatt and Tony E. Adams (Rotterdam: Sense Publishers, 2014), 95–102.

47 Arthur P. Bochner, and Nicholas A. Riggs, 'Practicing Narrative Inquiry,' in *The Oxford Handbook of Qualitative Research*, ed. Patricia Leavy (Oxford: Oxford University Press, 2014), 195–222.

48 H.L. (Bud) Goodall, 'Narrative Inheritance: A Nuclear Family with Toxic Secrets,' *Qualitative Inquiry* 11, no. 4 (2005): 492–513, https://doi.org/10.1177/1077800405276769.

49 Christopher Poulos, *Accidental Autoethnography: An Inquiry into Family Secrecy* (New York and London: Routledge, 2019).

50 H.L. (Bud) Goodall, 'Narrative Inheritance: A Nuclear Family with Toxic Secrets,' *Qualitative Inquiry* 11, no. 4 (2005): 492–513, https://doi.org/10.1177/1077800405276769.

51 Stacy Holman Jones, 'Always Strange: Transforming Loss,' in *On (Writing) Families: Autoethnographies of Presence and Absence, Love and Loss*, eds. Jonathon Wyatt and Tony E. Adams (Rotterdam: Sense Publishers, 2014), 13–21.

52 Alec Grant, 'Drinking to Relax: An Autoethnography of a Highland Family Viewed through a New Materialist Lens,' in *Auto/Biography Yearbook 2017*, ed. Andrew Sparkes (Nottingham: Russell Press, 2018), 33–46.

53 Tony E. Adams, 'Ties that Bind, Ties that Scar,' in *On (Writing) Families: Autoethnographies of Presence and Absence, Love and Loss*, eds. Jonathon Wyatt and Tony E. Adams (Rotterdam: Sense Publishers, 2014), 149–150; Craig Gingrich-Philbrook, 'On Gratitude, for My Father,' in *On (Writing) Families: Autoethnographies of Presence and Absence, Love and Loss*, eds. Jonathon Wyatt and Tony E. Adams (Rotterdam: Sense Publishers, 2014), 23–29; Stacy Holman Jones, 'Always Strange:

Transforming Loss,' in *On (Writing) Families: Autoethnographies of Presence and Absence, Love and Loss*, eds. Jonathon Wyatt and Tony E. Adams (Rotterdam: Sense Publishers, 2014), 13–21; Alec Grant, 'Drinking to Relax: An Autoethnography of a Highland Family Viewed through a New Materialist Lens,' in *Auto/Biography Yearbook 2017*, ed. Andrew Sparkes (Nottingham: Russell Press, 2018), 33–46; Alec Grant, and Laetitia Zeeman, 'Whose Story Is It? An Autoethnography Concerning Narrative Identity,' *The Qualitative Report (TQR)* 17, no. 72, 1–12. http://doi.org/10.46743/2160-3715/2012.1735; Colette Szczepaniak, 'Mental Health and the Body: An Autoethnography of Neuralgia, Migraine and Insulin Resistance,' in *Autoethnography in Psychology and Mental Health: New Voices*, eds. Alec Grant and Jerome Carson (London and New York: Routledge, 2024), X–X.

54 Jeannette Winterson, *Why Be Happy When You Could Be Normal?* (London: Vintage Books), 9.

55 Alec Grant, 'Drinking to Relax: An Autoethnography of a Highland Family Viewed through a New Materialist Lens,' in *Auto/Biography Yearbook 2017*, ed. Andrew Sparkes (Nottingham: Russell Press, 2018), 33–46; Alec Grant, 'In Search of My Narrative Character: A Philosophical Autoethnography,' in *Writing Philosophical Autoethnography*, ed. Alec Grant (New York and London: Routledge, 2024), 114–132; Alec Grant and Laetitia Zeeman, 'Whose Story Is It? An Autoethnography Concerning Narrative Identity,' *The Qualitative Report (TQR)* 17, no. 72, 1–12. http://doi.org/10.46743/2160-3715/2012.1735.

56 Alec Grant, 'How does Nietzschean Self-deceiving Moral Identity in a Modern Context Relate to Lukes' Third Dimension of Power?' (MA Dissertation, Open University, 2020), 39.

57 Alec Grant, 'Drinking to Relax: An Autoethnography of a Highland Family Viewed through a New Materialist Lens,' in *Auto/Biography Yearbook 2017*, ed. Andrew Sparkes (Nottingham: Russell Press, 2018), 33–46.

58 Alec Grant, 'Drinking to Relax: An Autoethnography of a Highland Family Viewed through a New Materialist Lens,' in *Auto/Biography Yearbook 2017*, ed. Andrew Sparkes (Nottingham: Russell Press, 2018), 33–46; Alec Grant, and Laetitia Zeeman, 'Whose Story Is It? An Autoethnography Concerning Narrative Identity,' *The Qualitative Report (TQR)* 17, no. 72, 1–12. http://doi.org/10.46743/2160-3715/2012.1735; Colette Szczepaniak, 'Mental Health and the Body: An Autoethnography of Neuralgia, Migraine and Insulin Resistance,' in *Autoethnography in Psychology and Mental Health: New Voices*, eds. Alec Grant and Jerome Carson (London and New York: Routledge, 2024), X–X.

59 W.H. Auden, 'In Transit,' in *W.H. Auden: Collected Poems*, ed. EdwardMendelson (London: Faber & Faber, 1994), 539–540.

60 Alec Grant, 'In Search of My Narrative Character: A Philosophical Autoethnography,' in *Writing Philosophical Autoethnography*, ed. Alec Grant (New York and London: Routledge, 2024), 117.

61 Alec Grant, 'In Search of My Narrative Character: A Philosophical Autoethnography,' in *Writing Philosophical Autoethnography*, ed. Alec Grant (New York and London: Routledge, 2024), 127.

62 Alec Grant, 'In Search of My Narrative Character: A Philosophical Autoethnography,' in *Writing Philosophical Autoethnography*, ed. Alec Grant (New York and London: Routledge, 2024), 121.

63 Dieter Ferring, 'Memory in Old Age: A Lifespan Perspective,' in *Handbook of Culture and Memory*, ed. Brady Wagoner (New York: Oxford University Press, 2018), 240.

64 Mark Freeman, *Hindsight: The Promise and Peril of Looking Backward* (Oxford: Oxford University Press, 2010); Alec Grant, 'In Search of My Narrative Character: A Philosophical Autoethnography,' in *Writing Philosophical Autoethnography*, ed. Alec Grant (New York and London: Routledge, 2024).

65 Andrew Thacker, 'Lost Cities and Found Lives: The 'Geographical Emotions' of Bryher and Walter Benjamin,' in *Life Writing and Space*, eds. Eveline Kilian and Hope Wolf (London and New York: Routledge), 41.

66 Mark Freeman, *Hindsight: The Promise and Peril of Looking Backward* (Oxford: Oxford University Press, 2010); Alec Grant, 'In Search of My Narrative Character: A Philosophical Autoethnography,' in *Writing Philosophical Autoethnography*, ed. Alec Grant (New York and London: Routledge, 2024), 114–132.

67 Mark Freeman, *Hindsight: The Promise and Peril of Looking Backward* (Oxford: Oxford University Press, 2010); Alec Grant, 'In Search of My Narrative Character: A Philosophical Autoethnography,' in *Writing Philosophical Autoethnography*, ed. Alec Grant (New York and London: Routledge, 2024), 114–132.

68 Craig Gingrich-Philbrook, 'On Gratitude, for My Father,' in *On (Writing) Families: Autoethnographies of Presence and Absence, Love and Loss*, eds. Jonathon Wyatt and Tony E. Adams (Rotterdam: Sense Publishers, 2014), 23–29.

69 Craig Gingrich-Philbrook, 'On Gratitude, for My Father,' in *On (Writing) Families: Autoethnographies of Presence and Absence, Love and Loss*, eds. Jonathon Wyatt and Tony E. Adams (Rotterdam: Sense Publishers, 2014), 25.

70 Alec Grant, 'Drinking to Relax: An Autoethnography of a Highland Family Viewed through a New Materialist Lens,' in *Auto/Biography Yearbook 2017*, ed. Andrew Sparkes (Nottingham: Russell Press, 2018), 33–46; Alec Grant, 'In Search of My Narrative Character: A Philosophical Autoethnography,' in *Writing Philosophical Autoethnography*, ed. Alec Grant (New York and London: Routledge, 2024), 114–132.

71 Mark Freeman, 'Discerning the History Inscribed Within: Significant Sites of the Narrative Unconscious,' in *Handbook of Culture and Memory*, ed. Brady Wagoner (New York: Oxford University Press, 2018).

72 Mark Freeman, 'Discerning the History Inscribed Within: Significant Sites of the Narrative Unconscious,' in *Handbook of Culture and Memory*, ed. Brady Wagoner (New York: Oxford University Press, 2018).

73 Mark Freeman, 'Discerning the History Inscribed Within: Significant Sites of the Narrative Unconscious,' in *Handbook of Culture and Memory*, ed. Brady Wagoner (New York: Oxford University Press, 2018), 80.

74 Mark Freeman, 'Discerning the History Inscribed Within: Significant Sites of the Narrative Unconscious,' in *Handbook of Culture and Memory*, ed. Brady Wagoner (New York: Oxford University Press, 2018), 70.

75 Mark Freeman, *Hindsight: The Promise and Peril of Looking Backward* (Oxford: Oxford University Press, 2010); Mark Freeman, 'Discerning the History Inscribed Within: Significant Sites of the Narrative Unconscious,' in *Handbook of Culture and Memory*, ed. Brady Wagoner (New York: Oxford University Press, 2018); Alec Grant, 'In Search of My Narrative Character: A Philosophical Autoethnography,' in *Writing Philosophical Autoethnography*, ed. Alec Grant (New York and London: Routledge, 2024), 114–132.

76 Mark Freeman, 'Discerning the History Inscribed Within: Significant Sites of the Narrative Unconscious,' in *Handbook of Culture and Memory*, ed. Brady Wagoner (New York: Oxford University Press, 2018).

77 Alec Grant, 'In Search of My Narrative Character: A Philosophical Autoethnography,' in *Writing Philosophical Autoethnography*, ed. Alec Grant (New York and London: Routledge, 2024), 114–132.

78 John Christman, 'Telling Our Own Stories: Narrative Selves and Oppressive Circumstance,' in *The Philosophy of Autobiography*, ed. Christopher Cowley (Chicago and London: The University of Chicago Press, 2015), 122.

79 Grant, A, Young, S. 2021. Troubling Tolichism in Several Voices: Resisting Epistemic Violence in Creative Analytical and Critical Autoethnographic Practices. *Journal of Autoethnography*. 3(1): pp. 103–117. E-ISSN 2637-5192. https://doi.org/10.1525/joae.2022.3.1.103

80 Paul Willis, *Learning to Labour: How Working-class Kids Get Working-class Jobs* (Aldershot, Hants: Gower Publishing 1988[1977]); Raymond Williams, 'Culture is Ordinary,' in *Resources of Hope: Culture, Democracy, Socialism*, ed. Robin Gable (London and New York: Verso, 1989 [1958]), 3–18.

81 Miranda Fricker, *Epistemic Injustice: Power and the Ethics of Knowing* (Oxford: Oxford University Press, 2007).

82 John Christman, 'Telling Our Own Stories: Narrative Selves and Oppressive Circumstance,' in *The Philosophy of Autobiography*, ed. Christopher Cowley (Chicago and London: The University of Chicago Press, 2015), 127.

83 Matthew Ingleby, 'Multiple Occupancy: Residency and Retrospection in Trollope's *Orley Farm* and *An Autobiography*,' in *Life Writing and Space*, eds. Eveline Kilian and Hope Wolf (London and New York: Routledge, 2016), 29.

84 Gaston Bachelard, *The Poetics of Space*. Tans. Maria Jolas (New York: Penguin Books, 2014 [1958]), 66–67.

85 Alec Grant, 'Toilets are the Proper Place for 'Outputs'! A Tale of Knowledge Production and Publishing with Students in Higher Education,' in *Self-Narrative and Pedagogy: Stories of Experience within Teaching and Learning*, eds. Mike Hayler and Jess Moriarty (Rotterdam: Sense Publishers, 2017), 45–57; Alec Grant, 'Drinking to Relax: An Autoethnography of a Highland Family Viewed through a New Materialist Lens,' in *Auto/Biography Yearbook 2017*, ed. Andrew Sparkes (Nottingham: Russell Press, 2018), 33–46; Grant 2024b; Alec Grant and Laetitia Zeeman, 'Whose Story Is It? An Autoethnography Concerning Narrative Identity,' *The Qualitative Report (TQR)* 17, no. 72, 1–12. http://doi.org/10.46743/2160-3715/2012.1735.

86 Lynn P. Nygaard and Kristin Solli, *Strategies for Writing a Thesis by Publication in the Social Sciences and Humanities* (London and New York: Routledge, 2021), 123.

87 Alec Grant, 'In Search of My Narrative Character: A Philosophical Autoethnography,' in *Writing Philosophical Autoethnography*, ed. Alec Grant (New York and London: Routledge, 2024), 114–132.

88 John Tosh, *The Pursuit of History: Aims. Methods and New Directions in the Study of History*. Seventh Edition (London and New York: Routledge, 2022), 277.

89 John Tosh, *The Pursuit of History: Aims. Methods and New Directions in the Study of History*. Seventh Edition (London and New York: Routledge, 2022), 278.

90 Alec Grant, 'In Search of My Narrative Character: A Philosophical Autoethnography,' in *Writing Philosophical Autoethnography*, ed. Alec Grant (New York and London: Routledge, 2024), 122.

91 Alec Grant, 'In Search of My Narrative Character: A Philosophical Autoethnography,' in *Writing Philosophical Autoethnography*, ed. Alec Grant (New York and London: Routledge, 2024), 122.

92 Alec Grant, 'Drinking to Relax: An Autoethnography of a Highland Family Viewed through a New Materialist Lens,' in *Auto/Biography Yearbook 2017*, ed. Andrew Sparkes (Nottingham: Russell Press, 2018), 33–46.

93 Jay L. Garfield, *Losing Ourselves: Learning to Live Without a Self* (Princeton and Oxford: Princeton University Press, 2022), 23.

94 Jay L. Garfield, *Losing Ourselves: Learning to Live Without a Self* (Princeton and Oxford: Princeton University Press, 2022), 23.

95 David Hume, *A Treatise of Human Nature*. Edited by Ernest C. Mossner (London: Penguin Books. 1969 [1739–1740]), 300.

4

SILENCING

Ash: Picking up on what we were talking about in the last two chapters, I refuse to go along with the idea that I'm culturally determined.

Alec: Let me quote you something from a great David Lodge novel: 'the truly determined subject is he who is not aware of the discursive formations that determine him. Or her.'[1]

Ash: Here we go again! You've always got to have the dialogic upper hand! I also realised a while back that you're trapping me in your own celebratory story of yourself and in your own culture for one – of belief in something you call 'cultural narrative entrapment.'

Alec: (At long bloody last!) You're right here, Ash! In fact, it's so obvious. So, hats off to you for spotting this! You got me bang to rights! Is my entrapment trickery working? And do you also think I'm being vainglorious?

Ash: (Bastard) No it's bl**dy well not, and I think you're patronising, and a vocabulary show-off. In fact, you're sick!

Alec: I am, Ash. Trude Klevan, my dear friend and sometimes co-writer, is currently trying to cure me of a bad dose of hybris and a touch of besserwisserness. I've been given a dual dia(logue)nosis (ha ha!).

Ash: AND YOU'RE AFFECTED!

Alec: Could've been much worse, Ash. At least I didn't talk with you in Scots through the chapters.[2] (I might do a bit of this next chapter.) Gin this wis a Scotoethnographic dialogue, fit wid ye hae done then? Ye'd've been richt confoonded.[3] That would've shut you up! Quite appropriate for this chapter!

DOI: 10.4324/9781003518594-4

Ash: (I can't believe this man!) … You really should learn a bit of humility, Alec. Why don't you grow up!!!???

Alec: (Oh shit, gone too far!) I apologise, Ash. I should and I need to. Right again! I can't seem to help myself (really must try harder).

Ash: Another thing – the big elephant in the room so far in the book: POWER!

Alec: (Better late than never, Ash!) Say more?

Ash: Okay. There's your age, your gender, your experience, your publishing track record, your reputation. All these things contribute to the accumulation of power. Then there's the fact that you call on philosophy to help you. Old white men with beards laying down the law for at least two and a half thousand years. And you're an old white man with a beard (ha f*ck*ng ha!).

Alec: (Here we sodding well go again. Philosophy belongs to aged European beardies, so I don't like it, despite knowing next to bugger all about it!) Yes. I've accrued a lot of capital over the years, which puts me at an advantage. But, regarding your comment about – implied Western – philosophy and patriarchy, it's certainly true that the pre- and post-Socratic philosophers were men, such was the status of women in those days. However, it's important not to commit what's known in philosophy as the 'genetic fallacy': judging something – in this case ancient philosophy – by the circumstances of its historical origin rather than in the merits of its content. In formal terms, Nigel Warburton describes this fallacy as: 'x originated from y, therefore x must now have some features in common with y.'[4]

There's lots of feminist intellectual writing that values the legacy of ancient philosophy – I'm thinking right now of Martha Nussbaum on ethics in Greek philosophy,[5] and Emily Wilson on the relevance of Socrates for our times, for example.[6] There are also great 20th-century, and current, women philosophers – too many to mention by name – many of whose books are in my home library.

Ash: (Blowhard!!) Okay, but the original male origins of philosophy impact on thinking today.

Alec: I agree with you here. Patriarchy colonises much of philosophy, one way or another. Someone once wrote – a man of course – that all the philosophy emerging out of the European tradition constitutes 'a series of footnotes to Plato.'[7] We're indebted to Gerda Lerner for informing us in great historical detail about patriarchy's very long history.[8] It's not surprising that it's seeped into canonical texts throughout the centuries and has crossed over into the misogyny of institutional and organisational life in our times. In this regard, Susan Young and I recently made the case that patriarchy and misogyny has colonised relational ethics in autoethnography.⁹ As a point of logic, doesn't all this more than imply that although autoethnography emerged as a reaction to patriarchy in the specific form of opposition to malestream, positivistic science, and has done this job very well in many respects, it's still likely to suffer from some patriarchal, subsuming positivistic, traces? In this regard, Gayle Letherby argues that much of the early critiques of positivism, including that emerging from qualitative inquiry, was gender-blinkered and sexist in failing to recognise the significance of the work, and leisure for that matter, of women and girls.¹⁰ I wonder to what extent this can still often be the case, including in autoethnography?

Ash: I'm not necessarily suggesting that patriarchy and male perspectives seeping in is problematic, more that it's interesting to think about what kind of effect it might have, rather than putting a value on it – thinking it good or bad.

Alec: Yes, it is interesting, Ash, but you seem to be contradicting yourself in what you've just said, because you're taking an evaluative stance, which I'm fully in sympathy with. People will and do make judgements about such things, and rightly so because what we're talking about is important at the levels of metaphysics and gender politics. Despite all the feminist pushbacks, the way women, and of course men, think about and act on the world is still often shaped by male assumptions, categories, pre-suppositions, and desires. To give you an example, I recently had an argument with a self-identifying feminist, autoethnographic colleague about British television political women news reporters wearing stiletto heeled shoes in their programmes. She maintained it was simply their choice. I rebutted by saying that this particular choice is shaped by patriarchal expectations and desires.

Ash: Okay then, so shouldn't you be helping more by taking much less of an overtly powerful, male hierarchical stance? The language you use in Chapter 1 of *Writing Philosophical Autoethnography* binaries autoethnographers. It's all about the more and less sophisticated, the more and less prepared and skilled?

Alec: (Fuck me down dead! You've actually gone and read that chapter!) What I wrote there – thanks very much for reading it, Ash, by the way – is both descriptive and evaluative. I talk about what I've seen and experienced and what I think is wrong about this. It would be disingenuous for me not to do so. But if you can consider it from my standpoint, there's an awful lot of power in the kind of support that autoethnographic unsophisticates, who exhibit little evidence of practise, preparation or skill, get at conferences – or at least the conferences I've been too virtually and in the flesh. I'm talking about the power of unconditional social support – a bit like when an unrehearsed person who fancies her-, him-, or their-self as a standup comedian performs at a club to an audience of family and friends, with hecklers barred from entry. After they've finished their act, they get a standing ovation, which makes them imagine they're top-notch. I'm exaggerating, obviously, but I think this is a useful hyperbolic analogy.

Ash: (B*st*rd!) You're very unkind, you know ... and what you say is obviously rubbish. Apart from the obvious fact that 'hyperbolic analogy' is a contradiction in terms, it's not nearly as bad as that. In any case, new people need encouragement.

Alec: It really can be as bad as all that, at least at the conferences I've been too, and in what I've seen as a journal reviewer of autoethnography. However, I should qualify this point. I'm with Gayle Letherby here. There's great work to be seen and heard at conferences, other places, and in manuscript review work – from new and not so new people. But, to quote from Gayle,

> there's some dreadful stuff too ... I've just reviewed an autoethnography piece for a journal. The author outed themselves as a senior researcher but included no methodological justification and very few substantive references. I'm absolutely sure they wouldn't do that in their other work, but because it's autoethnography they think it's okay and that they can get away with it.[11]

Of course, new people need encouragement, but they also need accurate reality feedback. My ten-year-old grandson lives, eats, sleeps, and breathes football, and wants to play in goal for Manchester City. Right now, he plays for his school team. He might never get beyond this. He might lose interest when he's a bit older and stop practising. He might never be other than mediocre, and mediocrity never excels. Do you see where I'm going with this?

Ash: I see another rubbish analogy coming up, and you don't sound like a very supportive grandad.

Alec: Fuck you, Ash. I love my grandson. I just don't have evidence of his footballing genius right now. So, he gets my encouragement for regular practice, but I would never leap up and down on the side of the pitch chanting his name and waving my arms about in an ecstasy of geriatric stupidity. Look, apropos autoethnography, reality feedback should happen pre-conference and pre-attempts at publication, in order to get people match-fit. That's what mentorship and supervision is all about, and I've done a lot of each of these things, if you want to check my curriculum vitae/resume, or my Research Gate pages, or the book on autoethnographic mentoring I co-wrote with Trude Klevan?[12]

Ash: You're being incredibly defensive now.

Alec: Is there a level of credible defensiveness? Seriously, I know, I know. I do this when I feel under attack. Don't we all? Maybe we should just move on?

Ash: Okay. I'm not over-keen, but let's see what's next…

***

Introduction

In Chapters 1–3, from the literature explored and with my first two inquiry questions in focus, I mapped out my take on the autoethnographic, conceptual, philosophical, and social scientific basis of critical cultural narrative identity. This enabled me to discuss cultural narrative entrapment in terms of the tension between acceptance and resistance. I argued that this tension needed to be considered in the broader socio-philosophical context of understanding the concept of culture in either qualified positive terms or in recognising its oppressive aspects.

While making direct reference to it and related writing, in this chapter I situate my selected work contained and described in the appendix to this book in the critical theoretical context of *Silencing*. In doing so, I try to strike a balance between telling a story that highlights the relevance of the philosophical and social scientific ideas and concepts associated with the Silencing concept, while avoiding the unnecessary duplication that would come from evidentially quoting from, and over-describing, my work. The number of the texts I cite would make doing this cumbersome in any case and would, I believe, serve to obscure the theoretical position I put forward. Readers can access descriptions of the texts cited in greater levels of detail in the appendix and follow up on reading them in full form if they so choose.

This chapter speaks to my third and fourth inquiry questions:

- What philosophical and related conceptual, theoretical, social scientific, and related issues emerge from the ways in which I've addressed resistance to cultural narrative entrapment across the last decade?
- What are the implications arising from these issues for the development of philosophical autoethnography?

The third question is thoroughly addressed and answered throughout this chapter. The fourth will be answered at its end.

Clarifying Narrative Compliance and Narrative Entrapment

In setting the scene for what follows, I should restate the clarificatory distinction between *cultural narrative compliance* and *cultural narrative entrapment*. Narrative compliance might be thought of as a reasonable voluntary act when culture is regarded as unproblematic. The need for resistance creeps in when culture is experienced as oppressively entrapping. In this regard, with Howard Becker and Sara Ahmed, respectively, in mind,[13] it's useful to consider the metaphorical straight line of cultural narrative acceptance pitted against the slanted line of resistance. According to Becker, social groups 'create deviance by making the rules whose infraction constitutes deviance.'[14] Those perceived as deviant according to this definition are seen as off-kilter and a poor fit with their socio-material environment. Ahmed argues that bodies and the spaces they occupy become straight because of repetition. In her terms, ordinary human perception functions in harmony with this – as a straightening device having a corresponding effect on bodies and spaces.[15]

As demonstrated in conformity studies,[16] a person so labelled can willingly or otherwise go along with the group consensus about their deviant status. Equally, illustrated in the stories by Helen Leigh-Phippard and Nigel Short in our 'Re-storying Narrative Identity' article,[17] and in my own in the *Writing Philosophical Autoethnography* volume,[18] they may appear to comply with dominant organisational narratives while subverting and ultimately resisting these. Or, as in Renata Ferdinand's story in the same volume,[19] they may oscillate – wavering between accepting and resisting their deviant status.

In whichever case, behind the centripetal pull to straighten up, there is always the related call to shut up.

The Impact of Silencing

If, in line with Becker, it is accepted that constructions of deviance are contingent rather than necessary and thus often unfair, resistance to cultural narrative entrapment becomes a legitimate moral response. However, resistance is made doubly difficult by the social power of *Silencing*. I have described and exposed how silencing negatively affects others throughout my selected work, described in the appendix to this book, and – as represented in some of this work – have personally experienced and resisted the impact of silencing.

In definitional terms, 'silencing' means *stopping or preventing individual or collective voice*. There are negative consequences for people who resist the power of silencing through not fully self-identifying with, or conforming to, hegemonic cultural beliefs and values. These consequences often ensue as a function of the power of institutions, organisations, professions, cultural traditions, and hierarchies. They include not being taken seriously, being disbelieved, dismissed, or seen as threatening and as a result of this being subjected to character- and body-shaming attacks.

Amply displayed across my work in the appendix, *Silencing* impacts on people entrapped in assumptions, macro and micro cultural policy-making, and writing, and in socio-material environments which are in various ways alien, unfriendly, and/or oppressive. This is specifically evidenced in the following ways:

My Mental Health-Related Work

I wrote about the failure of national UK mental health policy to acknowledge and listen to the lived realities and life contexts of people, because of policymakers' and policy advisors' entrapment in top-down, one-dimensional colonising assumptions about the nature of the cultural identities of people in 'recovery.'[20] I also addressed the plight of mental health service users caught up in cruel 'treatment' and 'care' environments who, with the complicity of mental health nurse educators, are left without stories that are taken seriously.[21] With their resistant voices dismissed,[22] service users can be subjected to ad hominem attacks on their morality, motives, or physical appearance.[23]

My Policy-, Research-, and Autoethnographic Discipline-Related Work

This work testifies to dominant policy and research discourses which display, promote, and reify simplistic, uncritical, or dismissive assumptions and perspectives about mental health service user populations,[24] research populations,[25] and researcher populations.[26] To the extent that these assumptions and perspectives are regarded as hegemonic, I argue they are unlikely to be sufficiently critiqued or challenged, thus depriving those written about, and sometimes those writing, of a voice, as follows:

- Regarding researcher populations, in addition to having a policing and silencing function, oppressive and gendered institutional and policy research cultural assumptions and prescriptions dismiss the contexts and imperatives of researchers' relational ethical challenges and dilemmas.[27]
- With specific reference to narrative autoethnographers, I contend that entrapment in insufficiently scrutinised assumptions about self and culture can result in methodological and cultural myopia and complacency. This eclipses and even prevents the development and emergence of critical scholarly voices.[28]
- In more global terms, I argue that the autoethnographic meta-community, innocently or by default through tacit 'gated community assumptions,' neglects and thus effectively silences the potential autoethnographic voice of excluded ethnogeographical populations.[29]

My Higher Education-Related Autoethnographic Work

Student and educator entrapment in epistemically constrained and limited curricular cultures functions to exclude often necessary alternative curricular content. This silences the voices of people who use mental health services.[30]

Entrapment in neoliberal or corporate academy cultures displaying implicit and sometimes explicit antagonism towards cultural outsiders and oppositional voices negatively impacts on, and trivialises, the voices of critical academics. Directly related to this issue, the oppressive power of life-limiting cultural stuckness and power-asymmetrical cultural values limit what can be spoken about.[31]

My Family-Related Autoethnographic Work

With obvious wider relevance, I write about scapegoating and identity entrapment within my birth family, where my oppositional voice was unrealised because of my then position in the family hierarchy. I contextualised my family entrapment in broader environmental, and historical life- and discourse-limiting, socio-material networks.[32]

My Philosophy-Related Autoethnographic Work

In the final chapter of my edited book, *Writing Philosophical Autoethnography*, I critically addressed the implicit silencing inherent in universalising claims about selfhood, methodological biases in autoethnographer positions on selfhood, arguably culturally racist biases evident in the privileging of Western philosophical cultures, autoethnography club cultures, and autoethnographic community unwillingness to address the arguable nurturance of ressentiment-based victimhood.[33]

My Linguistic-Related Autoethnographic Work

Lastly, in the first autoethnography co-written in large part in Scots, I write about the issue of cultural narrative entrapment inherent in dominant cultural discourses which both oppose the voice of a national language and are alien to its expression of passion and nuance.[34]

The Broader Political Implications of Silencing

As well as being a culturally contingent and situated phenomenon, silencing is more broadly political when mediated by *disparaging subjectivity, epistemic injustice, discursive policing, curriculum control, organisational stupidity, social conformity*, and *political power*. I will now deal with each of these categories in turn.

Silencing through Disparaging Subjectivity

Subjectivity is prized in all my work described in the appendix to this book. To recapitulate from Chapter 2, autoethnography emerged in the social sciences precisely as a critical pushback to the neglect and, by implication, disparagement of subjectivity. To counter this, in the late 1950s, Charles Wright Mills urged researchers to actively demonstrate their 'sociological imagination' by writing about their historically situated cultural lives.[35] Over three decades later, in 1992, a further sociological provocation against silencing came from Carolyn Ellis and Michael Flaherty, who believed that the avoidance of attention to subjectivity by social scientists was linked to its 'unpleasant' and 'dangerous' associations. As these authors argued then, and which is still the case now, 'unpleasant' translates as the inappropriateness of writing about emotional, cognitive, and bodily lived-through experiences, while 'dangerous' refers to the threat to rational-actor world views that continue to remain stickily hegemonic in the social sciences.[36]

Despite the turn towards the subjective voice, the presupposed superiority of objectivist reason over emotion continues to hold sway. This links to negative epistemic judgements about the moral significance of subjectivity-driven texts.

Silencing through Epistemic Injustice

The moral philosophical position of epistemic injustice speaks to silencing oppositional voices throughout much of my work in the appendix. As component parts of epistemic injustice, Miranda Fricker's key analytical concepts of *hermeneutical injustice* and *testimonial injustice* are of central importance here.[37] According to Fricker, hermeneutical injustice occurs when people are unfairly disadvantaged through lacking the knowledge resources required to make sense of their experiences. Testimonial injustice happens when a low level of credibility is accorded to a person's account of their experiences, because of prejudice held against them.

Fricker's analytical framework casts light on several of my articles. It can explain the inability of my family, and myself at the time represented in 'Drinking to Relax...', to make both interpretative and testimonial sense of our respective proximal and distal levels of cultural narrative entrapment.[38] Hermeneutical injustice also impacts on student mental health nurses, their educators, and the public they serve in not having the critical interpretive resources to challenge their curricular entrapment.[39] Testimonial injustice is apparent in Nigel's account of the dismissal of his objections to being called a 'cunt' by a young male staff nurse, during his time in an acute mental health ward in London.[40] Both testimonial injustice and hermeneutical injustice can be read off in the two autoethnographic articles I co-wrote with Susan Young. In 'Troubling Tolichism...',[41] researcher integrity is called into question at several levels, while dominant, hegemonic, and monologic institutional authority claims exhaustive interpretation, leaving little space for critical oppositional voices. In our '...Scotoethnography' text,[42] I argue that the diglossic prejudice about the Scots language from childhood socialisation to adult academic expression constitutes an act of testimonial injustice. I further contend that this is compounded by autoethnographers' general lack of access to historical, textual, and sociolinguistic exemplars to adequately challenge the dismissal or de-privileging of their national languages or dialects.

Silencing through Discursive Policing

Testimonial injustice in turn points to the availability of narrative resources to effectively counter silencing, and to narrative resource unavailability in reinforcing silencing. To put this another way, it points to the importance of having both *discursive* resources and the necessary levels of sophistication to use these resources intelligently, and to its opposite: a lack of discourses, thus zero possibility of their effective deployment. I regard all my work in the appendix as making a significant contribution to increasing the availability of sophisticated discourses.

My long-term position on discourse theory derives from Foucault, who, to recapitulate from Chapter 3, described discourses as 'practices that systematically form the objects of which they speak.'[43] In Foucauldian terms, discourses are historically contingent (thus changing over time) social practices that produce knowledge and meaning. More than a simple relationship between words and things, as sets of paradigms, or 'windows on the world,' discourses set limits for what can reasonably be done and spoken about, and the language and linguistic resources deployed in this regard. In relation to cultural silencing, it follows that some discourses are dominant in attracting majority social support. Conversely, others are marginal in not only failing to attract such a level support, and often triggering responses that range from indifference and disinterest to hostile social opprobrium.

Mediating the relative power of dominant and marginal discourses is the tendency throughout society for what Foucault called 'discursive policing.'[44] This term refers to the reinforcing and reification of hegemonic discourses in social exchanges at any one time and place. Discourses may either flourish and be prolific through people constantly speaking, writing, thus bringing into being, hegemonically valued social 'truths,' or may, if marginal, be constrained and limited in their influential range. The resultant cultural conformism based on the acceptance of dominant discourses used in the service of silencing cuts across all levels of academic ability and sophistication. My challenge to dominant discourses is exemplified across all my appendix texts, from policy enactment,[45] the neoliberal academy,[46] family and smalltown life,[47] mental health nursing academe,[48] relational ethics in autoethnography,[49] autoethnographic social and club cultures,[50] autoethnographic views on the self and culture,[51] and linguistic cultural convention.[52]

Of further interest to me, and with direct relevance to my work in the appendix, are two specific mediators of cultural conformism, in which Silencing is played out in some of my chosen texts. These are curricular narrative entrapment and the power of organisational discourses to trap people in forms of collective stupidity.

Silencing through Curriculum Control

Elliot Eisner and Shereen Bejamin describe the insidious effects of the 'hidden curriculum.'[53] This concept speaks to the ways in which educational establishments inscribe their cultural values and expectations within explicit, or formal, curricula. In this context, the 'hidden curriculum' constitutes the moral dimension of what Eisner describes as 'the null curriculum.'[54] This latter concept refers to important knowledge – knowledge which, from a critical pedagogical standpoint position, should be there, but which is excluded from conventional pedagogical teaching and writing. Null curriculum knowledge can be omitted through innocence or wilful ignorance, or because the neoliberal turn in contemporary academic life excludes that which threatens the imperatives of advanced capitalism.[55] At this political level, it seems likely that important knowledge is excluded precisely because it challenges related taken-for-granted assumptions and the policy- and professional-led principles informing dominant curricula.[56] The net result of this is that technical-rational and policy-led training can substitute for critical education.[57] Neglect of the null curriculum and a failure to remedy this is either explicitly flagged up or alluded to in my 'Living my Narrative,' 'Storying the World,' and co-written 'Re-storying Narrative Identity' articles, and in my 'Toilets Are the Proper Place for 'Outputs'!' chapter.[58]

Silencing through Organisational Stupidity

What mediates such curriculum deficiency at the level of local organisations? With a focus on work environments, one answer to this question can be found in the various related forms of learning failure apparent in collective organisational life, described in my own writing.[59] Mats Alvesson and André Spicer define such 'organisational functional stupidity' as a cognitively and affectively informed unwillingness or inability to employ reflexivity, justification, and substantive reasoning in work organisations.[60] In this context, reflexivity refers to the need for organisational members to actively question tacit and explicit, routinely accepted, organisational knowledge claims and norms. Justification entails these members demanding and being given plausible and acceptable reasons and explanations for decisions made within organisations that negatively impact on work practices, beliefs, and values. Substantive reasoning (which I believe also corresponds with critically reflexive reasoning) constitutes the act of engaging thinking as broadly as possible in relation to professional practices and related work problems. This contrasts with thinking myopically about such practices and problems, thus paying insufficient attention to their wider contextual implications. Whereas substantive reasoning leads in the direction of progressive social change and social justice, myopic thinking maintains the organisational status quo through error repetition, and a corresponding failure to pay sufficient attention to learn from, or even acknowledge, marginalised oppositional voices.

Silencing mediated by organisational stupidity begs deeper exploration of the sociological nature of conformity and corresponding perceptions of deviance from conventionally accepted ways of being in the world.

Silencing through Social Conformity

The significance of social influence on conformity needs to be understood against the backdrop of seminal social psychological experiments held between the 1930s and the 1960s: from Muzafer Sherif's experiments demonstrating the power of group judgements to internalise individual beliefs, to Solomon Asch's work on the power of groups to influence sensory perception, to the Stanley Milgram study on obedience conformity with delivering what was believed by participants as dangerous levels of electric shocks. Based on those experiments and work on conformity more generally, Cass Sunstein concludes and emphasises that people are strongly influenced by views unanimously held at the group level.[61] Not surprisingly, marginal or 'out' groups are far less likely to influence people, especially given the fact that people representing marginal groups may be seen as morally suspect by the conforming majority. This points back to Becker's concept of 'deviance.' To recapitulate, from his standpoint at the interface of philosophy with sociology, Becker asserts that 'Whether an act is deviant depends on how other people react to it.'[62]

The reaction of people tacitly policing discursively and culturally agreed rules is key to understanding deviance in relation to the silencing function of cultural narrative entrapment. In my co-written article, 'Re-storying Narrative Identity,'[63] for example, rule breaking was acceptable up to the point at which it was made public. Helen and Nigel could covertly undermine the rules of their mental health in- and out-patient environments through deceit or subterfuge, making them appear obedient and passive as opposed to culturally antagonistically and reactive. This contrasts with the unfriendly and critical reactions of nursing staff when they publicly broke the rules, or violated rules they were not aware of in the first place, or, in Nigel's case, were too depressed to adhere to.

Conformism, and its undermining, points in turn to my last Silencing-related issue – the significance of, often non-obvious, political power.

Silencing through Political Power

The political theorist Steven Lukes theorises the concept of power in terms of three dimensions. 'One-dimensional power' constitutes overt, observable conflicts of subjective interests within a bounded system, when people consciously exert force over others to get them to do things they would not otherwise do.[64] 'Two-dimensional power' constitutes the power inherent in non-decision-making. Issues and concerns held by stakeholders outside of the dominant bounded system of decision-making, threatening its agenda, are stifled.[65]

The third dimension is characterised by the 'securing (of) consent (and) … compliance to domination … of *willing* subjects.'[66] Across both my cited work and the arguments I've deployed throughout this book, this is reflected in people taking for granted and accepting cultural norms.

Althusser's writing around the role of 'ideological state apparatuses' adds theoretic weight to Lukes' third dimension.[67] At the socio-material level, subsuming embodied trans-generational behavioural, attitudinal dispositions, and with direct significance to cultural narrative entrapment, ideological state apparatuses constrain and shape preferences. They function to mislead people into engaging with the world in life-limiting ways, undermining the possibilities of them aspiring to more rewarding forms of self-determination.

Althusser theorises ideological state apparatuses as systems and practices carried out at institutional and organisational levels.[68] These systems and practices contain and reproduce elements of what he describes as 'State Ideology.' In Althusser's terms, complementing Lukes's thesis, State Ideology can be conceptually understood as that which brings together the dominant themes from the various ideological 'regions,' or areas of a state political system. These themes contain the values upon which consent to domination is predicated. In terms of their local appearance, application, and function, and with direct relevance to my cited work, Althusser subdivides ideological state apparatuses into several sites. The site of Schooling and Education is clearly theoretically linked to my higher education autoethnographies,[69] while the Family, and Information and News sites speak to my 'Drinking to Relax' article.[70]

In broader terms, it seems reasonable to me to assert that ideological mediation is behind all the variants of cultural acceptance argued throughout this book and described in my cited work. In Althusser's terms, all the sites of ideological state apparatuses play a part in ensuring formative socialisation to dominant cultural values, and value transmission. This implies a corresponding need to silence resistant voices in the face of ideology accepted as absolute truth, raising the question of why ideology has such hegemonic power. Terry Eagleton makes the point that, in the sense Althusser uses the concept, ideology has both affective and cognitive components that impact on shared interpersonal subjectivity.[71] Ideological attitudes and behaviour both illustrate and inform people's identities, at the levels of their cultural lived experiences and relationships, in the social orders they have been socialised to adaptively function within. From cradle to grave, people are subjected to systemic, identity-shaping socialisation pressures. These inculcate adherence to locally conventional, socially normative ways of feeling, thinking, and behaving – thus, in Lukes's terms by implication, willing compliance to culturally dominant ways of engaging with the world.

The Metaphysics of Power and Resistance

In considering resistance in relation to Silencing through a deeper, metaphysical lens, Friedrich Nietzsche argued that in the face of life's vicissitudes, autonomous, life-affirming moral agents who are indifferent to moral conformity draw on strength and resilience to sublimate their natural drives.[72] They reject the moral tendencies of the crowd in fate-loving and creative rather than onerous ways through engaging in projects that cohere with crafting singularly stylish identities.[73] I believe I have displayed exactly this in my own work, specifically in my 'Drinking to Relax' article, the chapter 'In Search of My Narrative Character' in my edited volume *Writing Philosophical Autoethnography*, and in the co-written '… Scotoethnography' essay.[74]

In contrast, in Nietzschean terms, moral self-deception entails an abdication of creativity. When power is rejected as a relevant cultural narrative issue and denied rather than affirmed, natural drive range is also necessarily denied and refused. Consequently, moral, and by extension social, conformity substitutes for creative resistance to cultural narrative entrapment. Taking the more passive line of least resistance by accepting conventional cultural narratives is a useful prerequisite for fitting in with the moral sensibilities of the crowd.

Within-group moral conformity implies a tendency to oppose non-conforming groups. In sympathy with Becker's standpoint on deviance, such opposition extends to events, people, and aspects of life that offend the moral assumptions of the judging group.[75] Sympathetic curiosity about the legitimacy of other possible, *different*, ways of living and being, proceeding from an alternative range, nuance, and configuration of moral goods, is relatively absent. Nietzschean self-deceiving morality depends on a negative reaction of one group directed towards another, disparagingly regarded as 'not like me/us.' My work in the appendix exemplifies this tendency. When *othering* reaches morally reprehensible extremes, people are stigmatised based on their perceived disorders or defects of character, even if this is rationalised away in a rhetoric of benevolence.[76] I argue that such *empathic violence* constitutes keeping people firmly in their *othered*, dependent status.[77] I also contend that *othering* is evident in the need to label individuals or groups in culturally stereotypical ways that confer a positive identity and moral superiority on those doing the labelling.[78]

Othering, pulling on stigmatisation, labelling, and moral superiority, serves to create a distance between cultural narrative-accepting conformists and those with a different moral register and resistant style of being in the world. However, unsurprisingly, the gap between the two groups can narrow when the autonomous moral agency of resistant people is undermined by centripetal pressures to conform to hegemonic cultural narratives. This can happen when individuals are caught up in shifting external circumstances that outweigh their individual wills.[79] To recapitulate, MacIntyre illustrates this in the question that points to the fundamental significance and danger of cultural narrative entrapment: 'Of what story or stories do I find myself a part?'[80] This question has more salience and carries more risks for moral life-affirmers given that conformists, by definition, arguably more willingly slot into pre-existing or pre-given life stories.

However, to press a point home, despite the likelihood of life-affirmers engaging in a greater degree of reflexive thinking about their shifting moral agency, they are not immune from social pressures to conform. I have shown in my co-writing that moral identity can, over time, come to overlap with stigmatised identity in those who – in a 'capture and tame' way – are systematically socially coerced into unwilling moral conformism through cultural narrative entrapment.[81] In related terms, transposed to mental health cultures, my co-written work shows that individuals perceived as damaged by more powerful others can sometimes be made to feel that they should accept rather than refuse this subordinate moral status, as a consequence of social pressure.[82]

Research Question Four

What are the implications arising from these issues for the development of philosophical autoethnography?

> Based on my discussion to this point, in developing philosophical autoethnography narrative, and arts- and performance-based autoethnographers might:
>
> - In the context of careful consideration about the maintenance of their integrity, and their relational ethical position, write/craft/ perform against cultural narrative entrapment mediated by Silencing, across areas including, but not limited to:
>   - Personal and relational subjectivity;
>   - Epistemic injustice;
>   - Discursive positioning;
>   - Academic curriculum control;
>   - Organisational stupidity;
>   - Cultural conformity;
>   - Political and ideological socialisation.

As well as having therapeutic value and the level of the individual writer/crafter/ performer, this might hopefully positively contribute to the development of philosophical autoethnographic identity grounded in life-affirming critical autoethnographicity. Furthermore, this will implicate:

- Adding to the cultural capital stock of life-affirming autoethnographic stories;
- Resisting the centripetal pull of cultural narratives which prove restrictive, oppressive, or toxic, thus,
- Changing the interiority of the self, including rejecting as many historically embedded and residual stories as is possible.

Regarding the last bullet point, in Part 2 of my literature exploration, I presented the argument that shifting environments can bring aspects of the narrative unconscious into consciousness. This might also result in corresponding changes in the meaning of this material, which I believe I've evidenced in my autoethnographic chapter in my co-edited volume, *Writing Philosophical Autoethnography*.[83] In this regard, in shifting the balance between cultural acceptance and cultural resistance, creative narrative truth takes priority over historical truth.

Conclusion

Developing philosophical autoethnography mediated by the nurturance of critical autoethnographicity is – in line with the view expressed by Marcin Kafar,[84] quoted in Chapter 2 – always likely to be promoted by the few not the many. The few will take autoethnography seriously by recognising the distinction between the kind of method-based 'autoethnography,' often proceeding from superficial understandings of the craft, and used to bolster the hegemonic power of the neoliberal academy, and living according to the values of critical autoethnographicity. Dominant cultural narratives are sustained by the power of the centripetal pull into the straight line of conformity and acceptance. Externally imposed or internally assumed inscription within cultural narratives which are, or have the potential to be, oppressive is accepted by some and resisted by others. In a Nietzschean sense, acceptance – the safer option – signals life-denial, while resistance – risky but worth it – signals life-affirmation.

Having selectively explored the literature relevant to my doctoral topic and first two research questions in Chapters 2 and 3, and having discussed the corresponding philosophical, conceptual, and social scientific issues related to my portfolio of work in this chapter, I am now able to restate my answers to my research questions before turning to the autocritique of my standpoint position in Chapter 5.

To recapitulate, with cultural narrative entrapment defined as:

The insufficiently reflexive autoethnographic display of stuckness, complacency, or indifference in accepting potentially, or actually, life-limiting auto/biographical storied constructions of the cultural narrative identity of oneself and others as ontologically and epistemologically adequate, whether these constructions are individually or socially assumed, or externally conferred or imposed,

- **What constitutes resistance to cultural narrative entrapment in autoethnography?**

  Resistance to cultural narrative entrapment is constituted by continual reflexive alertness to the seductive power of culture, through the exercise of critical autoethnographicity. This alertness can be enhanced by discursive sophistication, and critical sensitivity to the narrative surround, narrative inheritance, and the corresponding impact of distal, narrative identity-shaping forces.

- **Why is it important to resist this cultural narrative entrapment in autoethnography?**

  When and while assumed to be benign, culture can often be oppressive and life-limiting. It is therefore often important to resist the centripetal pull into cultural entrapment, through the exercise of queering sensibilities. This can contribute to re-storying narrative identity in life-affirming ways, to moral character development, and to bringing awareness of distal forces more into consciousness.

- **What philosophical and related conceptual, theoretical, and social scientific issues emerge from the ways in which I address resistance to cultural narrative entrapment across my autoethnographic scholarship over the years?**

  Silencing critical narrative identity across the following areas: the disparaging of subjectivity in the social sciences, epistemic injustice, discursive policing, curriculum control, organisational stupidity, social conformity, and political power.

- **What implications arise from these issues for the development of philosophical autoethnography?**

  Through the exercise of critical autoethnographicity, writers of philosophical autoethnography may exemplify:

  - Resisting the centripetal pull of cultural narratives which prove restrictive, oppressive, or toxic, thus,
  - Changing the interiority of the self, by rejecting as many life-denying historically embedded and residual stories and discourses as possible;
  - Consolidating existing, and developing new, life-affirming, discourses;
  - Writing against entrapment mediated by the silencing of critical cultural narrative identity, thus adding to the cultural capital stock of life-affirming autoethnographic stories.

***

Ash: You seem to be living in a fantasy world, in which you believe that your claim to embracing 'life-affirming morality' gives you some sort of transcendental power. Isn't that as mad as the belief in the power of Astrology, which you lampoon in your 'In Search of My Narrative Character...' chapter in your *Writing Philosophical Autoethnography* book?[85]

Alec: (Read that too? Great! Must be doing something right!) Dodgy comparison there, Ash!

Ash: Why?

Alec: Because Nietzsche's life-affirming morality concept is grounded in respectable metaphysical and aphoristic philosophy, whereas the Astrology I refer to in 'The Talking Tomcats of Totnes' story in that chapter[86] amounts to consistently unverifiable pseudo-scientific nonsense. If you check out Wikipedia, you'll find that Astrology's been rejected by the scientific communities because of the numerous studies conducted over the years that repeatedly demonstrate its lack of explanatory power to ever explain or make sense of the universe.[87]

Ash: Loads of people in Asia still believe in Astrology.

Alec: As I described in story, so do loads of people in Totnes, Devon. Loads of people in Britain also believed in magic and witchcraft, including distinguished members of the Royal Society in the Early Modern period, even up to the 20th century.[88] Didn't make that true either!

Ash: Shouldn't people be allowed to believe in what they want to believe in?

Alec: Does that include me being allowed to believe in life-affirming morality?

Ash: (Tw*t!) You make such a big thing of it!

Alec: You're deflecting now, Ash. You've shifted from expressing a liberal attitude towards having beliefs in things generally to a criticism of what you perceive as the strength of my specific belief. So, it's okay to believe in anything, including rubbish, providing you don't express this in strong terms?

Ash: That's not what I meant.

Alec: What did you mean then?

Ash: Look, people have believed in Astrology for many thousands of years. Nietzsche comes along in the second half of the 19th century and pontificates on morality.

Alec: You're deflecting again, Ash, throwing in red herrings. So, you're saying that a belief gains in respectability the longer it's held by a group of people?

Ash: (B*st*rd!) No, I'm not saying that!

Alec: What are you saying then?

Ash: Look, there's got to be some sort of profundity to Astrology for people to have believed in it for so long!

Alec: (Back we go to genetic fallacy) Have you ever read Nietzsche?

Ash: No.

Alec: Know much about Astrology, do you Ash?

Ash: No! (Rank puller!) What's your bl**dy point?

Alec: Let's do a little thought experiment. Imagine a world where Astrology (Arsetrology) has taken off big time, despite its pseudo-scientific status, with lots of Astrologers offering their services to people. In this world, there are roughly the same number of people who, with an academic background in Nietzschean philosophy, are available to help people embark on a journey towards life-affirming morality. Which group of people do you think would make the world a better, more creative, less unquestioning, less conventional cultural rule-following, more morally sound, less batshit crazy place – Astrologers or Nietzschean Life Affirmers?

Ash: Your question is loaded. In any case, it would be up to the public to choose between the two groups. They'd be free to do so.

Alec: You didn't answer my question. What my thought experiment was intended to show, Ash, was a refutation of the moral equivalence of Astrology and Nietszchean Life-Affirmation in a counterfactual future by using what's known as the 'absurd consequences move.'[89] You might want to check out Nigel Warburton's helpful little book sometime (you won't).[90] In the longer term, if you ever buy a swimming pool, you're not going to need a deep end. Save you a bit of money, and good for the planet.

Ash: As well as the sarcasm, you're resorting to the ad hominem tactics you say you despise. Hypocrite!

Alec: (Shit! Yep!) Guilty as charged, Ash. Unreserved apologies.

Ash: Not accepted! I'm so angry with you. Let's just move on to the next chapter.

Alec: (Fuck. I've gone too far. I was cruel and my apology was no apology at all. Done it again!).

Notes

1 David Lodge, *Nice Work* (London: Secker & Warburg, 1988), 22.
2 Alec Grant and Susan Young, 'A Scot an' a Sassenach Scrieve Aboot leid: A Three Pairt Scotoethnography (A Scot and an English Person Write about Language: A Scotoethnography in Three Parts),' *Journal of Autoethnography* 5, no. 1 (Winter 2024): 39–55, https://doi.org/10.1525/joae.2024.5.1.39; Alec Grant and Susan Young, 'A Scot an' a Sassenach Scrieve Aboot Leid: A Three Pairt Scotoethnography (A Scot and an English Person Write about Language: A Scotoethnography in Three Parts,' in *Meaningful journeys: Autoethnographies of Quest and Identity Transformation*, eds. Alec Grant and Elizabeth Lloyd-Parkes (London and New York: Routledge, 2024), 96–116.
3 Translation: If I'd conducted a Scotoethnographic dialogue, what would you have done? It would have left you confounded.
4 Nigel Warburon, *Thinking from A to Z*. Third Edition (London and New York: Routledge, 2007), 74.
5 Martha C. Nussbaum, *The Fragility of Goodness: Luck and Ethics in Greek Tragedy and Philosophy*. Updated Edition (New York: Cambridge University Press, 2001).
6 Emily Wilson, *The Death of Socrates* (Cambridge, MA: Harvard University Press, 2007).
7 Alfred North Whitehead, *Process and Reality* (New York: Free Press, 1979), 39.
8 Gerda Lerner, *The Creation of Patriarchy* (New York: Oxford University Press, 1986).
9 Alec Grant and SusanYoung, 'Troubling Tolichism in Several Voices: Resisting Epistemic Violence in Creative Analytical and Critical Autoethnographic Practices,' *Journal of Autoethnography* 3, no. 1 (Winter 2022): 103–117, https://doi.org/10.1525/joae.2022.3.1.103
10 Gayle Letherby, *Feminist Research in Theory and Practice* (Buckingham and Philadelphia: Open University Press.
11 Gayle Letherby, Email message to author, July 28, 2024.
12 Trude Klevan and Alec Grant, *An Autoethnography of Becoming a Qualitative Researcher: A Dialogic View of Academic Development* (London and New York: Routledge, 2022).
13 Howard Becker, *Outsiders: Studies in the Sociology of Deviance* (New York: Free Press, 2018 [1963]): Sara Ahmed, *Queer Phenomenology: Orientations, Objects, Others* (Durham, NC: Duke University Press, 2006).
14 Howard Becker, *Outsiders: Studies in the Sociology of Deviance* (New York: Free Press, 2018 [1963]), 8.
15 Sara Ahmed, *Queer Phenomenology: Orientations, Objects, Others* (Durham, NC: Duke University Press, 2006), 92.
16 Cass R. Sunstein, *Conformity: The Power of Social Influences* (New York: New York University Press, 2019).
17 Alec Grant, Helen Leigh-Phippard, and Nigel P. Short, 'Re-storying Narrative Identity: A Dialogical Study of Mental Health Recovery and Survival,' *Journal of Psychiatric and Mental Health Nursing* 22, no. 4 (February 2015): 278–286, https://doi.org/10.1111/jpm.12188.
18 Alec Grant, 'In Search of my Narrative Character,' in *Writing Philosophical Autoethnography*, ed. Alec Grant (New York and London: Routledge, 2024), 114–132.
19 Renata Ferdinand, 'Which Way Is Up? A Philosophical Autoethnography of Trying to Stand in a "Crooked Room",' in *Writing Philosophical Autoethnography*, ed. Alec Grant (New York and London: Routledge, 2024), 80–95.
20 Alec Grant, Helen Leigh-Phippard, and Nigel P. Short, 'Re-storying Narrative Identity: A Dialogical Study of Mental Health Recovery and Survival,' *Journal*

of Psychiatric and Mental Health Nursing 22, no. 4 (February 2015): 278–286, https://doi.org/10.1111/jpm.12188

21 Alec Grant, Helen Leigh-Phippard, and Nigel P. Short, 'Re-storying Narrative Identity: A Dialogical Study of Mental Health Recovery and Survival,' *Journal of Psychiatric and Mental Health Nursing* 22, no. 4 (February 2015): 278–286, https://doi.org/10.1111/jpm.12188; Alec Grant, 'Living my Narrative: Storying Dishonesty and Deception in Mental Health Nursing,' *Nursing Philosophy* 17, no. 3 (May 2016): 194–201, https://doi.org/10.1111/nup.12127; Alec Grant, 'Storying the World: A Post-Humanist Critique of Phenomenological-Humanist Representational Practices in Mental Health Nurse Qualitative Inquiry,' *Nursing Philosophy* 17, no. 4 (June 2016): 290–297, https://doi.org/10.1111/nup.12135; Alec Grant, 'Moving Around the Hyphens: A Critical Meta-Autoethnographic Performance,' in *Critical Mental Health Nursing: Observations from the Inside*, eds. Pete Bull, Jonathan Gadsby, and Stephen Williams S. (Monmouth: PCCS Books, 2018), 30–50.

22 Alec Grant, Helen Leigh-Phippard, and Nigel P. Short, 'Re-storying Narrative Identity: A Dialogical Study of Mental Health Recovery and Survival,' *Journal of Psychiatric and Mental Health Nursing* 22, no. 4 (February 2015): 278–286, https://doi.org/10.1111/jpm.12188

23 Alec Grant, Helen Leigh-Phippard, and Nigel P. Short, 'Re-storying Narrative Identity: A Dialogical Study of Mental Health Recovery and Survival,' *Journal of Psychiatric and Mental Health Nursing* 22, no. 4 (February 2015): 278–286, https://doi.org/10.1111/jpm.12188; Alec Grant, 'Living my Narrative: Storying Dishonesty and Deception in Mental Health Nursing,' *Nursing Philosophy* 17, no. 3 (May 2016): 194–201, https://doi.org/10.1111/nup.12127

24 Alec Grant, Helen Leigh-Phippard, and Nigel P. Short, 'Re-storying Narrative Identity: A Dialogical Study of Mental Health Recovery and Survival,' *Journal of Psychiatric and Mental Health Nursing* 22, no. 4 (February 2015): 278–286, https://doi.org/10.1111/jpm.12188

25 Alec Grant, 'Storying the World: A Post-Humanist Critique of Phenomenological-Humanist Representational Practices in Mental Health Nurse Qualitative Inquiry,' *Nursing Philosophy* 17, no. 4 (June 2016): 290–297, https://doi.org/10.1111/nup.12135

26 Alec Grant and SusanYoung, 'Troubling Tolichism in Several Voices: Resisting Epistemic Violence in Creative Analytical and Critical Autoethnographic Practices,' *Journal of Autoethnography* 3, no. 1 (Winter 2022): 103–117, https://doi.org/10.1525/joae.2022.3.1.103

27 Alec Grant and SusanYoung, 'Troubling Tolichism in Several Voices: Resisting Epistemic Violence in Creative Analytical and Critical Autoethnographic Practices,' *Journal of Autoethnography* 3, no. 1 (Winter 2022): 103–117, https://doi.org/10.1525/joae.2022.3.1.103

28 Alec Grant, 'The Philosophical Autoethnographer,' in *Writing Philosophical Autoethnography*, ed. Alec Grant (New York and London: Routledge, 2024), 1–22.

29 Alec Grant, 'Concluding Thoughts: Selves, Cultures, Limitations, Futures,' in *Writing Philosophical Autoethnography*, ed. Alec Grant (New York and London: Routledge, 2024), 249–269.

30 Alec Grant, 'Living my Narrative: Storying Dishonesty and Deception in Mental Health Nursing,' *Nursing Philosophy* 17, no. 3 (May 2016): 194–201, https://doi.org/10.1111/nup.12127; Alec Grant, 'Moving Around the Hyphens: A Critical Meta-Autoethnographic Performance,' in *Critical Mental Health Nursing: Observations from the Inside*, eds. Pete Bull, Jonathan Gadsby, and Stephen Williams S. (Monmouth: PCCS Books, 2018), 30–50.

31 Alec Grant, 'Toilets are the Proper Place for 'Outputs'! A Tale of Knowledge Production and Publishing with Students in Higher Education,' in *Self-narrative and*

Pedagogy: Stories of Experience within Teaching and Learning, eds. Mike Hayler, and Jess Moriarty (Rotterdam: Sense Publishers, 2017), 45–57; Alec Grant, 'In Search of my Narrative Character,' in *Writing Philosophical Autoethnography*, ed. Alec Grant (New York and London: Routledge, 2024), 114–132.

32 Alec Grant, 'Drinking to Relax: An Autoethnography of a Highland Family Viewed through a New Materialist lens,' in *Auto/Biography Yearbook 2017*, ed. Andrew Sparkes (Nottingham: Russell Press, 2018), 33–46. (6) (PDF) Paper for British Sociological Association Yearbook 2017, Drinking to Relax. (researchgate.net).

33 Alec Grant, 'Concluding Thoughts: Selves, Cultures, Limitations, Futures,' in *Writing Philosophical Autoethnography*, ed. Alec Grant (New York and London: Routledge, 2024), 249–269.

34 Alec Grant and Susan Young, 'A Scot an' a Sassenach Scrieve Aboot leid: A Three Pairt Scotoethnography (A Scot and an English Person Write about Language: A Scotoethnography in Three Parts),' *Journal of Autoethnography* 5, no. 1 (Winter 2024): 39–55, https://doi.org/10.1525/joae.2024.5.1.39

35 Charles Wright Mills, *The Sociological Imagination. Fortieth Anniversary Edition* (New York: Oxford University Press, Inc., 2000 [1959]).

36 Carolyn Ellis and Michael Flaherty, 'An Agenda for the Interpretation of Lived Experience,' in *Investigating Subjectivity: Research on Lived Experience*, eds. Carolyn Ellis and Michael Flaherty (Newbury Park, CA: Sage Publications, Inc., 1992), 1–13, quoted words on page 1.

37 Miranda Fricker, *Epistemic Injustice: Power and the Ethics of Knowing* (Oxford: Oxford University Press, 2007).

38 Alec Grant, 'Drinking to Relax: An Autoethnography of a Highland Family Viewed through a New Materialist lens,' in *Auto/Biography Yearbook 2017*, ed. Andrew Sparkes (Nottingham: Russell Press, 2018), 33–46.

39 Alec Grant, 'Living my Narrative: Storying Dishonesty and Deception in Mental Health Nursing,' *Nursing Philosophy* 17, no. 3 (May 2016): 194–201, https://doi.org/10.1111/nup.12127; Alec Grant, 'Storying the World: A Post-Humanist Critique of Phenomenological-Humanist Representational Practices in Mental Health Nurse Qualitative Inquiry,' *Nursing Philosophy* 17, no. 4 (June 2016): 290–297, https://doi.org/10.1111/nup.12135; Alec Grant, 'Toilets are the Proper Place for 'Outputs'! A Tale of Knowledge Production and Publishing with Students in Higher Education,' in *Self-narrative and Pedagogy: Stories of Experience within Teaching and Learning*, eds. Mike Hayler, and Jess Moriarty (Rotterdam: Sense Publishers, 2017), 45–57.

40 Alec Grant, Helen Leigh-Phippard, and Nigel P. Short, 'Re-storying Narrative Identity: A Dialogical Study of Mental Health Recovery and Survival,' *Journal of Psychiatric and Mental Health Nursing* 22, no. 4 (February 2015): 283, https://doi.org/10.1111/jpm.12188

41 Alec Grant and SusanYoung, 'Troubling Tolichism in Several Voices: Resisting Epistemic Violence in Creative Analytical and Critical Autoethnographic Practices,' *Journal of Autoethnography* 3, no. 1 (Winter 2022): 103–117, https://doi.org/10.1525/joae.2022.3.1.103

42 Alec Grant and Susan Young, 'A Scot an' a Sassenach Scrieve Aboot leid: A Three Pairt Scotoethnography (A Scot and an English Person Write about Language: A Scotoethnography in Three Parts),' *Journal of Autoethnography* 5, no. 1 (Winter 2024): 39–55, https://doi.org/10.1525/joae.2024.5.1.39

43 Michel Foucault, *The Archaeology of Knowledge and the Discourse on Language* (London: Vintage Books, 2010 [1972]), 49.

44 Michel Foucault, 'The Order of Discourse: Inaugural Lecture at the Collège de France, given 2 December 1970,' in *Untying the Text: A Post-Structuralist Reader*, ed. Robert Young (Boston, MA: Routledge & Kegan Paul, 1981 [1970]), 48–78.

45 Alec Grant, Helen Leigh-Phippard, and Nigel P. Short, 'Re-storying Narrative Identity: A Dialogical Study of Mental Health Recovery and Survival,' *Journal of Psychiatric and Mental Health Nursing* 22, no. 4 (February 2015): 278–286, https://doi.org/10.1111/jpm.12188

46 Alec Grant, 'Toilets are the Proper Place for 'Outputs'! A Tale of Knowledge Production and Publishing with Students in Higher Education,' in *Self-narrative and Pedagogy: Stories of Experience within Teaching and Learning*, eds. Mike Hayler, and Jess Moriarty (Rotterdam: Sense Publishers, 2017), 45–57; Alec Grant, 'Moving Around the Hyphens: A Critical Meta-Autoethnographic Performance,' in *Critical Mental Health Nursing: Observations from the Inside*, eds. Pete Bull, Jonathan Gadsby, and Stephen Williams S. (Monmouth: PCCS Books, 2018), 30–50.

47 Alec Grant, 'Drinking to Relax: An Autoethnography of a Highland Family Viewed through a New Materialist lens,' in *Auto/Biography Yearbook 2017*, ed. Andrew Sparkes (Nottingham: Russell Press, 2018), 33–46.

48 Alec Grant, 'Living my Narrative: Storying Dishonesty and Deception in Mental Health Nursing,' *Nursing Philosophy* 17, no. 3 (May 2016): 194–201, https://doi.org/10.1111/nup.12127; Alec Grant, 'Storying the World: A Post-Humanist Critique of Phenomenological-Humanist Representational Practices in Mental Health Nurse Qualitative Inquiry,' *Nursing Philosophy* 17, no. 4 (June 2016): 290–297, https://doi.org/10.1111/nup.12135; Alec Grant, 'Toilets are the Proper Place for 'Outputs'! A Tale of Knowledge Production and Publishing with Students in Higher Education,' in *Self-narrative and Pedagogy: Stories of Experience within Teaching and Learning*, eds. Mike Hayler, and Jess Moriarty (Rotterdam: Sense Publishers, 2017), 45–57; Alec Grant, 'Moving Around the Hyphens: A Critical Meta-Autoethnographic Performance,' in *Critical Mental Health Nursing: Observations from the Inside*, eds. Pete Bull, Jonathan Gadsby, and Stephen Williams S. (Monmouth: PCCS Books, 2018), 30–50.

49 Alec Grant and SusanYoung, 'Troubling Tolichism in Several Voices: Resisting Epistemic Violence in Creative Analytical and Critical Autoethnographic Practices,' *Journal of Autoethnography* 3, no. 1 (Winter 2022): 103–117, https://doi.org/10.1525/joae.2022.3.1.103

50 Alec Grant, 'Concluding Thoughts: Selves, Cultures, Limitations, Futures,' in *Writing Philosophical Autoethnography*, ed. Alec Grant (New York and London: Routledge, 2024), 249–269.

51 Alec Grant, 'The Philosophical Autoethnographer,' in *Writing Philosophical Autoethnography*, ed. Alec Grant (New York and London: Routledge, 2024), 1–22.

52 Alec Grant and Susan Young, 'A Scot an' a Sassenach Scrieve Aboot Leid: A Three Pairt Scotoethnography (A Scot and an English Person Write about Language: A Scotoethnography in Three Parts),' *Journal of Autoethnography* 5, no. 1 (Winter 2024): 39–55, https://doi.org/10.1525/joae.2024.5.1.39

53 Elliot W. Eisner, *The Educational Imagination: On the Design and Evaluation of School Programs* (New York: Macmillan Publishing Co., 1979); Shereen Benjamin, 'Schools, Feminism and Gender-Identity Theory,' in *Sex and Gender: A Contemporary Reader*, eds. Alice Sullivan, and Selina Todd (London and New York: Routledge, 2024), 194–213.

54 Elliot W. Eisner, *The Educational Imagination: On the Design and Evaluation of School Programs* (New York: Macmillan Publishing Co., 1979), 83–92.

55 Bill Readings, *The University in Ruins* (Cambridge, MA: Harvard University Press, 1996); Gary Rolfe. *The university in Dissent: Scholarship in the Corporate University* (London and New York: Routledge, 2013).

56 Alec Grant and Mark Radcliffe, 'Resisting Technical Rationality in Mental Health Nurse Higher Education: A Duoethnography,' *The Qualitative Report (TQR)* 20, no. 6 (June 2015): 815–825. https://doi.org/10.46743/2160-3715/2015.2157.

57 Alec Grant and Mark Radcliffe, 'Resisting Technical Rationality in Mental Health Nurse Higher Education: A Duoethnography,' *The Qualitative Report (TQR)* 20, no. 6 (June 2015): 815–825. http://doi.org/10.46743/2160-3715/2015.2157; Alec Grant and Benny Goodman, *Communication & Interpersonal Skills in Nursing*. Fourth Edition (London: Learning Matters/SAGE Publications Ltd, 2018).

58 Alec Grant, 'Living my Narrative: Storying Dishonesty and Deception in Mental Health Nursing,' *Nursing Philosophy* 17, no. 3 (May 2016): 194–201, https://doi.org/10.1111/nup.12127; Alec Grant, 'Storying the World: A Post-Humanist Critique of Phenomenological-Humanist Representational Practices in Mental Health Nurse Qualitative Inquiry,' *Nursing Philosophy* 17, no. 4 (June 2016): 290–297, https://doi.org/10.1111/nup.12135; Alec Grant, 'Toilets are the Proper Place for 'Outputs'! A Tale of Knowledge Production and Publishing with Students in Higher Education,' in *Self-narrative and Pedagogy: Stories of Experience within Teaching and Learning*, eds. Mike Hayler, and Jess Moriarty (Rotterdam: Sense Publishers, 2017), 45–57; Alec Grant, Helen Leigh-Phippard, and Nigel P. Short, 'Re-storying Narrative Identity: A Dialogical Study of Mental Health Recovery and Survival,' *Journal of Psychiatric and Mental Health Nursing* 22, no. 4 (February 2015): 278–286, https://doi.org/10.1111/jpm.12188.

59 Alec Grant, 'Moving Around the Hyphens: A Critical Meta-Autoethnographic Performance,' in *Critical Mental Health Nursing: Observations from the Inside*, eds. Pete Bull, Jonathan Gadsby, and Stephen Williams S. (Monmouth: PCCS Books, 2018), 30–50; Alec Grant and Mark Radcliffe, 'Resisting Technical Rationality in Mental Health Nurse Higher Education: A Duoethnography,' *The Qualitative Report (TQR)* 20, no. 6 (June 2015): 815–825. http://doi.org/10.46743/2160-3715/2015.2157.

60 Mats Alvesson and Andrè Spicer, 'A Stupidity-Based Theory of Organizations,' *Journal of Management Studies* 49, no. 7 (June 2012), 1194–1220, https://doi.org/10.1111/j.1467-6486.2012.01072.x; Mats Alvesson and Andrè Spicer, *The Stupidity Paradox: The Power and Pitfalls of Functional Stupidity at Work* (London: Profile Books, 2016).

61 Cass R. Sunstein, *Conformity: The Power of Social Influences* (New York: New York University Press, 2019).

62 Howard Becker, *Outsiders: Studies in the Sociology of Deviance* (New York: Free Press, 2018 [1963]), 11.

63 Alec Grant, Helen Leigh-Phippard, and Nigel P. Short, 'Re-storying Narrative Identity: A Dialogical Study of Mental Health Recovery and Survival,' *Journal of Psychiatric and Mental Health Nursing* 22, no. 4 (February 2015): 278–286, https://doi.org/10.1111/jpm.12188.

64 Steven Lukes, *Power: A Radical View*. Second Edition (London: Red Globe Press, 2005), 16–19.

65 Steven Lukes, *Power: A Radical View*. Second Edition (London: Red Globe Press, 2005), 20–25.

66 Steven Lukes, *Power: A Radical View*. Second Edition (London: Red Globe Press, 2005), 109, my brackets and italics.

67 Louis Althusser, *On the Reproduction of Capitalism: Ideology and Ideological State Apparatuses*, translated by G.M. Goshgarian (London: Verso, 2014).

68 Louis Althusser, *On the Reproduction of Capitalism: Ideology and Ideological State Apparatuses*, translated by G.M. Goshgarian (London: Verso, 2014), 74–77.

69 Alec Grant, 'Toilets are the Proper Place for "Outputs"! A Tale of Knowledge Production and Publishing with Students in Higher Education,' in *Self-narrative and Pedagogy: Stories of Experience within Teaching and Learning*, eds. Mike Hayler, and Jess Moriarty (Rotterdam: Sense Publishers, 2017), 45–57; Alec Grant, 'Moving Around the Hyphens: A Critical Meta-Autoethnographic Performance,' in

Critical Mental Health Nursing: Observations from the Inside, eds. Pete Bull, Jonathan Gadsby, and Stephen Williams S. (Monmouth: PCCS Books, 2018), 30–50.

70 Alec Grant, 'Drinking to Relax: An Autoethnography of a Highland Family Viewed through a New Materialist lens,' in *Auto/Biography Yearbook 2017*, ed. Andrew Sparkes (Nottingham: Russell Press, 2018), 33–46.

71 Terry Eagleton, *Ideology: An Introduction* (London: Verso, 1991), 19–20.

72 Freidrich Nietzsche, *Beyond Good and Evil: Prelude to a Philosophy of the Future.* Translated Reginald J. Hollingdale (London: Penguin Books (2003 [1886]); Freidrich Nietzsche, *The will to Power: Selections from the Notebooks of the 1880s.* Translated R. Kevin Hill, and Michael A. Scarpitti (London: Penguin Books, 2017 [1901/6]).

73 Brian Leiter, *Nietzsche on Morality*, 2nd edn. (London: Routledge, 2014), 96; Simon May, *Nietzsche's Ethics and his 'War on Morality'* (Oxford: Clarendon Press, 1999), 26–29.

74 Alec Grant, 'Drinking to Relax: An Autoethnography of a Highland Family Viewed through a New Materialist lens,' in *Auto/Biography Yearbook 2017*, ed. Andrew Sparkes (Nottingham: Russell Press, 2018), 33–46. Alec Grant, 'In Search of my Narrative Character,' in *Writing Philosophical Autoethnography*, ed. Alec Grant (New York and London: Routledge, 2024), 114–132. Alec Grant and Susan Young, 'A Scot an' a Sassenach Scrieve Aboot Leid: A Three Pairt Scotoethnography (A Scot and an English Person Write about Language: A Scotoethnography in Three Parts),' *Journal of Autoethnography* 5, no. 1 (Winter 2024): 39–55, https://doi.org/10.1525/joae.2024.5.1.39

75 Simon May, *Nietzsche's Ethics and his 'War on Morality'* (Oxford: Clarendon Press, 1999), 105.

76 Alec Grant, 'Living my Narrative: Storying Dishonesty and Deception in Mental Health Nursing,' *Nursing Philosophy* 17, no. 3 (May 2016): 194–201, https://doi.org/10.1111/nup.12127; Alec Grant, Helen Leigh-Phippard, and Nigel P. Short, 'Re-storying Narrative Identity: A Dialogical Study of Mental Health Recovery and Survival,' *Journal of Psychiatric and Mental Health Nursing* 22, no. 4 (February 2015): 278–286, https://doi.org/10.1111/jpm.12188.

77 Alec Grant, 'Storying the World: A Post-Humanist Critique of Phenomenological-Humanist Representational Practices in Mental Health Nurse Qualitative Inquiry,' *Nursing Philosophy* 17, no. 4 (June 2016): 290–297, https://doi.org/10.1111/nup.12135; Alec Grant and SusanYoung, 'Troubling Tolichism in Several Voices: Resisting Epistemic Violence in Creative Analytical and Critical Autoethnographic Practices,' *Journal of Autoethnography* 3, no. 1 (Winter 2022): 103–117, https://doi.org/10.1525/joae.2022.3.1.103; Alec Grant, Helen Leigh-Phippard, and Nigel P. Short, 'Re-storying Narrative Identity: A Dialogical Study of Mental Health Recovery and Survival,' *Journal of Psychiatric and Mental Health Nursing* 22, no. 4 (February 2015): 278–286, https://doi.org/10.1111/jpm.12188.

78 Alec Grant, 'Living my Narrative: Storying Dishonesty and Deception in Mental Health Nursing,' *Nursing Philosophy* 17, no. 3 (May 2016): 194–201, https://doi.org/10.1111/nup.12127; Alec Grant, 'Storying the World: A Post-Humanist Critique of Phenomenological-Humanist Representational Practices in Mental Health Nurse Qualitative Inquiry,' *Nursing Philosophy* 17, no. 4 (June 2016): 290–297, https://doi.org/10.1111/nup.12135; Alec Grant and SusanYoung, 'Troubling Tolichism in Several Voices: Resisting Epistemic Violence in Creative Analytical and Critical Autoethnographic Practices,' *Journal of Autoethnography* 3, no. 1 (Winter 2022): 103–117, https://doi.org/10.1525/joae.2022.3.1.103; Alec Grant, Helen Leigh-Phippard, and Nigel P. Short, 'Re-storying Narrative Identity: A Dialogical Study of Mental Health Recovery and Survival,' *Journal of Psychiatric*

and Mental Health Nursing 22, no. 4 (February 2015): 278–286, https://doi.
org/10.1111/jpm.12188.

79 Martha C. Nussbaum, *The Fragility of Goodness: Luck and Ethics in Greek Tragedy
and Philosophy.* Updated Edition (New York: Cambridge University Press, 2001), 35.

80 Alasdair MacIntyre, *After Virtue: A Study in Moral Virtue.* Third Edition (with
Prologue) (London and New York: Bloomsbury, 2007), 250.

81 Alec Grant and SusanYoung, 'Troubling Tolichism in Several Voices: Resisting
Epistemic Violence in Creative Analytical and Critical Autoethnographic Practices,' *Journal of Autoethnography* 3, no. 1 (Winter 2022): 103–117, https://doi.
org/10.1525/joae.2022.3.1.103; Alec Grant and Susan Young, 'A Scot an' a Sassenach Scrieve Aboot leid: A Three Pairt Scotoethnography (A Scot and an English Person Write about Language: A Scotoethnography in Three Parts),' *Journal
of Autoethnography* 5, no. 1 (Winter 2024): 39–55, https://doi.org/10.1525/
joae.2024.5.1.39.

82 Alec Grant, Helen Leigh-Phippard, and Nigel P. Short, 'Re-storying Narrative
Identity: A Dialogical Study of Mental Health Recovery and Survival,' *Journal
of Psychiatric and Mental Health Nursing* 22, no. 4 (February 2015): 278–286,
https://doi.org/10.1111/jpm.12188

83 Alec Grant, 'In Search of my Narrative Character,' in *Writing Philosophical Autoethnography*, ed. Alec Grant (New York and London: Routledge, 2024), 114–132.

84 Marcin Kafar, 'Traveling with Carolyn Ellis and Art Bochner, or How I became Harmonized with the Autoethnographic Life: An Autoformative Story,' in *Advances in
Autoethnography and Narrative Inquiry: Reflections on the Legacy of Carolyn Ellis
and Arthur Bochner*, eds. Tony E. Adams, Robin M. Boylorn, and Lisa M. Tillmann (New York and London: Routledge, 2021), 48–63.

85 Alec Grant, 'In Search of my Narrative Character,' in *Writing Philosophical Autoethnography*, ed. Alec Grant (New York and London: Routledge, 2024), 114–132.

86 Alec Grant, 'In Search of my Narrative Character,' in *Writing Philosophical Autoethnography*, ed. Alec Grant (New York and London: Routledge, 2024), 114–132.

87 Astrology and Science – Wikipedia.

88 Michael Hunter, *The Decline of Magic: Britain in the Enlightenment* (New Haven
and London: Yale University Press, 2020).

89 Nigel Warburon, *Thinking from A to Z.* Third Edition (London and New York:
Routledge, 2007), 1–2.

90 Nigel Warburon, *Thinking from A to Z.* Third Edition (London and New York:
Routledge, 2007), 1–2.

5
AUTO-CRITIQUE

Ash: At the end of the day, who are you anyway?

Alec: Who are any of us? I think of Stacy Holman Jones's words: 'I am in process ... My language, both in learning and in use, is a movement of becomings.'[1]

Ash: So you believe that we're all trapped in language, flowing along it like an object in a river?

Alec: Trapped and enabled – at least potentially – at the same time. Some just passively flow along and change without noticing. Others flow along and work towards transformation as much as they can. As objects with agency, they move with the flow but resist the currents.

Ash: (Here we go! Mystic bl**dy philosopher!) Explain!

Alec: Think of memes: words, phrases, and concepts that are argued to come into circulation and rapidly become popular.[2] Humans imitate each other. We say these words, phrases, and concepts as meme clusters, or 'memeplexes,' as Susan Blackmore puts it,[3] and act in accord with them in creating the 'ordinary culture' I've spoken about earlier in the book.

Ash: People always have choice about which words, phrases, and concepts they use and live up to.

Alec: Yes, of course, but that choice has limits, and for many is more battery farm than free-range. To put it simply, the question for me is: to what extent do we speak words as opposed to words speaking us? To put this another way, how much choice do we have in creating our worlds

DOI: 10.4324/9781003518594-5

through the concepts we use when, and if, the concepts are off the peg rather than personally crafted?

Ash: Lots of choice. And stop patronising me.

Alec: Okay Ash, sorry. To explain what I mean a bit more, let me read you something from one of my co-written articles in the appendix:

> Fowk's ideas bide in waardrobes,
> Nately hingin up,
> Chinged aften tae meet
> The current style.
> Wird claes eyways
> Fair an' balanced.
> Naethin that clashes
> Gings in there.
> Beige an' bland
> Gings wi' athin.[4]

Ash: (What!!!!????) How the hell am I supposed to understand that?

Alec: Exactly! I've just proven my point! You're trapped in the giant meme, metameme rather, of Standard English.

Ash: Duh! So are you! Except for your poem in Scots, you use Standard English in our exchange throughout this book.

Alec: You're duhing me again, Ash. Spoke to you about this before. You know I don't like it.

Ash: Don't talk to me like a headmaster. And you don't bl**dy well tell me what words to use!

Alec: Who does then?

Ash: Nobody does! I'm the boss of my own language use.

Alec: Do you get the fucking irony in what you're saying?

Ash: NO!! It's a statement of fact. Nothing ironic about it. What does your sodding 'poem' even mean anyway?

Alec: Here's the Standard English translation:

> People's ideas kept in wardrobes
> Neatly hanging up,
> Changed often to meet
> The current style.

> Conceptual garb always
> Fair and balanced.
> Nothing that clashes
> Goes in there.
> Beige and bland
> Goes with everything.[5]

The poem speaks to my beef that what people present and write about in the name of autoethnography often tends to follow current memeplex trends. Reflecting wider patterns in society more generally, this is often done in ways that won't cause offence because people's words rest comfortably within the bandwidth of cultural acceptability of what can and can't be said. I believe that in autoethnography this applies not just to the choice of topic but also to the choice of the words used in representing topics. Regarding the former, it's difficult to tease out the extent to which spates of single topic autoethnography writing are due to reasonable concerns about world events, for example, COVID lockdown, or whether they're happening because of the proliferation of memeplexes. I suspect a bit of both, but with memeplexes sometimes in the lead, leading unfortunately to the 'So what?' point, whereby the possibilities for new autoethnographic perspectives on a topic are in danger of drying up.[6] That links to what I meant earlier when I used the phrase 'going with the flow.' Too many people fail to resist memeplex currents.

Ash: You're being bl**dy well reductive here – putting this all down to language rather than shared human concerns.

Alec: Okay Ash, let's come at this from a political angle. Think about the silencing power of dominant discourses argument, which I discussed in the previous chapter: more and more words – and, in terms of their contextual application, phrases, and topics – become acceptable and popular. When that happens, other words, phrases, and topics are subjected to the linguistic equivalent of **othering** to the extent that they're, often unfairly, categorized as offensive, irrespective of their context of use. For example, I was recently invited to do an article re-write for a journal because I'd described myself as a morally compromised 'whore' in the first submitted version, for selling myself to aspects of culture which I found simultaneously entrapping and in my interest to go along with. One of the reviewers said that my use of the whore word was offensive to sex workers. The editors agreed.

Ash: Quite right too!

Alec: (Predictable) Hang on! I can accept that many, perhaps most, women would find the whore word demeaning, degrading, insulting to women, across all times and places. But in this regard the reviewer was displaying a double standard in saying that the word would be offensive to women sex workers but, by omission, not to – most – women who don't sell sex. In any case, rightly or wrongly, I responded by defending my informed polysemic choice over the meaning of the word, which I was clearly using outside of its sexual context. This didn't cut any ice with the editors, so as a matter of principle I declined the re-write invitation.

Ash: Your loss!

Alec: (I bet you're a peer-reviewer. Write next to/fuck all, but poke your nose in and pontificate all over the place!). Maybe. But I think that my polysemic choice standpoint directly links to a related problem displayed in an editorial assessment perspective recently expressed by Andrew Herrmann and Tony Adams, co-editors of the *Journal of Autoethnography.* In their words, this is that authors should not use 'an insensitive word instead of a more inclusive term.'[7]

Ash: Absolutely they shouldn't!

Alec: Hang on! Deciding that particular words are insensitive in terms of their anticipated reception by readers, as well as ignoring polysemy and word use-context arguments, might link to a few other possible problems.

Ash: Such as?

Alec: Okay, given what I've already said, how about linguistic cultural entrapment, and the history of the legitimate re-appropriation of words previously regarded as offensive – think of 'queer' and 'cunt.' The Herrmann-Adams position also implies a related blanket lack of semantic sophistication among readers. This is forgivable to the extent that their book is a boon to newbie autoethnographers. However, when monosemy, or one meaning per word, rules the day, the worthy aim of inclusivity is stretched way beyond its range of appropriateness. It's a short step in my view from this form of linguistic cultural entrapment to linguistic cultural fascism.

Ash: Oh, come on! You're going too far!

Alec: Moreover, given what Andrew and Tony write elsewhere in their book, their views on language sensitivity seem to me to be as much political – in terms of being shaped by a need to survive and thrive in the broader culture of publishing and the politics of market forces – as they are valued on the basis of their shared background in communication studies.[8]

Ash: Hmmm!

Alec: And it's ironic that monosemic assumptions themselves can be offensive and inclusivity-breaching, especially when they're based on a poorly informed prejudice on the part of the assumer. Once, years back on Twitter/X, I was accused by a woman, who up to that point had been a friend, of not being a feminist because I used the word 'cunt' in connection with a politician reviled by cosmopolitan liberals across the world.

Ash: She was quite right to accuse you of this.

Alec: Well, the power of the cunt word to cause offence across our islands and beyond is uneven, but it's given the blanket 'nasty and forbidden' tag. It's only become offensive and associated with misogyny among some, but not all, cultural groups in relatively recent British history. 'Cunt' was a descriptive, not obscene, term in late medieval England. The philosopher Rebecca Roache writes that quite a few English towns and cities, including Shrewsbury, Oxford, and London, had streets by the name of 'Gropecunt Lane,' because of the prostitution that took place in them.[9] Roache also informs us that the word appeared in people's names, describing 13- and 14th-century English records that testify to the existence of 'Gunoka Cuntles,' 'John Fillecunt,' and 'Robert Clevecunt.'[10] She also points to an English translation of a 15th-century Italian surgery textbook that contained teachings such as the 'necke of the bladder is schort & is maad fast to the cunte.'[11]

Ash: People have become more civilised in the last 500 years.

Alec: Have they? Okay. What do you have to say about cultures where the cunt word remains relatively inoffensive,[12] or, as in parts of my homeland of Scotland, where it's still used as a term of endearment, as in 'he's a lovely cunt,' or 'God I miss the cunt.'?[13] Or about contemporary literary fiction where the cunt word appears in different contexts? How about Kevin Barry's wonderful *The Heart in Winter*, for example? Barry, a multi award-winning author, uses the cunt word lots of times – sometimes sexualised, sometimes antagonistically social, sometimes barroom anecdotal. For example, '... he gazed with mild dismay across the lid of her cunt'; 'Kathleen at once roused herself from the floor – The fuck is cuntface sayin?'; and 'No better boy for the letterwritin ... The cunt would take medals for it.'[14]

Ash: Okay but educated Scottish people are less likely to use that word, I'm sure. And they certainly wouldn't say 'f*ck' as much as your do, especially not in their work if they're academic writers. It's not professional!

Alec: (Fucking typical!) My reference to Roache's work above shows that what's deemed 'professional' shifts over time. I personally think it disingenuous and unprofessional to semi-bowdlerise expletives by substituting asterisks for the vowels in them, as lots of qualitative, including autoethnographic, writers do. It's coy, patronising, and childish – akin to swearing behind a partially closed door with a handkerchief stuffed in your mouth, when the people on the other side of the door know exactly what you're saying.

Furthermore, I'm Scottish, and I'm highly educated. So, cunt, cunt, cunt, cunt, fuck, fuck, fuck, fuck, fuckity fuck! Moreover, if you want an historical precedent...

Ash: I don't, and grow up!

Alec: (The fucking irony!) I'm going to give you one anyway, Ash. The late medieval Scots poet William Dunbar, who was the Scottish 'Makar' or court poet to King James IV, and whose work is currently well respected in both literary and historical circles, used the 'fuck' word in his great poem *In Secreit Place This Hyndir Nycht*:

> ...His bony beird wes kemmit and croppit,
> But all with cale it was bedroppit,
> And he wes townysche, peirt and gukit.
> He clappit fast, he kist and chukkit,
> As with the glaikis he wer ovirgane.
> Yit be his feirris he wald haue fukkit –
> 'Ye brek my hart, my bony ane.'[15]

(His pretty beard was combed and trimmed, but it was spattered with broth, and he was a towny, pushy, and foolish. He held her fast; he kissed and fondled her, as if he were overpowered by passion. Yet what he was doing showed that he wanted to fuck – 'You're breaking my heart, my pretty').[16]

Ash: So what?! You're just saying all this to be provocative.

Alec: No, I'm not. I'm saying all this to inform and challenge. Don't you want to find out more about the words – the use of which you revile, or is it just enough for you to hate them because it's *de rigueur* to do so, and you're quite happy to be linguistically culturally entrapped in the assumption that they're globally, unconditionally, and essentially offensive? The relative status of the 'cunt' and 'fuck' words is an issue of respectable philosophical, historical, and literary interest,[17] but for you it's better to cut your linguistic and conceptual cloth to suit this year's fashion?

Ash: I'm growing rapidly tired of this conversation, so let's have a look at your auto-critique.

***

Introduction

While studying for an MA in Philosophy, I learned the value of rigorously arguing against one's standpoint position and of equally rigorously responding to this argument, and we've got to the chapter in the book where I need to do this. So, in this auto-critique of the formal parts of Chapters 1–4, and in the exchange with Ash below that ends the book, I present and answer arguments that might already have occurred to some readers, about: implicit biases in my perceptual experience, my tendency to engage in representational stereotyping, the value of conformity, and the danger of binary thinking. I end the chapter by addressing in greater depth: the metaphysical problem around my claim to an enduring trickster identity in my work, the limited scope of my position in preaching to the converted, and the problem emerging from my own entrapment in 'strong individualism.'

Biases in my Perceptual Experiences

Interpreting and clarifying Mikhail Bakhtin,[18] Daphna Erdinast-Vulcan[19] argues that people have two modes of perceptual experience: 'I-for-myself' and 'I-for-the-other.' The former is lived experiential and representational and is always partial. Confined to an inside perspective of itself, my I-for-myself does not have access to an external vantage point. Thus, with reference to my published work represented in this book, contra Mark Freeman[20] and myself,[21] according to Bakhtin, 'I myself cannot be the author of my own value, just as I cannot lift myself by my own hair.'[22]

Blinkered by limitations of lived-through experiences and the interpretation of these, onto-epistemological entrapment is, however, an intractable problem in all self-representational autoethnographic work. As for all others working with this approach, this does not undermine my argument about the value of subjectivity as an epistemic resource.[23] However, my I-for-myself position needs some important qualification. There is a middle ground between the impact of distal forces on cultural identity, discussed in Chapters 2 and 3, and proximal forces. I'm with Judith Butler in accepting that, at a perceptual level, my resistance to cultural narrative entrapment will always be compromised by the fact that 'I am not fully known to myself, because part of what I am is the enigmatic traces of others.'[24]

My Representational Stereotyping

The above quote from Butler has implications for my tendency to use representational stereotyping as a (always failing) defensive strategy. Howard Becker argues that 'the othered' is not a homogeneous category.[25] Similarly, from a socio-philosophical standpoint, Raymond Williams reminds us that 'there are in fact no masses, but only ways of seeing people as masses.'[26] This signals both a weakness and a strength in my standpoint position. At the points at which my work constitutes a critique of externally imposed cultural narrative entrapment, I clearly display such homogeneous categorical thinking. However, accepting the fact that probably most other humans display this too, there is at least one general counterargument in favour of the deployment of representational stereotyping useful to my standpoint position. From a literary-philosophical standpoint that both speaks to metaphysics and honours the aesthetic, humanities dimension of autoethnography, Henry Miller wrote:

> The language of society is conformity; the language of the creative individual is freedom. Life will continue to be hell as long as people who make up the world *shut their eyes to reality.*[27]

The Value of Conformity and the Danger of Binary Thinking

Questions emerge, of course: what makes people accept cultural narratives? What is the value in so doing? And what are the implications of these two issues for the worth of my overall standpoint position? At a general level, from the argument emerging in Chapters 3 and 4, acceptance of culture as the reassuring space of the known and familiar arguably corresponds with a need for many to avoid rocking the cultural boat. Thinking with Michel Foucault here, there are those who live in states of discursive poverty in the face of dominant discourses, and others with hegemonic discourses and related cultural stories as their default attitudinal, emotional, and behavioural resources. As Jerome Bruner and Anthony Giddens argue, ordinary, 'just so,' purposeful, predictable, and routinised cultures co-evolve and are co-extensive with individual and collective lives, in myriad ongoing stories.

Moreover, in terms of the arguments and positions of Giddens and Paul Willis, there are people who lack sophistication about discursive possibilities beyond their local class and reference group bases, and those who, after Pierre Bourdieu, have an inherited class habitus tendency to defer to cultural tradition and authority. Dominant cultural stories function to enforce cultural conformity, and the difficulties in resisting the centripetal pull of culture are therefore better understood if it is accepted that culture has agency at social and material levels rather than simply constituting a benign backdrop to living. In addition to these points, it's tempting also to speculate that many may invest in adherence to dominant cultural discourses as a form of ongoing life therapy. By this, I mean that the tendency towards believing and adhering to dominant and conventional beliefs and actions might serve to increase feelings of existential certainty and safety.

So, at a metaphysical level with Galen Strawson in mind, it's equally tempting to speculate that some, with an investment in the extension of their lives as a coherent narrative, might perhaps be less likely to challenge the cultures informing their lives compared with those of an anti-narrative persuasion. As Eric Eisenberg and Bud Goodall maintain, the strength of the narrative surround and people's narrative inheritance seems to have a logical fit here, especially if it is accepted, as Alasdair MacIntyre contends, that human lives are pre-existing stories waiting to be invested in. This in turn points, as Mark Freeman argues, to unconscious drivers on narrative compliance. The pull towards Nietzschean life-affirmation is clearly not there for everybody, even presupposing the availability of personal, environmental, and cultural resources to exercise such life-affirmation. Dominant and entrapping socio-environmental stories trump individual emancipatory stories, John Christman reminds us, and, as Miranda Fricker argues, this is especially true for those lacking epistemic resources.

From a more general sociological instrumentalist perspective, Becker speaks of the 'process of commitment' whereby people become socialised to, and invested in, conventional, conformist institutional life. He argues that conformity becomes the more likely option when doing so corresponds with their interests, and the costs of deviating are too offputting. Consequently:

> The 'normal' person, when he (sic) discovers a deviant impulse in himself, is able to check that impulse by thinking of the ... consequences. He has staked too much on continuing to be normal to allow himself to be swayed by unconventional impulses.
>
> *(p. 26)*[28]

My sustained resistance to cultural narrative entrapment is grounded on the premise that my creativity co-entails my individual freedom, and at least at a conscious level, I'm by no means troubled by or frightened by this. However, I still need to address the danger of binary thinking threatening the integrity of my resistance thesis. Framing moral identity in relation to *either* acceptance *or* rejection of cultural narrative entrapment can be regarded as simplistic in failing to account for the variety of positions across a spectrum of possibilities. Perhaps my overall thesis may be seen to be too 'black and white,' too rigidly categorical? To recapitulate from Chapter 1, there must surely be shades of grey between acceptance and resistance, and, extrapolating from this, between autoethnography-as-method and critical autoethnographicity.

However, my overall intention throughout my doctoral thesis was to portray an accentuation of general tendencies, in line with Max Weber's 'ideal type' concept. According to Sung Ho Kim,[29] the ideal type constitutes a one-sided analytical construct, where rhetorical adequacy and standing up for one's ideals are privileged over strict correspondence with reality. It is also arguably the case that my construction of an acceptance-resistance binary *does* cohere with objective moral reality to the extent that from a Nietzschean perspective 'objectivity means the intersubjective agreement about judgements from within a specific type.'[30] Objectivity defined in this way explains how, in the face of shared thinking and feeling, an approximate unity will be felt and held by people of a particular moral psychological persuasion.

In related terms, there is the issue of the Nietzschean argument that, from a naturalistic perspective, shifting lifeforces or drives lies behind the self-construction of moral identity. This must logically impinge on either accepting or resisting cultural narratives. If this naturalistic argument is accepted, it is equally reasonable to suppose that these forces might constantly threaten to undermine my identity construction. Thinking with Nietzsche, maintaining coherent autonomous moral agency in the face of shifting drives requires drive mastery, in the indeterminate and interminable process of resisting cultural narrative entrapment. This process in turn entails unavoidable suffering.[31] Creative drive mastery, resting as it does on sustained respect for personal integrity, is clearly a difficult but not impossible task. With the image of Socrates in mind, in the face of centripetal cultural pressures to come back into line, can I sustain a consistent belief in myself and follow through on this?

From a secular reading, Socrates's 'daimonion' concept – partly grounded in reason and partly on personal intuition[32] – can be understood as a guiding internal voice of integrity, specifically regarding what *not* to do:

> ...whenever it speaks it turns me away from something I am about to do, But it never encourages me to do anything.[33]

If understood as an injunction to avoid, when necessary, toeing the normative cultural line rather than a license for capriciousness, clearly those who follow through on the daimonion voice threaten the smooth running of conventional society. It's always safer to conform because it's customary, but 'tradition can never be a sufficient guide for moral action.'[34] Curtis Johnson gives voice to Socrates's position here in more provocative terms: 'The many ... have never given much careful thought to anything of real importance.'[35] No matter how worthy ordinary culture is – as represented by Williams, Giddens, Willis, and Bruner – unscrutinised, un-reflexive adherence to proximal and distal culture, through either reliance on tradition, custom and practice, or habit, is an excuse for not thinking for oneself. On the other hand, thinking for oneself can threaten one's wider community:

> It is easy to see why the idea of a personal *daimonion* might (seem) dangerous. The deity authorised Socrates to cross-question even the most highly respected citizens of Athens ... A city in which every citizen followed the instructions of his own divine sign, could easily slip into anarchy.[36]

Descriptions from primary and secondary sources of the death of Socrates are metaphorically useful to illustrate the tension between cultural resistance and cultural acceptance, and their moral implications. In Plato's *Apology*, when facing his death, Socrates valued his duty to obey his daimonion, in the context of his role as a public philosopher, over his duty to his fellow citizens. However, in summarising the conversation that took place between Socrates and his friend Crito, Emily Wilson writes that, in justifying his decision not to go along with the suggestion that his friends rescue him from execution by taking him to a place of safety, Socrates maintained that it was his duty to obey the laws of Athens irrespective of whether they were just or unjust.[37]

At the level of political philosophy, the contradiction apparent in the above starkly reflects the struggle between integrity-grounded individualism versus unquestioning adherence to conventional morality. In terms of my standpoint position, this is played out in the issue of the extent to which hegemonic cultural narratives should be accepted or resisted.[38] Clearly, one person's entrapment is another's respect for cultural authority, legacy, tradition, and of course time- and place-bound contingent mores. This is not to suggest a kind of moral relativistic 'anything goes.' Freedom to think for oneself should always claim moral ascendency. The risk of cultural isolation and opprobrium must be set against the fact that cultural acceptance must entail integrity compromise:

Concluding thoughts: Trickster Identity, Preaching to the Converted, and Strong Individualism

There remains a problem with an aspect of my narrative identity claim. In the chapter 'In Search of my Narrative Character,' I argued after Freeman that my moral character enduring through time and space is that of a 'trickster,' while asserting the converse – that my life narrative was discontinuous.[39] I'm sympathetic to Galen Strawson's anti-narrative position, which I described in Chapter 3, and in related terms I'm also with David Hume's argument that there is no essential self under the fleeting, shifting impressions and ideas we constantly experience.[40] These pose onto-epistemological problems for any claim I might make to having an enduring, extensive trickster identity.

If, after Hume, my identity is simply the social psychological site where experiences happen, I do not need recourse to an assumption of continuous selfhood, especially if – following Jay Garfield's lead – I replace 'selfhood' with 'personhood' (see my discussion about this in the preface).[41] However, because these experiences are ones that *I* have had, which have been incorporated into my story of *my* life, it seems reasonable to assume that in a conventional sense 'I' exist as a psychological unity.[42] That said, looking back in time from my vantage point as a 72-year-old man, I regard my shifting identities throughout my life as in many respects discontinuous.[43] Although I have been biologically extended and continuous since my birth in 1952, because of repeated identity re-inventions I do not identify much – ontologically, epistemologically, or ethically – with who 'I' was as an adolescent, then young man, then middle-aged man.

My response to this contradiction is that while it is psychologically, morally, and ethically true for me that I have experienced all my identities as a discontinuous series, I regard my trickster persona more as sustained dispositional tendency than unifying 'essence.' In this regard, with relevance to my first research question, *What constitutes resistance to cultural narrative entrapment?*, this tendency complements my critical autoethnographicity standpoing in helping me recognise and deal with such entrapment, when and where necessary.

Tricksters thrive on the margins of cultures. I argued in my edited volume *Writing Philosophical Autoethnography*, that Thomas Frentz captures my own trickster agenda well. His argument is that being a trickster amounts to learning cultural rules, then avoiding and disrupting them in the service of rescuing critical scholarship.[44] In completely identifying with this, I believe my own trickster disposition to be morally and ethically justified. In related terms, in line with Lewis Hyde,[45] as culturally antagonistic trickster I believe myself to be fulfilling an essential duty: cultural advancement needs people whose role is to uncover and disrupt the assumptions that cultures are based on.

However, cultural tricksters don't exactly abound. I argued earlier in this book, in support of Marcin Kafar's standpoint position, that more people are likely to be engaged in *autoethnography as method* rather than in *critical autoethnographicity*. For this reason, given the hegemonic strength of normative neoliberal academic culture, the development of the latter is likely to be both limited in reach and – bearing in mind Becker's argument about why people conform, discussed earlier – perceived rewardingness. I might be preaching to the already converted, or the convertible. My answer to this is that promoting a morally ideal agenda is always more an issue of personal integrity than foolhardiness.

However, my claimed trickster status will not remedy my entrapment in the contemporary cultural narrative of *strong individualism*. It might reasonably be argued that I'm stuck in my existential story and justification of my personhood throughout this book in my display of what Hannah Kim labels 'main character syndrome.'[46] Two tricky questions occur to me here: first, is there a possibility that I have over-extended the relevance of my 'resisting cultural narrative entrapment' concept to all the texts in my portfolio simply because I claim this to be case? To put this in psychoanalytic terms, am I indulging in narcissistic projection? Second, if my autoethnographic work is premised on strong individualism, how can I credibly call for the 'no-self' development of philosophical autoethnography in the direction of incorporating Eastern philosophy?[47]

The first question must remain troublingly open, while the second betrays my inconsistency. That said, Eisenberg argues that, when conceived in terms of performance, identity is a significant accomplishment.[48] I agree, and in this regard, because of the lack of a felt need to doff my impression managing cap to mainstream culture, as a fairly sophisticated performance, writing this book and pulling off the second PhD informing it compensates for the trepidation I have about the public reception of my work. For many years now I have had little concern that my 'sense of self … professional identity and future are put at risk.'[49] All I have at my disposal are the trans-discursive 'small stories,'[50] which I've deployed down the years to resist cultural narrative entrapment. And in doing so, like Walt Whitman, I'm not always consistent:

'Do I contradict myself/
Very well then I contradict myself,
(I am large, I contain multitudes).'[51]

* * *

Ash: I don't really care about your pretentious auto-critique, but you've gone way beyond the remit of autoethnography in it and throughout the entire book.

Alec: What's the remit of autoethnography?

Ash: Stop being stupid. You know what it is!

Alec: No I don't, not really. I used to think I did. Take 'Evocative Autoethnography,' for example. Everything seems to count as that these days. I haven't changed my mind about this since I critiqued its coherence as a concept in my *Writing Philosophical Autoethnography* edited volume, where I argued that the respective works of Devin the Dude and Dostoevsky could be regarded as autoethnography.[52]

Ash: Dostoevsky and Devin the Dude don't count as autoethnographers.

Alec: How so?

Ash: Because Dostoevsky's work is in novels and Devin the Dude is a rapper.

Alec: So, novels and rap music don't count?

Ash: No.

Alec: What about Carolyn Ellis's novel about autoethnography?[53]

Ash: That's different. That's a novel with autoethnography as its topic.

Alec: Autoethnography's about writing subjectivity and speaking to culture, is it not?

Ash: Yes.

Alec: Doestoevsky does that, doesn't he?

Ash: Yes, but he's outside the frame of autoethnography given that he died a century or more before autoethnography formally emerged as a method. Anyway, his novels are not social science (obviously!!).

Alec: (Fuck! Unbelievable!) What you say about Dostoevsky's work not counting as social science is moot, and you're forgetting that both social science **and** the humanities, subsuming literary fiction, are part of the purview of autoethnography. Furthermore, if what counts as autoethnography is historically contingent, if people were writing in autoethnographic ways, in terms of honouring each component of the fundamental concept of auto-ethno-graphy,[54] but not calling it 'autoethnography' because the term hadn't yet emerged as a qualitative inquiry category label, their work can't be counted as autoethnography?

Ash: I'm not saying that (you smug b*st*rd), but Devin the Dude definitely doesn't do autoethnography!!!!

Alec: Exasperation marks again, Ash. Is our conversation rattling you? And doesn't rap music, packaged as autoethnography, happen at autoethnography conferences?

Ash: Yes it does, but that's entirely different!

Alec: How is it different?

Ash: The organizational and environmental contexts are different (obviously!!!).

Alec: So if, for argument's sake, Devin the Dude applied to do a performance presentation at an autoethnography conference, and it was accepted, and he did it. Would what he performed be rap music or autoethnography, or both?

Ash: Shut the f**k up!!!!!!!

Alec: I won't! Don't you think it interesting that, on the one hand, there's work in the public domain about good practice in autoethnography,[55] and, on the other, it sometimes looks as though anything goes at some conferences?

Ash: No it doesn't. You've got no evidence for that apart from your deeply unpleasant, biased opinion! This book is total revenge autoethnography! And you've come across as an intellectual snob throughout it!

Alec: Yes, I sort of own up to these accusations. The book is a kind of payback for all the time I've tuned out, and been bored or angry, at conferences and other events during autoethnography-lite sessions, while people around me are shouting encouraging superlatives. Or when I'm reading autoethnography-lite articles and book chapters as a reviewer or editor.

Ash: What do you mean by 'autoethnography-lite'?

Alec: 'Lite' translates as 'containing less of an ingredient,' or 'being less complex.'[56] Contrasted with what might be described as critical autoethnographicity-heavy, autoethnography-lite 'autoethnography' contains significantly less of the ingredients necessary for autoethnography, and less of its equally necessary complexities to be seriously regarded as such. Autoethnography-lite 'autoethnographers' don't think it important to know much about autoethnography to do autoethnography. They don't get beyond the bits about writing about yourself in the first person. They display evidence that they neither read nor write enough. They are theory-averse, so don't engage with the social sciences or the humanities. They think that autoethnography is just about writing stories. Some have told me this without any hint of embarrassment.

Ash: You'll alienate soooo many people (you a***hole). Who's actually going to read this book!?

Alec: Great points, Ash. It's least likely that the people who need to will. And would they get it even if they did? Perhaps you might like to do the world a service and review it when it's published? Have you any experience of autoethnography book reviewing, perchance?

Ash: You're being f**ck*ng superior again. You believe you're smarter than most people in the autoethnography world.

Alec: What I believe is that it's great that I read a lot, write a lot, and have over the course of this book tried to make some critical sense of myself as a person associated with something called 'autoethnography.' Can you say the same, Ash?

Notes

1 Stacy Holman Jones, 'Am I that Name?', in *Language and Culture: Reflective Narratives and the Emergence of Identity*, eds. David Nunan and Julie Choi (New York and Abingdon: Routledge, 2010), 116.

2 Susan Blackmore, *The Meme Machine* (New York: Oxford University Press, 1999).

3 Susan Blackmore, *The Meme Machine* (New York: Oxford University Press, 1999), 19.

4 Alec Grant and Susan Young, 'A Scot an' a Sassenach Scrieve Aboot Leid: A Three Pairt Scotoethnography (A Scot and an English Person Write about Language: A Scotoethnography in Three Parts),' *Journal of Autoethnography* 5, no. 1 (Winter 2024): 42–43, https://doi.org/10.1525/joae.2024.5.1.39; Also published as: Alec Grant and Susan Young, 'A Scot an' a Sassenach Scrieve Aboot Leid: A Three Pairt Scotoethnography (A Scot and an English Person Write about Language: A Scotoethnography in Three Parts,' in *Meaningful Journeys: Autoethnographies of Quest and Identity Transformation*, eds. Alec Grant and Elizabeth Lloyd-Parkes (London and New York: Routledge, 2024), 100–101.

5 Alec Grant and Susan Young, 'A Scot an' a Sassenach Scrieve Aboot Leid: A Three Pairt Scotoethnography (A Scot and an English Person Write about Language: A Scotoethnography in Three Parts,' in *Meaningful Journeys: Autoethnographies of Quest and Identity Transformation*, eds. Alec Grant and Elizabeth Lloyd-Parkes (London and New York: Routledge, 2024), 43.

6 Andrew F. Herrmann, and Tony E. Adams, *Assessing Autoethnography: Notes on Analysis, Evaluation, and Craft* (New York and London: Routledge, 2024), 31–34.

7 Andrew F. Herrmann, and Tony E. Adams, *Assessing Autoethnography: Notes on Analysis, Evaluation, and Craft* (New York and London: Routledge, 2024), 25.

8 Andrew F. Herrmann, and Tony E. Adams, *Assessing Autoethnography: Notes on Analysis, Evaluation, and Craft* (New York and London: Routledge, 2024), 25–31.

9 Rebecca Roache, *For F*cks Sake: Why Swearing is Shocking, Rude and Fun* (New York: Oxford University Press, 2024).

10 Rebecca Roache, *For F*cks Sake: Why Swearing is Shocking, Rude and Fun* (New York: Oxford University Press, 2024), 164.

11 Rebecca Roache, *For F*cks Sake: Why Swearing is Shocking, Rude and Fun* (New York: Oxford University Press, 2024), 165.

12 Rebecca Roache, *For F*cks Sake: Why Swearing is Shocking, Rude and Fun* (New York: Oxford University Press, 2024), 175.

13 Rebecca Roache, *For F*cks Sake: Why Swearing is Shocking, Rude and Fun* (New York: Oxford University Press, 2024), 176.

14 Kevin Barry, *The Heart in Winter* (Edinburgh: Canongate, 2024), 17, 182, 195.

15 William Dunbar, 'In Secret Place this Hyndir Nycht,' in *Selected Poems of Robert Henryson and William Dunbar*, ed. Douglas Gray (London: Penguin Books, 1998), 278–281.

16 Standard English translation: Sally Mapstone Dunbar's Disappearance: William Dunbar (lrb.co.uk).

17 Rebecca Roache, *For F*cks Sake: Why Swearing is Shocking, Rude and Fun* (New York: Oxford University Press, 2024), 176; Melissa Mohr, *Holy Sh*t: A Brief History of Swearing* (New York: Oxford University Press, 2013).

18 Mikhail M. Bakhtin, *Art and Answerability: Early Philosophical Essays by M.M. Bakhtin*. Edited by M. Holquist and Vadim Liapunov. Translated by Vadim Liapunove. Supplement translated by Kenneth Brostrom (Austin: University of Texas Press, 1990).

19 Daphna Erdinast-Vulcan, 'Heterobiography: A Bakhtinian Perspective on Autobiographical Writing,' in *Philosophy and Life Writing*, eds. D.L. LeMahieu, and Christopher Cowley (London and New York: Routledge, 2019), 111–112.

20 Mark Freeman, *Hindsight: The Promise and Peril of Looking Backward* (New York: Oxford University Press, 2010).

21 Alec Grant, 'In Search of my Narrative Character: A Philosophical Autoethnography,' in *Writing Philosophical Autoethnography*, ed. Alec Grant (New York and London: Routledge, 2024), 114–132.

22 Mikhail M. Bakhtin, *Art and Answerability: Early Philosophical Essays by M.M. Bakhtin*. Edited by M. Holquist and Vadim Liapunov. Translated by Vadim Liapunove. Supplement translated by Kenneth Brostrom (Austin: University of Texas Press, 1990), 55.

23 Alec Grant, 'In Search of my Narrative Character: A Philosophical Autoethnography,' in *Writing Philosophical Autoethnography*, ed. Alec Grant (New York and London: Routledge, 2024), 114–132.

24 Judith Butler, *Precarious Life: The Powers of Mourning and Violence* (London: Verso, 2004), 46.

25 Howard S. Becker, *Outsiders: Studies in the Sociology of Deviance* (London: Free Press, 2018 [1963]), 8–9.

26 Raymond Williams, 'Culture Is Ordinary,' in Raymond Williams, *Resources of Hope*. Edited Robin Gable (London: Verso, 1989 [1958]), 11.

27 Henry Miller, *Stand Still Like the Hummingbird* (New York: New Directions, 1962), ix.

28 Howard S. Becker, *Outsiders: Studies in the Sociology of Deviance* (London: Free Press, 2018 [1963]), 26, my brackets.

29 Sung Ho Kim and Max Weber, *Stanford Encyclopedia of Philosophy* (Winter 2019 Edition), Edward N. Zalta (Ed.), https://plato.stanford.edu/archives/win2019/entries/weber/, 25–26.

30 Anthony K. Jensen, *Nietzsche's Philosophy of History* (Cambridge: Cambridge University Press, 2013), 127.

31 Bernard Reginster, 'The Will to Power and the Ethics of Creativity,' in *Nietzsche and Morality*, ed. Brian Leiter, and Neil Sinhababu (New York: Oxford University Press. 2007), 32–56.

32 Curtis Johnson, '"Socrates" Political Philosophy,' in *The Bloomsbury Handbook of Socrates*, eds. Russell E. Jones, Ravi Sharma, and Nicholas D. Smith (London and New York: Bloomsbury Academic, 2024), 275–298.

33 Plato, 'Apology 31d,' in Plato, *Five Dialogues: Euthyphro, Apology, Crito, Meno, Phaedo*. Second Edition. Translated. Georges M.A. Grube (Indianapolis and Cambridge: Hackett Publishing Company, Inc., 2002), 36.

34 Emily Wilson, *The Death of Socrates: Hero, Villain, Chatterbox, Saint* (London: Profile Books), 33.

35 Curtis Johnson, '"Socrates" Political Philosophy,' in *The Bloomsbury Handbook of Socrates*, eds. Russell E. Jones, Ravi Sharma, and Nicholas D. Smith (London and New York: Bloomsbury Academic, 2024), 279.

36 Emily Wilson, *The Death of Socrates: Hero, Villain, Chatterbox, Saint* (London: Profile Books), 33.

37 Emily Wilson, *The Death of Socrates: Hero, Villain, Chatterbox, Saint* (London: Profile Books), 63.

38 For a more detailed discussion of this at the level of political philosophy, see Emily Wilson, *The Death of Socrates: Hero, Villain, Chatterbox, Saint* (London: Profile Books), 195–197.

39 Alec Grant, 'In Search of my Narrative Character: A Philosophical Autoethnography,' in *Writing Philosophical Autoethnography*, ed. Alec Grant (New York and London: Routledge, 2024), 114–132.

40 David Hume, 'Appendix,' in David Hume, *A Treatise of Human Nature*. Edited Ernest C. Mossner (London: Penguin Books, 1969 [1739–40]), 671–678.

41 Jay L. Garfield, *Losing Ourselves: Learning to Live Without a Self* (Princeton and Oxford: Princeton University Press, 2022).

42 Marya Schechtman, *The Constitution of Selves* (Ithaca and London: Cornell University Press, 1996), 96–99.

43 Alec Grant, 'In Search of my Narrative Character: A Philosophical Autoethnography,' in *Writing Philosophical Autoethnography*, ed. Alec Grant (New York and London: Routledge, 2024), 114–132.

44 Thomas Frentz, *Trickster in Tweed: My Quest for Quality in Faculty Life* (London and New York: Routledge, 2008).

45 Lewis Hyde, *Trickster Makes this World: How Disruptive Imagination Creates Culture* (Edinburgh: Canongate Books Ltd, 2017), 9.

46 Hannah H. Kim, 'Life as "Non-Standard" Narrative,' *The Philosopher* 111, no. 2 (2023): 80–84, 80 for quote page, "Life as a 'Non-standard' Narrative" By Hannah Kim (Keywords: Selfhood; Identity; Literature; East-Asian Fiction; Collectivity) (thephilosopher1923.org).

47 Alec Grant, 'Concluding Thoughts: Selves, Cultures, Limitations, Futures,' in *Writing Philosophical Autoethnography*, ed. Alec Grant (New York and London: Routledge, 2024), 264–265.

48 Eric M. Eisenberg, 'Building a Mystery: Toward a New Theory of Communication and Identity,' *Journal of Communication* 51, no. 3 (September 2001, 2006): 534–552. https://doi.org/10.1111/j.1460-2466.2001.tb02895.x

49 Gayle Letherby, 'Dangerous Liaisons: Auto/biography in Research and Research Writing,' in *Danger in the Field: Ethics and Risk in Social Research*, eds. Geraldine Lee-Traweek, and Stephanie Linkogle (London and New York: Routledge, 2000), 109.

50 Siv H. Tønnessen, 'The Meaningfulness of Challenging the Controlled Drinking Discourse: An autoethnographic study,' *Qualitative Social Work*. Online First (2023): 1–16, http://doi.org/10.1177/14733250231200499.

51 Walt Whitman, 'Song of Myself,' in Walt Whitman, *The Complete Poems of Walt Whitman*. Introduction and notes by Stephen Matterson (Ware: Wordsworth Editions, 1995), 67.

52 Alec Grant, 'The Philosophical Autoethnographer,' in *Writing Philosophical Autoethnography*, ed. Alec Grant (New York and London: Routledge, 2024), 3.

53 Carolyn Ellis, *The Ethnographic I: A Methodological Novel about Autoethnography* (Walnut Creek, CA: AltaMira Press, 2004).

54 Alec Grant, 'The Philosophical Autoethnographer,' in *Writing Philosophical Autoethnography*, ed. Alec Grant (New York and London: Routledge, 2024), 4–5.

55 See, for example, Alec Grant, 'Crafting and Recognising Good Enough Autoethnographies: A Practical Guide and Checklist,' *Mental Health and Social Inclusion* 27, no. 3 (2023): 196–209, https://doi.org/10.1108/MHSI-01-2023-0009; Andrew F. Herrmann, and Tony E. Adams, *Assessing Autoethnography: Notes on Analysis, Evaluation, and Craft* (New York and London: Routledge, 2024), 25–31; Andrew C. Sparkes, 'Autoethnography as an Ethically Contested Terrain: Some Thinking Points for Consideration,' *Qualitative Research in Psychology* 21, no. 1 (2024): 107–139, https://doi.org/10.1080/14780887.2023.2293073; Alec Grant and Susan Young, 'Troubling Tolichism in Several Voices: Resisting Epistemic Violence in Creative Analytical and Critical Autoethnographic Practices,' *Journal of Autoethnography* 3, no. 1 (Winter 2022): 103–117, https://doi.org/10.1525/joae.2022.3.1.103

56 http://www.grammarly.com blog entry for 'lite.'

APPENDIX

Texts Chosen for my PhD in Published Work (Retrospective) Thesis[1]

Section 1: Introduction

I began my personal project of resisting cultural narrative entrapment when I started writing autoethnographically in the mid-1990s. My earliest publications reflecting this gradually evolving position drew on my first PhD (by Research), the thesis of which had the title *Clinical Supervision Activity among Mental Health Nurses: A Critical Organizational Ethnography*. Although the term 'autoethnography' hadn't really taken off at that time – the mid-1990s – my style of crafting this thesis was inspired by a growing interest in, and celebration of, subjectivity. Deeply influenced by the opening chapter of the then recently published and groundbreaking *Investigating Subjectivity: Research on Lived Experience*,[2] I wrote my thesis entirely in the first person. My reflexive analytic lens shifted between my participants' and my own thoughts, feelings, and behaviour, and I included a final, meta-reflexive, auto-critique chapter. My university doctoral supervisors and senior managers took a dim view of this at first and wanted me to switch to a tradidional methodology (Grounded Theory was their favourite). I stood my ground and, aided by a change to the constitution of the team supervising my doctoral research, all stakeholders eventually came round, or at least let me get on with following my own path. I was awarded my first PhD in the autumn of 1999.

The experience of being tenacious in the face of opposition in my university school usefully sensitised me to the phenomena of 'organisational mediation,' which I theorised, analysed, and discussed in my first doctoral thesis and emerging publications.[3] I used this term to refer to the ways in which organisational cultures, from macro institutional to shop floor levels, have agency that shapes the thinking of its members. For example, while doing my fieldwork I became more and more interested in the ways in which mental health service and academic participants seemed to me to be entrapped within the assumptions and corresponding behaviour of their work settings. In relation to my doctoral topic, I argued that this undermined their policy-led aim of developing effective forms of clinical supervision. At the time, this was an emerging intervention which was regarded as essential in supporting nurses in their practice, while maintaining their professionalism and ethical standards.

*

Section 2: Articles and Book Chapters Used as the Basis for My PhD by Publication (Retrospective), in Date Order of Publication

After completing my first PhD in 1999, my engagement with clinical supervision quickly waned, but my interest in the idea of cultural mediation did not. Since then, I've moved on to autoethnographically challenge what I've come to formally label 'cultural narrative entrapment' from shifting standpoint positions, as follows:

In 2015, I co-critiqued colonising, top-down policy-to-practice assumptions, conceptions, and enactments of 'mental health recovery.'[4] I later argued that mental health nurses and educators at disciplinary and institutional and practice levels, me included, have been entrapped in large and small oppressive cultural discourses, or stories.[5]

This was linked to the challenge I made in the following year, from postcolonial, critical qualitative inquiry, and critical autoethnographic standpoints, to the methodological culture of phenomenological-humanism in mental health nursing qualitative research. I took issue with the abusive representational practices of *othering*, cultural colonisation, and cultural misappropriation.[6]

In 2017, I wrote 'Toilets are the proper place for "outputs"!...'[7] This irreverently titled book chapter represented my resistance to the neoliberal, or more precisely 'new public management' university agenda around organisational reputational entrapment in the narrative of 'excellence.' I critically lampooned the audit culture, in favour of more meaningful measures of 'impact.' Being thoroughly involved with, and championing, curricular development locally, I also voiced resistance to conformity with conventional mental health curricular and service practice and assumptions.

A year later, I wrote an autoethnographic article storying my own upbringing and family.[8] Part 1 of this begins with the suicide of my mother and the immediate impact this had on my father and brother, and on me. The narrative broadens to describe my experience of home and local community life while growing up in a small town in the Scottish Highlands. This gives environmental context to my troubled relationship with my family, with a local culture of working-class drinking and its short- and long-term consequences constantly in focus. The second part of the article analytically draws on New Materialism theory, which gives my story sociological and philosophical depth.

That same year (2018), I discussed cultural narrative entrapment in the mental health nursing classroom in a more developed critique of the 'custom and practice' cultures on wards and in nursing academe.[9] I argue that there are cognitive biases held by students and, by implication, their educators, which remain unaddressed because of a lack of sufficient levels of critical reflexivity within and between these groups. These biases feed into the simple 'well' versus 'ill' stories nurses tell about themselves in relation to the people they purportedly care for. From my own developing hybrid educator position as 'mental health-academic-practitioner-system survivor,' I refuse these stories, grounded as they are in assumptions of mono-identity. Instead, I promote the idea of more complex lived experiential narratives, reflecting what I described as 'hyphenated' identities.

After this period, I gradually became increasingly interested in relational ethics in autoethnography, and in 2022 went on to co-write against what I regarded as the most serious form of cultural narrative entrapment in this area, which I coined as 'Tolichism.'[10] I use this term to critically refer to the position taken by the sociologist Martin Tolich: that autoethnographers *must* conform to a particular code of relational ethics, which can silence their work and even undermine the likelihood of them producing such work in the first place. I argue that this form of entrapment rhetorically proceeds from authorial and disciplinary authority and claims institutional support at the level of ethical review structures and professional researcher practice.

In the article, which draws on traditional and contemporary philosophical work, Susan Young and I also take to task the insidious patriarchy, misogyny, silencing, imposition of inflexible rules, and dogmatic 'mansplaining' that we read off from Tolich's writing, regarding this as epistemic violence targeted at (mostly women) researchers.

Moving up to date (2024), my edited volume, *Writing Philosophical Autoethnography* represents, I believe, a major step in the maturation of my thinking around cultural narrative entrapment. In Chapters 1 and 14, and implicitly in Chapter 7, I critique autoethnographic communities and writers within these communities for their complacency in the areas of culture and selfhood.[11] Among other issues, I argue that cultural narrative entrapment is often evident in work written by autoethnographers who accept conventional psychological notions of the self and represent culture in 'taken-for-granted' ways. I trouble the idea of narrative identity (identity as continuous story), which is commonly accepted in the autoethnographic communities. I also challenge the equally pervading assumptions of liberal-humanist selfhood and cultural determinism around how identity is both produced and constituted. I argue that autoethnographers need to resist regarding culture too comfortably as 'the space of the familiar' through queering it, and identifying and critically responding to the ideological bases of their cultural location and positioning.

The final co-authored contribution for my PhD by Published Work (Retrospective) is an autoethnographic challenge to my experience of scholarly linguistic cultural entrapment in writing academic texts in Standard English.[12] In this co-written text, simultaneously published as an article and book chapter, I draw on my early upbringing to chart my socialisation away from the Scots language towards Standard English. I use historical, literary, and linguistic theoretical and empirical material to back up my argument of the need to resist cultural narrative entrapment in imposed and dominant linguistic cultures. I conclude by suggesting that the article/chapter could function as a helpful exemplar for autoethnographers internationally who wish to write more in their own dialects, with less of a need to comply with normative entrapment in Standard English.

*

Section 3: A More Detailed Summary of the Articles Described in Section 2

Alec Grant, Helen Leigh-Phippard, and Nigel P. Short, 'Re-storying narrative identity: A dialogical study of mental health recovery and survival,' *Journal of Psychiatric and Mental Health Nursing* 22, no. 4 (February 2015): 278–286, https://doi.org/10.1111/jpm.12188

The complexities of recovery and survival were neglected in the 'Chief Nursing Officer's Review of Mental Health Nursing in England' (2006) and, by association and implication, in nursing research and practice. To redress this, this critical theoretical and methodological article – part of larger research project – presents two short stories, written by co-authors Dr Nigel P. Short and Dr Helen Leigh-Phippard, respectively, about their lived-through experiences of their times as in-patients in acute psychiatric wards. The overall significance of the article is in its emerging benefits and implications for users of mental health services, practitioners, and researchers. Its central, orienting principle is 'narrative re-storying.'

The article is structured in three parts. The first reviews selected relevant background policy and related literature, the contextual and theoretical bases of the paper, and related methodological and ethical issues. The second presents the two stories. The third brings the article to a close in discussing specific and global emerging implications for mental health nursing practice and research, around narrative re-storying as a recovery tool and methodological innovations that include 'hybrid' writing.

As lead author, I challenge the cultural narrative entrapment implicit in policy enactment and interpretation of the 2006 Chief Nursing Officer's Review, and its colonising, top-down policy-to-practice assumptions and conceptions around what constitutes 'mental health recovery.' I also take to task the biomedical story of 'mental illness,' and tacit organisational rules around 'good patient' attitudes and behaviour. I analyse how Helen and Nigel effectively resist all the above in their storied accounts, through privileging mental health system survival above institutional psychiatric expectations imposed on them about what it means to be 'in recovery.'

Moreover, my taking the lead role in conceiving the need for the article in the first place, and in its construction and writing and editing, constituted an act of meta-resistance. From a critical social and human science standpoint perspective, I wanted to show in stark concrete detail how complex psycho-social lived realities were erased in and by the 2006 Review. It presented a simplistic, 'top-down' colonising account of distress and 'recovery' through the construction of gender-neutral, homogenised, and compliant users, excised from their life contexts. Because of this, as a power-silent story, the review failed to acknowledge and reflect the ways in which people caught up in oppressive institutional psychiatric cultural narrative entrapment may often resist this. Resistance is exemplified in our article in the stories written by Helen and Nigel.

Alec Grant, 'Living my narrative: Storying dishonesty and deception in mental health nursing,' *Nursing Philosophy* 17, no. 3 (May 2016): 194–201, https://doi.org/10.1111/nup.12127

This article is theoretically grounded in the position put forward by the moral philosopher Alasdair MacIntyre: that individual human lives constitute unifying and unified narratives, in the context of the master narratives within which they are inscribed. From this position, specific episodes in people's lives are argued as important in shaping and developing their storied and enacted individual histories.

From this philosophical base, I used autoethnographic principles in crafting accounts from significant periods in my own professional life as a mental health nurse educator. These speak to the issue of institutionalised dishonesty and deception in mental health nursing education and practice, within which I was complicit.

Based on my pre-existing experience of publishing in nursing journals, and my developing scholarly identity, I begin my argument by contesting the idea of an imagined stable foundational professional ethos underpinning mental health nursing practice against which to judge professional dishonesty and deception. I go on to use illustrative short stories, drawn from my recent lived-through experiences as a mental health nurse educator, to show that dishonesty and deception are always an inevitable part of the lives of mental health nurses and mental health nurse academics. This is because of the constant disconnect between the nursing rhetoric and ideology that both groups espouse and how they actually behave on a day-to-day level, in and out of work and/or classroom. This disconnect makes the public front of what mental health nursing is claimed to be about amount to dishonest and deceitful window dressing.

I assert that the many first-person, experience-based accounts in mental health nursing publications are important educational resources in reducing this gap at professional practice, academic, and informal levels. Such storied accounts may also be useful in moving nurses and their educators towards more morally and ethically sensitive and reflexively attuned positions around what they talk and write into existence.

My overarching aim in writing the article was to argue that mental health nurses and mental health nurse academics – me included – were entrapped in large (institutional, professional) and small (local organisational) cultural stories. These stories highlight the cruelty often displayed by those educators and practitioners. In Goffman's terms, they starkly display the gap between the positive frontstage impression management of the mental health nursing discipline and the off-duty attitudes and behaviours of its members. Further related aims in writing the article included calling out entrapment in professional cultural dishonesty and deception; entrapment in assumptions of professional stability; implicit entrapment in categorical rather than hybrid identities; and entrapment in conventional curricular and practice assumptions and expectations.

Alec Grant, 'Storying the world: A posthumanist critique of phenomenological-humanist representational practices in mental health nurse qualitative inquiry,' Nursing Philosophy 17, no. 4 (June 2016): 290–297, https://doi.org/10.1111/nup.12135

The purpose of this essay was to build on my critique of phenomenological-humanist representational practices in mental health nursing qualitative inquiry, already in the public domain. I further unpacked and troubled those practices from an explicitly posthumanist philosophical position, based both on seminal texts and on my own single- and co-authored work.

My argument is that I see researchers in mental health nurse qualitative inquiry, specifically those displaying a phenomenological-humanist narrative bent in their writing, often tending to endorse the validity of oppressive institutional psychiatric assumptions, practices, and related ways of representing human psychological distress. I explicitly reject such writing in favour of more critical forms of qualitative inquiry, which includes my own work. My position is that the use of phenomenological humanist representational practices in mental health nursing, and by implication and extension possibly in other healthcare disciplines, is unethical, un-empathic, and morally compromised.

In this regard, I specifically aimed to trouble the methodological culture of phenomenological-humanism in mental health nursing qualitative inquiry by voicing resistance from postcolonial, critical qualitative inquiry, and critical autoethnographic standpoints. This amounts to taking issue with the abusive representational practices of *othering*, cultural colonisation, and cultural misappropriation in such writing. I argue that mental health nursing qualitative research academics are entrapped in academic representational worlds lacking necessary and sufficient levels of criticality, context, and the experiences of survivors of institutional mental health. Regarding this latter point, my position is that 'top-down' phenomenological-humanist theory is privileged over 'bottom-out' lived experience epistemic knowledge.

In challenging the objectivist and positivist premises informing representational practices by using posthumanist writing as a resistance strategy, I also argue in favour of subjectivist scholarship. This enables me to critically call out 'well or ill' binary assumptions, and the presentation of apolitical, power-silent worlds. My overall aim at the time was to use critically reflexive autoethnogaphic writing to champion resistance against unscrutinised and naïve realist normative assumptions and writing practices.

Alec Grant, 'Toilets are the proper place for "outputs"! A tale of knowledge production and publishing with students in higher education, in *Self-narrative and pedagogy: Stories of experience within teaching and learning,'* **eds. Mike Hayler, and Jess Moriarty (Rotterdam: Sense Publishers, 2017), 45–57**

I began this book chapter by setting the scene for readers in describing that it is mid-July 2016, and I am presenting my work at the University of Brighton's annual Teaching and Learning Conference. Its title that year was 'Nurturing Co-construction,' and the 30 or so delegates at my session were mostly University of Brighton academics, some of whom I knew very well as they work in my school.

The chapter represented my resistance to the neoliberal, new public management agenda in my university, around reputational management and related organisational entrapment in the implicit neoliberal academy narrative of 'excellence.' It was written and published prior to my retirement from my position of *Reader in Narrative Mental Health* in the School of Health Sciences at the University of Brighton.

Within it, I lampoon the audit culture of my school, in favour of more meaningful measures of 'impact.' Being thoroughly involved with, and leading, curricular development locally, I also voice resistance to conformity with conventional mental health curricular and service practice, and related assumptions. I particularly challenge assumptions of mono-identity binaries in pedagogic practices – for example, that one can be either a mental health academic/practitioner or a mental health service user, but not both – in favour of celebrating the concept of 'hybrid identity' in the overall service of undermining *othering*.

I also call out the acceptance of unchecked poor writing and grammatical skills evident in my school. I do so in the broader theoretical context of critically differentiating between technocratic *training* cultures and cultures favouring critical educational practices and consciousness.

I describe how I experienced the paraversity community of scholars much more rewarding than that which I found in my own institution. The friendship-based collegiate relationships I made in the former contrasted with the organisationally reptilian ways of relating I encountered in the latter. Finally, I challenge conventional, 'zombie-halal,' and liberal-humanist writing, in favour of creative, passionate, blood-saturated work, characterised by fractured and hybrid identities.

Alec Grant, 'Drinking to relax: An autoethnography of a highland family viewed through a New Materialist lens,' in *Auto/Biography Yearbook* 2017, ed. Andrew Sparkes (Nottingham: Russell Press, 2018), 33–46.

(6) (PDF) Paper for British Sociological Association Yearbook 2017, Drinking to Relax. (researchgate.net)

The first part of this article is an autoethnographic story, which I wrote several years before its publication, having revised it in the light of other of my, then, recently published work. It begins with a first-person, present-tense description of my father as he walks through the front door of the house I grew up in, seeing my mother – who had hanged herself a short time before – directly in front of him. I then describe the immediate impact of her suicide on my father, brother, and myself.

Following this, my story broadens to describe my experience of home and local community life while growing up in a small town in the Scottish Highlands. This gives context to my troubled relationship with my family, with the culture of Highland working-class drinking and its short- and long-term consequences constantly in focus.

I critique the culture of alcohol-related dysfunctional family life in the north of Scotland, within which my family was positioned. In related terms, I also explore my lived-through experiences of decades of narrative entrapment in imposed biographies and the negative impact this had on my psychological health. Part 1 of the article ends with my description of the ways in which I've used my scholarship in subsequent years to explore the cultural production of un-scrutinised, often stagnant and toxic, lives and relationships. In this regard, as expressed in the article, my constant aim has been to better understand and liberate myself from my past.

In Part 2 of the article, I utilise a New Materialist socio-philosophical conceptual toolkit as an analytic aid. This enables me to add a layer of meta-reflexive sociological depth to Part 1. Such further exploration of my family culture, in terms of its broader environmental and historical social and material connections, allows me to resist presenting simplistic causal connections and blaming individuals.

Alec Grant, 'Moving around the hyphens: A critical meta-autoethnographic performance,' in *Critical Mental Health Nursing: Observations from the Inside*, ed. Pete Bull, Jonathan Gadsby, and Steve Williams (Monmouth: PCCS Books, 2018), 30–50

I open this chapter as follows:

The important question
A classroom in a university in the south of England in 2016. Thirty-six BSc Mental Health Nurse students in the last months of their final year. Dr Grant, their teacher for the afternoon. The topic: Working in Partnership.
Alec: Okay, let me ask you a question. A very important question. In my view, the most important question. What is your understanding of the following social psychological phenomena: confirmation bias, fundamental attribution error, and actor-observer effect?
Feeling a little nervous, I pace around with a hint of a smile on my face. Most of them won't know the answer to this question. They never do...

I critically address cultural narrative entrapment in this autoethnographic performance piece in the context of my sustained questioning of the morality of trapping mental health service users in externally imposed, institutional mental health identities. In so doing, I also challenge organisational 'custom and practice' cultures, both on the wards and in nursing academe, and the difficulties involved in changing these cultures. Less explicitly addressed are the differences between front-stage rhetorical stories (how things are supposed to be) and lived experiential stories (how things really are). I also call out the curricular stories that weren't, but should have been, in circulation among students, which leaves them entrapped in dominant stories as a function of curricular design. This marks their classroom experience as one of 'training' rather than critical educational (my constant beef).

I describe students', and by implication their teachers', cognitive biases in my chapter and the lack of critical reflexivity of either group towards these biases. These biases shape the stories group members tell about themselves, their patients, and themselves in relation to their patients. With patients fitting into 'ill' rather than 'well' categories, students' stories also assume narrative identities which must be 'either-or' binary, rather than 'hyphenated' hybrid. In terms of the latter, from my own position as mental health-academic-educator-practitioner-system survivor, and my corresponding published work, challenging this tendency allows me to the deny the onto-epistemological viability of simplistic mono-identity cultural narratives. I'm also able to reject ideologically sanitised narratives about mental health nurse 'professional' identity. These give the lie to how people often actually experience mental health nurses and other mainstream mental health workers, and how mental health nurses really experience themselves.

Alec Grant, and Susan Young, 'Troubling Tolichism in Several Voices: Resisting Epistemic Violence in Creative Analytical and Critical Autoethnographic Practices,' *Journal of Autoethnography* 3, no. 1 (Winter 2022): 103–117, https://doi.org/10.1525/joae.2022.3.1.103

This article is dialogic, with several voices engaging and responding together from embodied, relational, and textual standpoints. Tacitly informed by the voices of friends, colleagues, and respected others, Susan Young and I have a conversation with ourselves and with readers. We conduct this around the presence of a boxed-text academic voice, written more formally and rhetorically by me.

The main story is our critical reaction to selected aspects of the 'Tolichist' voice, which we regard as promoting epistemic violence towards critical and creative analytical autoethnographers in the areas of relational ethics and methodology. The other related – back, subsidiary, and implicit – stories emerging include alienation from the insidious cultural backdrop of patriarchy and misogyny, two conceptions of 'autonomy', the development of a neophyte critical autoethnographer, colonisation and resistance, the bifurcation of assumptions about autoethnographic writing, and the importance of philosophy for autoethnographic scholarship. The article ends in a meta-reflexive exchange between Susan and me about its content.

The premise behind the most insidious and serious form of critical narrative entrapment we critique in this article is represented by the sociologist Martin Tolich's admonition in his influential paper, 'A Critique of Current Practice: Ten Foundational Guidelines for Autoethnographers.' This is that autoethnographers *must* conform to a code of relational ethics that silences their work and, at worst, threatens the potential for them producing this work in the first place.

This form of admonition rhetorically proceeds from authorial and disciplinary authority, resting on claims of institutional support at the level of ethical review structures, and professional social science researcher practice. Susan and I resist this form of entrapment, coined by us as 'Tolichism,' in several ways. We take to task the insidious and implicit patriarchy, misogyny, silencing, imposition of inflexible rules, and dogmatic 'mansplaining' evident in Tolich's article, regarding all this as epistemic violence targeted at (implicitly mostly women) autoethnographic researchers. We do this from the perspectives of feminist relational, autonomy-based ethics; the situated relational knowledge that only occurs in the *doing* of autoethnography[13]; and the growing international pushback against the 'managerialism' of institutional ethical review bodies. Finally, as first author and a man, I seek feedback from Susan about whether my behaviour during the writing process was in any way entrapping for her, in terms of my own potential for 'mansplaining.' She reassures me that this was not the case.

Alec Grant, 'The Philosophical Autoethnographer,' in *Writing Philosophical Autoethnography*, ed. Alec Grant (New York and London: Routledge, 2024), 1–22

At the outset of this opening chapter, I describe the overall aim of the edited volume. This is to promote the idea of *philosophical autoethnography* across the autoethnographic and related communities, as a basis for writing lives. Accordingly, I assert that the volume is the first collection of narrative autoethnographic work, in which

> Authors autoethnographically explore their issues, concerns and topics about human society, cultures, and the nonhuman and material worlds through an explicitly philosophical lens. In specific terms, this means that each chapter – while written as first-person autoethnography (not precluding the use of second- and third-person narrative, as relevant) – will showcase sustained engagement with philosophical arguments, ideas, concepts, theories, and corresponding ethical positions. This philosophical basis will be fundamental to the content, topic, focus, and context of each autoethnography chapter, rather than supplementary.

Throughout the chapter, I critique the autoethnographic communities and autoethnographic writers for complacency around cultural narrative entrapment. I argue that this is often evident in the acceptance of lay psychological notions of the self and taking culture as represented, or 'ordinary culture,' for granted. I write in resistance to this by troubling the idea of unitary and sustained narrative identities, in my view commonly accepted in the autoethnographic communities; challenging the equally pervading assumption of liberal-humanist selfhood; and taking to task the cultural determinism linked to the production of identity. I go on to discuss the need to resist regarding culture too comfortably as 'the space of the familiar,' through the need to both 'queer' culture, and identify and respond to the ideological bases of cultural location and positioning.

Alec Grant, 'In Search of My Narrative Character: A Philosophical Autoethnography,' in *Writing Philosophical Autoethnography*, ed. Alec Grant (New York and London: Routledge, 2024), 114–132

My main aim in this autoethnographic chapter is to show that engaging in hindsight work is a productive way of uncovering the nature of our individual characters over time, the purpose of which is to demystify the manifest content of seemingly disparate memories. This enables the reflexive discernment of how these memories may in fact be connected, which in turn might point to deeper, increasingly sophisticated understandings about the meaning and moral significance of our individual lives.

I go on to present, as short stories, three memories which have stood out in my consciousness over the years. I argue that these are connected thematically to other less significant memories in my life, in terms of my enduring dispositional and behavioural tendencies, and that they have 'punctuated the grammar of my existence' in simultaneously disturbing and instructive ways. I end each story with a discussion – gradually developing throughout the chapter – in which I address emerging philosophical issues. This enables me to reach the provisional but personally compelling conclusion that my character is, after Bakhtin, effectively 'trickster-carnivalesque.' In bringing the chapter to a close, I critically evaluate its storied content against the relational ethical assumptions of mainstream qualitative inquiry informing what I regard as naive humanist-informed autoethnography. I then subject my discussion to critical scrutiny from the philosophy of autobiography. Finally, I briefly evaluate the moral status of my trickster identity in the context of dominant cultural narratives.

Implied in all of this are my aims for crafting the chapter. Over the course of writing it, approaching, and, at the time of writing, reaching the age of 70, I describe how I recognise, more acutely than earlier in my life, that narrative time is at the heart of my existence. Relatedly, I state that I *feel* the stark existential need to use autoethnography purposefully before that time, my time, runs out, and that I've a pressing developmental motivation to sharpen and deepen my philosophical awareness of the person I present to myself and the world. I say that, in so doing, I also wish – as much as is possible – to cleanse my memories of their lingering negative residue, particularly embarrassment, anger, and toxic time-wasting.

I deal with resistance to cultural narrative entrapment in this chapter in several ways. I challenge dominant cultures from a trickster standpoint, which, as I express in the chapter introduction, I do for therapeutic purposes. In the first story, I deploy autoethnography to call out the culture of the new public managed, or neoliberal, academy through exposing its administrivia, critiquing its training masquerading as education, and strongly voicing my oppositional need to pursue subjectivist research, despite, and to spite, the support of the academy. Following this, I proceed to a philosophical defence of narrative truth, a continuing critical theme throughout the chapter. Using satirical lampooning and magical realism, I then, in the next story, take to task the cultural stuckness and anachronistic cultural pretensions of 1980s British folk club culture. Continuing to defend narrative truth against the dominant academic culture of objectivism, I move on to a discussion of the philosophy of memory in the creative construction of narrative identity. In the final story, I caricature aspects of the 'New Age' culture of the 1960s–1970s. From this point on, I critically engage with the seriousness, pomposities, and absurdities of cultural values more generally, from Bakhtinian carnivalesque resistance and Bourdieusian sociological philosophical positions. This enables me to fully articulate my trickster, or critical cultural flaneur, position.

Alec Grant, 'Concluding Thoughts: Selves, Cultures, Limitations, Futures,' in *Writing Philosophical Autoethnography*, ed. Alec Grant (New York and London: Routledge, 2024), 249–269

I open this chapter by providing context: I describe how I argued in my opening chapter that autoethnographers, while accepting their intercorporeality or embodiment among other bodies, may also claim non-enduring and disconnected self-identities, and that my discussion of the interrelated concepts of *Selfhood* and *Culture* has definitional importance in autoethnography, and is thus in need of further scrutiny and unpacking from a philosophical autoethnographic standpoint.

This enables me to expand on this discussion in this, final, chapter of the volume.

My aim is not to give equal attention to all contributor essays. Instead, I make selective reference to aspects of them as and when I feel appropriate in the context of my developing discussion. Along the way, while also giving relevant space to the work of, and about, Virginia Woolf, I suggest some emerging implications for philosophical autoethnography. I finish the chapter by addressing what I regard as the philosophical limitations of the volume overall and argue for a future text, needed to articulate the philosophical basis of image- and performance-based autoethnography.

I categorise in the chapter what I regard as the range of selfhood types on which contributors' chapters are premised, and their corresponding philosophical foundations, in relation to the issues of contested selfhood raised throughout the volume. In so doing, I challenge the simplistic, naïve, culture-centric, universalising notions of selfhood represented in the kinds of autoethnographic work which I critique as lacking an adequate philosophical grounding. I also describe the ways in which I see cultural and ideological narrative entrapment resisted in my contributors' work, while equally suggesting that autoethnographic selfhood positions can, in and of themselves, be culturally narratively entrapping. Using the work of Virginia Woolf as an example, this leads me to argue again that the authors of life writing can be blinkered by their own privilege.

In this regard, I take the autoethnographic communities to task to the extent to which they exclude voices. I provide examples of such exclusion, arguing that this necessarily includes my own work and the *Writing Philosophical Autoethnography* volume itself, given that both are premised on the sufficiency of the Western philosophical tradition. I link this to a critique of the club culture I see in the autoethnographic world, and, more broadly, the 'happiness' culture understood in Western hedonistic terms. Focusing specifically on autoethnographic conference cultures, I argue that these might be tainted by a form of victim-celebrating ressentiment. I conclude by stressing the importance of queering cultural life to both deal with culture as the 'space of the familiar' and maintain writer self-integrity, while conceding that my entire argument might be premised on my dispositional inability to achieve full and happy membership of any cultural community.

Alec Grant and Susan Young, 'A Scot an' a Sassenach scrieve aboot leid: A three pairt Scotoethnography (A Scot and an English person write about language: A Scotoethnography in three parts),' *Journal of Autoethnography* 5, no. 1 (January 2024): 29–55, https://doi.org/10.1525/joae.2024.5.1.39

Also Published as:

Alec Grant and Susan Young, 'A Scot an' a Sassenach scrieve aboot leid: A three pairt Scotoethnography (A Scot and an English person write about language: A Scotoethnography in three parts),' in *Meaningful Journeys: Autoethnographies of Quest and Identity Transformation,* **ed. Alec Grant and Elizabeth Lloyd-Parkes (London and New York: Routledge, 2024), 96–116**

This article/chapter is structured in three parts. It is written in accordance with 'layered account' principles to reflect the underpinning of my emerging identity-transformative, quest standpoint position by social scientific, political, and historical and literary texts. In Part 1, my developing 'Scotoethnography' is written in a poetic and prose mixture of Scots and Standard English. Within it, I critically explore my early socialisation away from the Scots language towards Standard English. With examples from my published autoethnographic work, and drawing wider on literary texts and personal communication, I advocate for my use of Scots as an additional linguistic conceptual resource to represent my feelings and lived experiences.

In Part 2, I argue the historical, political, empirical, and sociolinguistic underpinning basis and justification for the text overall. The final part is a critically focused dialogue between myself and my co-writer, Susan Young. It ranges across defining 'Scotoethnography'; my motivation for crafting the paper; the emerging political and cultural implications of othering, colonisation, and related silencing of Scottish identity; the passion and creativity which I believe is both inherent in the Scots language and neglected Scots literature relative to Standard English; and, finally, the implications for autoethnographers around rescuing their regional dialects from monolinguistic entrapment in Standard English.

I begin this meta-autoethnographic text by challenging Susan's cultural Anglo-centrism about the Scots language which, like many people in the UK and beyond, she does not recognise as such. Coining the term 'Scotoethnography,' I write my own poetry and much of the text in Scots, as a challenge to the Anglo-American linguistic cultural entrapment I've felt myself inscribed within throughout my life. Because this has become an increasingly more pressing issue for me in recent years, I acknowledge that putting this text in the public domain constitutes one of my final major acts of cultural resistance in preparation for my death. From a personal perspective, justified by my own writing, work from Hugh MacDiarmid – a major figure in the 'Scottish Renaissance,' and other relevant Scots literature, I criticise Scottish Standard English and Standard English more generally for its inability to adequately convey passion and emotional nuance.

In the context of the sociopolitical strand to the text, I also take to task linguistic cultural erasure: the fact that I was schooled out of using my own regional variant of Scots from childhood onwards. In consequence, I describe how I find myself forced as a scholar to accept 'diglossia' – the privileging as one language as superior to another – by writing my work almost exclusively in Standard English, acknowledging its obvious cultural advantages and lingua franca status. As an antidote to this, I promote resistance to diglossia through autoethnographic polyglossia, or bilingualism. I acknowledge that my linguistic cultural resistance project is romantically driven and unlikely to fully succeed, given the politics of support behind the hegemony of Standard English. Yet, I contend that my text and argument could be used as an international exemplar by autoethnographers who wish to rescue their languages or regional dialects from marginalisation.

Notes

1 Alec Grant, *Developing Philosophical Autoethnography: Resisting Cultural Narrative Entrapment* (PhD thesis by Published Work (Retrospective), University of Bolton, 2024).
2 Carolyn Ellis and Michael G. Flaherty, 'An Agenda for the Interpretation of Lived Experience,' in *Investigating Subjectivity: Research on Lived Experience*, eds. Carolyn Ellis, and Michael G. Flaherty (Newbury Park, CA: SAGE Publications, Inc.), 1–13.
3 Alec Duncan-Grant, *Clinical Supervision Activity among Mental Health Nurses: A Critical Organizational Ethnography* (PhD by Research thesis, University of Brighton, 1999); Alec Duncan-Grant, *Clinical Supervision Activity among Mental Health Nurses: A Critical Organizational Ethnography* (Portsmouth: Nursing Praxis International, 2001); Alec Grant, 'Clinical Supervision in Mental Health Nursing: A Triumph of Hope Over Experience?' *Mental Health Practice* 6, no. 6 (2003): 22–23. No DOI. Clinical supervision in mental health nursing: a triumph of hope over experience? | Semantic Scholar.
4 Alec Grant, Helen Leigh-Phippard, and Nigel P. Short, 'Re-storying Narrative Identity: A Dialogical Study of Mental Health Recovery and Survival,' *Journal of Psychiatric and Mental Health Nursing* 22, no. 4 (May 2015): 278–286, https://doi.org/10.1111/jpm.12188.
5 Alec Grant, 'Living my Narrative: Storying Dishonesty and Deception in Mental Health Nursing,' *Nursing Philosophy* 17, no. 3 (May 2016): 194–201, https://doi.org/10.1111/nup.12127.
6 Alec Grant, 'Storying the World: A Post-humanist Critique of Phenomenological-Humanist Representational Practices in Mental Health Nurse Qualitative Inquiry,' *Nursing Philosophy* 17, no. 4 (June 2016): 290–297. https://doi.org/10.1111/nup.12135.
7 Alec Grant, 'Toilets are the Proper Place for "Outputs"! A Tale of Knowledge Production and Publishing with Students in Higher Education,' in *Self-Narrative and Pedagogy: Stories of Experience within Teaching and Learning*, eds. Mike Hayler and Jess Moriarty (Rotterdam: Sense Publishers, 2017), 45–57.
8 Alec Grant, 'Drinking to Relax: An Autoethnography of a Highland Family Viewed through a New Materialist lens,' in *Auto/Biography Yearbook 2017*, ed. Andrew Sparkes (Nottingham: Russell Press, 2018), 33–46. Grant, Alec. Paper for British Sociological Association Yearbook 2017, Drinking to Relax. ResearchGate. 2018. https://www.researchgate.net/publication/324861731_Paper_for_British_Sociological_Association_Yearbook_2017_Drinking_to_Relax.

9 Alec Grant, 'Moving around the Hyphens: A Critical Meta-autoethnographic Performance,' in *Critical Mental Health Nursing: Observations from the Inside*, eds. Pete Bull, Jonathan Gadsby, and Steve Williams (Monmouth: PCCS Books, 2018), 30–50.

10 Alec Grant, and Susan Young, 'Troubling Tolichism in Several Voices: Resisting Epistemic Violence in Creative Analytical and Critical Autoethnographic Practices,' *Journal of Autoethnography* 3, no. 1 (Winter 2022): 103–117, https://doi.org/10.1525/joae.2022.3.1.103.

11 Alec Grant, 'The Philosophical Autoethnographer,' in *Writing Philosophical Autoethnography*, ed. Alec Grant (New York and London: Routledge, 2024), 1–22; Alec Grant, 'In Search of My Narrative Character: A Philosophical Autoethnography,' in *Writing Philosophical Autoethnography*, ed. Alec Grant (New York and London: Routledge, 2024), 114–132; Alec Grant, 'Concluding Thoughts: Selves, Cultures, Limitations, Futures,' in *Writing Philosophical Autoethnography*, ed. Alec Grant (New York and London: Routledge, 2024), 249–269.

12 Alec Grant and Susan Young, 'A Scot an' a Sassenach Scrieve Aboot Leid: A Three Pairt Scotoethnography (A Scot and an English Person Write about Language: A Scotoethnography in Three Parts),' *Journal of Autoethnography* 5, no. 1 (January 2024): 29–55, https://doi.org/10.1525/joae.2024.5.1.39; Alec Grant and Susan Young, 'A Scot an' a Sassenach Scrieve Aboot Leid: A Three Pairt Scotoethnography (A Scot and an English Person Write about Language: A Scotoethnography in Three Parts),' in *Meaningful Journeys: Autoethnographies of Quest and Identity Transformation*, eds. Alec Grant and Elizabeth Lloyd-Parkes (London and New York: Routledge, 2024), 96–116.

13 It is worth noting that Martin Tolich, having never conducted autoethnographic research himself, is clearly *not* an autoethnographer.

BIBLIOGRAPHY

Adams, Tony E. 'Ties that Bind, Ties that Scar.' In *On (Writing) Families: Autoethnographies of Presence and Absence, Love and Loss*, edited by Jonathon Wyatt, and Tony E. Adams, 149–150. Rotterdam: Sense Publishers, 2014.

Ahmed, Sara. *Queer Phenomenology: Orientations, Objects, Others*. Durham, NNC: Duke University Press, 2006.

Althusser, Louis. *On the Reproduction of Capitalism: Ideology and Ideological State Apparatuses*, translated by G.M. Goshgarian. London: Verso, 2014.

Alvesson, Mats and Andrè Spicer. 'A Stupidity-Based Theory of Organizations.' *Journal of Management Studies* 49, no. 7 (June 2012), 1194–1220, https://doi.org/10.1111/j.1467-6486.2012.01072.x

Alvesson, Mats and Andrè Spicer. *The Stupidity Paradox: The Power and Pitfalls of Functional Stupidity at Work*. London: Profile Books, 2016.

Anderson, Benedict. *Imagined Communities: Reflections on the Origin and Spread of Nationalism*. London and New York: Verso, 1983.

Arendt, Hannah. *Eichmann in Jerusalem: A Report on the Banality of Evil*. London: Penguin Books, 2006 [1965].

Ásta. *Categories We Live By: The Construction of Sex, Gender, Race, and Other Social Categories*. New York: Oxford University Press, 2018.

Auden, Wystan H. 'In Transit.' In *W.H. Auden: Collected Poems*, edited by Edward Mendelson, 539–540. London: Faber and Faber, 1994.

Bachelard, Gaston. *The Poetics of Space*. Tans. Maria Jolas. New York: Penguin Books, 2014 [1958].

Bakhtin, Mikhail M. *Art and Answerability: Early Philosophical Essays by M.M. Bakhtin*. Edited by M. Holquist and Vadim Liapunov. Translated by Vadim Liapunove. Supplement translated by Kenneth Brostrom. Austin: University of Texas Press, 1990.

Barry, Kevin. *The Heart in Winter*. Edinburgh: Canongate, 2024.

Barthes, Roland. *The Semiotic Challenge*. Trans. Richard Howard. Berkeley and Los Angeles and London: University of California Press, 1988.

Becker, Howard. *Outsiders: Studies in the Sociology of Deviance*. New York: Free Press, 2018 [1963].

Benjamin, Shereen. 'Schools, Feminism and Gender-Identity Theory.' In *Sex and Gender: A Contemporary Reader*, edited by Alice Sullivan and Selina Todd, 194–213. London and New York: Routledge, 2024.

Bhaba, Homi K. 'Culture's In-Between.' In *Questions of Cultural Identity*, edited by Stuart Hall and Paul du Gay, 53–60. London: SAGE Publications, 1996.

Bhabha, Homi K. *The Location of Culture*. London and New York: Routledge Classics, 2004.

Bibler, Vladimir. 'Arche.' In *Vladimir Bibler (1918-2000), Filosofia: An Encyclopedia of Russian Thought*, edited by Alyssa DeBlasio and Mikhail Epstein, Filosofia: An Encyclopedia of Russian Thought (dickinson.edu)

Blackburn, Simon. *Truth: A Guide for the Perplexed*. London: Allen Lane, 2005.

Blackmore, Susan. *The Meme Machine*. New York: Oxford University Press, 1999.

Bochner, Arthur P. and Nicholas A. Riggs. 'Practicing Narrative Inquiry.' In *The Oxford Handbook of Qualitative Research*, edited by Patricia Leavy, 195–122. Oxford: Oxford University Press, 2014.

Bochner, Arthur P. and Carolyn Ellis. *Evocative Autoethnography: Writing Lives and Telling Stories*. New York and London: Routledge, 2016.

Boever, Arne De. *François Jullien's Unexceptional Thought: A Critical Introduction*. London and New York: Rowman & Littlefield, 2020.

Bourdieu, Pierre. 'The Forms of Capital.' In *Handbook of Theory and Research for the Sociology of Education*, edited by John G. Richardson, 241–258. London: Bloomsbury, 1986.

Brewer, Marilynn B. and Wendi Gardner. 'Who Is this "We"? Levels of Collective Identity and Self Representations.' *Journal of Personality and Social Psychology* 71, no. 1 (1996), 83–93, https://doi.org/10.1093/oso/9780199269464.003.0006

Brock, Gillian. *Global Justice: A Cosmopolitan Account*. New York: Oxford University Press, 2009.

Brock, Gillian. 'Cosmopolitanism Versus Noncosmopolitanism: The State of Play.' *The Monist* 94, no. 4 (October 2011), 455–465, https://doi.org/10.5840/monist201194423

Browning, Christopher R. *Ordinary Men: Reserve Police Battalion 101 and the Final Solution in Poland*. London: Penguin Books, 2001.

Bruner, Jerome. 'Life as Narrative.' *Social Research* 71, no. 3 (Fall 2004), 691–710, https://doi.org/10.1353/sor.2004.0045

Butler, Judith. *Precarious Life: The Powers of Mourning and Violence*. London: Verso, 2004.

Christman, John. 'Telling Our Own Stories: Narrative Selves and Oppressive Circumstance.' In *The Philosophy of Autobiography*, edited by Christopher Cowley, 122–140. Chicago and London: The University of Chicago Press, 2015.

Cobley, Paul. *Narrative*. 2nd Edition. London and New York: Routledge, 2014.

Dowling, William C. *Ricoeur on Time and Narrative: An Introduction to Temps et récit*. Notre Dame, IN: University of Notre Dame Press, 2011.

Dunbar, William. 'In Secret Place this Hyndir Nycht.' In *Selected Poems of Robert Henryson and William Dunbar*, edited by Douglas Gray, 103. London: Penguin Books, 1998.

Duncan-Grant, Alec. '*Clinical Supervision Activity among Mental Health Nurses: A Critical Organizational Ethnography*' (PhD by Research thesis, University of Brighton, 1999).

Duncan-Grant, Alec. *Clinical Supervision Activity among Mental Health Nurses: A Critical Organizational Ethnography.* Portsmouth: Nursing Praxis International, 2001.

Eagleton, Terry. *Ideology: An Introduction.* London: Verso, 1991.

Eisenberg, Eric M. 'Building a Mystery: Toward a New Theory of Communication and Identity.' *Journal of Communication* 51, no. 3 (January 2006), 534–552, https://doi.org/10.1111/j.1460-2466.2001.tb02895.x

Eisner, Elliot W. *The Educational Imagination: On the Design and Evaluation of School Programs.* New York: Macmillan Publishing Co., 1979.

Ellis, Carolyn. *The Ethnographic I: A Methodological Novel about Autoethnography.* Walnut Creek, CA: AltaMira Press.

Ellis, Carolyn and Michael G. Flaherty. 'An Agenda for the Interpretation of Lived Experience.' In *Investigating Subjectivity: Research on Lived Experience*, edited by Carolyn Ellis, and Michael G. Flaherty, 1–13. Newbury Park, CA: SAGE Publications, Inc, 1992.

Elon, Amos. 'Introduction.' Hannah Arendt, *Eichmann in Jerusalem: A Report on the Banality of Evil*, vii–xviii. London: Penguin Books, 2006 [1965].

Erdinast-Vulcan, Daphna. 'Heterobiography: A Bakhtinian Perspective on Autobiographical Writing.' In *Philosophy and Life Writing*, edited by D. L. LeMahieu, and Christopher Cowley, 108–125. London and New York: Routledge, 2019.

Ewing, Katherine P. 'The Illusion of Wholeness: Culture, Self, and the Experience of Inconsistency.' *Ethos* 18, no. 3 (1990), 251–278, https://www.jstor.org/stable/640337?origin=JSTOR-pdf.

Ferdinand, Renata. 'Which Way is Up: A Philosophical Autoethnoraphy of Trying to Stand in a "Crooked Room."' In *Writing Philosophical Autoethnography*, edited by Alec Grant, 80–95. New York and London: Routledge, 2024.

Ferring, Dieter. 'Memory in Old Age: A Lifespan Perspective.' In *Handbook of Culture and Memory*, edited by Brady Wagoner, 237–256. New York: Oxford University Press, 2018.

Fisher, Walter R. *Human Communication as Narration: Toward a Philosophy of Reason, Value, and Action.* Columbia: University of South Carolina Press, 1987.

Forster, Edwin M. *Aspects of the Novel*, edited by Oliver Stallybrass, 87. Harmondsworth: Penguin Books Ltd., 1962 [1927].

Foucault, Michel. *The Archaeology of Knowledge and the Discourse on Language.* New York: Vintage Books, 2010 [1972].

Foucault, Michel. 'The Order of Discourse: Inaugural Lecture at the Collège de France, given 2 December 1970.' In *Untying the Text: A Post-Structuralist Reader*, edited by Robert Young, 48–78. Boston, MA: Routledge & Kegan Paul, 1981 [1970].

Frank, Arthur W. *Letting Stories Breathe: A Socio-Narratology.* Chicago: University of Chicago Press, 2010.

Freeman, Mark. *Hindsight: The Promise and Peril of Looking Backward.* Oxford: Oxford University Press, 2010.

Freeman, Mark. 'Discerning the History Inscribed Within: Significant Sites of the Narrative Unconscious.' In *Handbook of Culture and Memory*, edited by Brady Wagoner, 65–82. New York: Oxford University Press, 2018.

Frentz, Thomas S. *Trickster in Tweed: My Quest for Quality in Faculty Life.* London and New York: Routledge, 2008.

Fricker, Miranda. *Epistemic Injustice: Power and the Ethics of Knowing.* Oxford: Oxford University Press, 2007.

Galal, Lise Paulsen. 'Interculturality in Ethnographic Practice: Noisy Silences.' In *Researching Identity and Interculturality*, edited by Fred Dervin and Karen Risager, 151–168. Abingdon and New York: Routledge, 2015.

Garfield, Jay L. *Losing Ourselves: Learning to Live Without a Self.* Princeton and Oxford: Princeton University Press, 2022.

Geertz, Clifford. *The Interpretation of Cultures.* 2000 Edition. New York: Basic Books, 1973.

Giddens, Anthony. *The Constitution of Society: Outline of the Theory of Structuration.* Cambridge: Polity Press, 1984.

Gingrich-Philbrook, Craig. 'On Gratitude, for My Father.' In *On (Writing) Families: Autoethnographies of Presence and Absence, Love and Loss*, edited by Jonathon Wyatt, and Tony E. Adams, 23–29. Rotterdam: Sense Publishers, 2014.

Goodall, Bud (H.L.). 'Narrative Inheritance: A Nuclear Family With Toxic Secrets.' *Qualitative Inquiry* 11, no. 4 (2005), 492–513, https://doi.org/10.1177/1077800405276769

Grant, Alec. 'Clinical Supervision in Mental Health Nursing: A Triumph of Hope Over Experience?' *Mental Health Practice* 6, no. 6 (2003), 22–23

Grant, Alec. 'Writing Teaching and Survival in Mental Health: A discordant quintet for one.' In *Contemporary British Autoethnography*, edited by Nigel P. Short, Lydia Turner, and Alec Grant, 33–48. Rotterdam: Sense Publishers, 2013.

Grant, Alec. 'Breaking the Grip: A Critical Insider Account of Representational Practices in Cognitive Behavioural Psychotherapy and Mental Health Nursing.' In *Queering Health: Critical Challenges to Normative Health and Healthcare*, edited by Laetitia Zeeman, Kay Aranda, and Alec Grant, 116–133. Ross-on-Wye: PCCS Books, 2014.

Grant, Alec. 'Troubling "Lived Experience": A Poststructural Critique of Mental Health Nursing Qualitative Research Assumptions.' *Journal of Psychiatric and Mental Health Nursing* 21 (2014), 544–549, https://doi.org/10.1111/jpm.12113

Grant, Alec. 'Living My Narrative: Storying Dishonesty and Deception in Mental Health Nursing.' *Nursing Philosophy* 17, no. 3 (2016), 194–201, https://doi.org/10.1111/nup.12127

Grant, Alec. 'Storying the World: A Posthumanist Critique of Phenomenological-Humanist Representational Practices in Mental Health Nurse Qualitative Inquiry.' *Nursing Philosophy* 17 (2016), 290–297, https://doi.org/10.1111/nup.12135

Grant, Alec. 'Toilets are the Proper Place for "Outputs"! A Tale of Knowledge Production and Publishing with Students in Higher Education.' In *Self-Narrative and Pedagogy: Stories of Experience within Teaching and Learning*, edited by Mike Hayler, and Jess Moriarty, 45–57. Rotterdam: Sense Publishers, 2017.

Grant, Alec. 'Drinking to Relax: An Autoethnography of a Highland Family Viewed through a New Materialist Lens.' In *Auto/Biography Yearbook 2017*, edited by Andrew Sparkes, 33–46. Nottingham: Russell Press, 2018.

Grant, Alec. 'Moving Around the Hyphens: A Critical Meta-Autoethnographic Performance.' In *Critical Mental Health Nursing: Observations from the Inside*, edited by Jonathan Gadsby Pete Bull, and S. Stephen Williams, 30–50. Monmouth: PCCS Books, 2018.

Grant, Alec. Paper for British Sociological Association Yearbook 2017, Drinking to Relax. ResearchGate. 2018. https://www.researchgate.net/publication/324861731_Paper_for_British_Sociological_Association_Yearbook_2017_Drinking_to_Relax

Grant, Alec. 'Dare to be a Wolf: Embracing Autoethnography in Nurse Educational Research.' *Nurse Education Today* 82 (2019), 88–92, https://doi.org/10.1016/j. nedt.2019.07.006

Grant, Alec. 'How does Nietzschean Self-deceiving Moral Identity in a Modern Context Relate to Lukes' Third Dimension of Power?' (MA Dissertation, Open University, 2020).

Grant, Alec. 'Crafting and Recognising Good Enough Autoethnographies: A Practical Guide and Checklist.' *Mental Health and Social Inclusion* 27, no. 3 (2023), 196–209. https://doi.org/10.1108/mhsi-01-2023-0009

Grant, Alec. 'In Praise of Subjectivity: My Involvement with Autoethnography, and Why I Think You should be Interested.' *Social Work and Social Sciences Review* 23, no. 3 (2023), 66–79, https://doi.org/10.1921/swssr.v23i3.2151

Grant, Alec. 'Concluding Thoughts: Selves, Cultures, Limitations, Futures.' In *Writing Philosophical Autoethnography*, edited by Alec Grant, 249–269. New York and London: Routledge, 2024.

Grant, Alec. '*Developing Philosophical Autoethnography: Resisting Cultural Narrative Entrapment*' (PhD thesis by Published Work (Retrospective), University of Bolton, 2024).

Grant, Alec. 'The Philosophical Autoethnographer.' In *Writing Philosophical Autoethnography*, edited by Alec Grant, 1–22. New York and London: Routledge, 2024.

Grant, Alec. 'In Search of My Narrative Character: A Philosophical Autoethnography.' In *Writing Philosophical Autoethnography*, edited by Alec Grant, 123–131. New York and London: Routledge, 2024.

Grant, Alec (editor). *Writing Philosophical Autoethnography*. New York and London: Routledge, 2024.

Grant, Alec and Benny Goodman. *Communication & Interpersonal Skills in Nursing*. 4th Edition. London: Learning Matters/SAGE Publications Ltd, 2018.

Grant, Alec and Helen Leigh-Phippard. 'Troubling the Normative Mental Health Recovery Project: The Silent Resistance of a Disappearing Doctor.' In *Queering Health: Critical Challenges to Normative Health and Healthcare*, edited by Laetitia Zeeman, Kay Aranda, and Alec Grant, 100–115. Ross-on-Wye: PCCS Books, 2014.

Grant, Alec and Elizabeth Lloyd-Parkes. 'Meaningful Journeys, Identity Transformation, and Autoethnographic Selfhood.' In *Meaningful Journeys: Autoethnographies of Quest and Identity Transformation*, edited by Alec Grant and Elizabeth Lloyd-Parkes, 1–16. London and New York: Routledge, 2024.

Grant, Alec and Mark Radcliffe. 'Resisting Technical Rationality in Mental Health Nurse Higher Education: A Duoethnography.' *The Qualitative Report (TQR)* 20, no. 6 (June 2015), 815–825, https://doi.org/10.46743/2160-3715/2015.2157

Grant, Alec and Susan Young. 'Troubling Tolichism in Several Voices: Resisting Epistemic Violence in Creative Analytical and Critical Autoethnographic Practices.' *Journal of Autoethnography* 3, no. 1 (Winter 2022), 103–117, https://doi. org/10.1525/joae.2022.3.1.103

Grant, Alec and Susan Young. 'A Scot an' a Sassenach Scrieve Aboot leid: A Three Pairt Scotoethnography (A Scot and an English Person Write about Language: A Scotoethnography in Three Parts).' *Journal of Autoethnography* 5, no. 1 (2024), 39–55. https://doi.org/10.1525/joae.2024.5.1.39

Grant, Alec and Susan Young. 'A Scot an' a Sassenach Scrieve Aboot Leid: A Three Pairt Scotoethnography (A Scot and an English Person Write about Language: A Scotoethnography in Three Parts).' In *Meaningful Journeys: Autoethnographies of Quest and Identity Transformation*, edited by Alec Grant and Elizabeth Lloyd-Parkes, 96–116. London and New York: Routledge, 2024.

Grant, Alec and Laetitia Zeeman. 'Whose Story Is It? An Autoethnography Concerning Narrative Identity.' *The Qualitative Report (TQR)* 17, no. 72 (2012), 1–12, https://doi.org/10.46743/2160-3715/2012.1735

Grant, Alec, Helen Leigh-Phippard, and Nigel P. Short. 'Re-storying Narrative Identity: A Dialogical Study of Mental Health Recovery and Survival.' *Journal of Psychiatric and Mental Health Nursing* 22, no. 4 (2015), 278–286, https://doi.org/10.1111/jpm.12188

Grant, Alec, Laetitia Zeeman, and Kay Aranda. 'Queering the Relationship between Evidence-based Mental Health and Psychiatric Diagnosis: Some Implications for International Mental Health Nurse Curricular Development.' *Nurse Education Today* 35, no. 10 (October 2015), e18–e20, https://doi.org/10.1016/j.nedt.2015.07.033

Heidegger, Martin. *Poetry, Language, Thought.* New York: Harper Perennial Modern Thought, 2013.

Herrmann, Andrew F. 'The Ghostwriter: Living a Father's Unfinished Narrative.' In *On (Writing) Families: Autoethnographies of Presence and Absence, Love and Loss*, edited by Jonathon Wyatt, and Tony E. Adams, 95–102. Rotterdam: Sense Publishers, 2014.

Herrmann, Andrew and Tony E. Adams. *Assessing Autoethnography: Notes on Analysis, Evaluation, and Craft.* London and New York: Routledge, 2025.

Hobsbawm, Eric and Terence Ranger. *The Invention of Tradition.* Cambridge: Cambridge University Press, 1983.

Holliday, Adrian. *Understanding Intercultural Communication: Negotiating a Grammar of Culture.* 2nd edn. London and New York: Routledge, 2019.

Holman Jones, Stacy. 'Am I that Name?' In *Language and Culture: Reflective Narratives and the Emergence of Identity*, edited by David Nunan and Julie Choi, 112–117. New York and Abingdon: Routledge, 2010.

Holman Jones, Stacy. 'Always Strange: Transforming Loss.' In *On (Writing) Families: Autoethnographies of Presence and Absence, Love and Loss*, edited by Jonathon Wyatt and Tony E. Adams, 13–21. Rotterdam: Sense Publishers, 2014.

Holman Jones, Stacy, Tony E. Adams, and Carolyn Ellis. 'Introduction: Coming to Know Autoethnography as more than a Method.' In *Handbook of Autoethnography*, edited by Stacy Holman Jones, Tony E. Adams, and Carolyn Ellis, 17–47. Walnut Creek, CA: Left Coast Press, Inc., 2013.

Hume, David. 'Appendix.' In David Hume, *A Treatise of Human Nature*, edited by Ernest C. Mossner, 671–678. London: Penguin Books, 1969.

Hunter, Michael. *The Decline of Magic: Britain in the Enlightenment.* New Haven and London: Yale University Press, 2020.

Hyde, Lewis. *Trickster Makes This World: How Disruptive Imagination Creates Culture.* Edinburgh: Canongate Books Ltd, 2017.

Ingleby, Matthew. 'Multiple Occupancy: Residency and Retrospection in Trollope's *Orley Farm* and *An Autobiography*.' In *Life Writing and Space*, edited by Eveline Kilian and Hope Wolf, 25–40. London and New York: Routledge, 2016.

Jensen, Anthony K. *Nietzsche's Philosophy of History.* Cambridge: Cambridge University Press, 2013.

Johnson, Curtis. 'Socrates' Political Philosophy.' In *The Bloomsbury Handbook of Socrates*, edited by Russell E. Jones, Ravi Sharma, and Nicholas D. Smith, 275–298. London and New York: Bloomsbury Academic, 2024.

Jullien, François. 'Between Is Not Being.' *Theory, Culture & Society* 40, no. 4–5 (December 2022), 239–249, https://doi.org/10.1177/02632764221111324

Kafar, Marcin. 'Traveling with Carolyn Ellis and Art Bochner, or How I became Harmonized with the Autoethnographic Life: An Autoformative Story.' In *Advances in Autoethnography and Narrative Inquiry: Reflections on the Legacy of Carolyn Ellis and Arthur Bochner*, edited by Tony E. Adams, Robin M. Boylorn, and Lisa M. Tillmann, 48–63. New York and London: Routledge, 2021.

Kafar, Marcin and Justyna Ratkowska-Pasikowska. 'Conversational Autoethnography on Experiencing Loss and Grief.' In *Autoethnographies in Psychology and Mental Health: New Voices*, edited by Alec Grant and Jerome Carson, PAGE NUMBERS. London and New York: Routledge.

Kim, Sung Ho. Max Weber, *Stanford Encyclopedia of Philosophy* (Winter 2019 Edition), Edward N. Zalta (Ed.), 25–26. https://plato.stanford.edu/archives/win2019/entries/weber/

Kim, Hannah H. 'Life as "Non-Standard" Narrative.' *The Philosopher* 111, no. 2 (2023), 80–84. "Life as a 'Non-standard' Narrative" By Hannah Kim (Keywords: Selfhood; Identity; Literature; East-Asian Fiction; Collectivity) (thephilosopher1923.org)

Klevan, Trude and Alec Grant. *An Autoethnography of Becoming a Qualitative Researcher: A Dialogic View of Academic Development*. London and New York: Routledge, 2022.

Leiter, Brian. *Nietzsche on Morality*, 2nd Edition. London: Routledge, 2014.

Leonard, Stephen T. *Critical Theory in Political Practice*. Princeton, NJ: Princeton University Press, 1990.

Lerner, Gerda. *The Creation of Patriarchy*. New York: Oxford University Press, 1986.

Letherby, Gayle. 'Dangerous Liaisons: Auto/biography in Research and Research Writing.' In *Danger in the Field: Ethics and Risk in Social Research*, edited by Geraldine Lee-Traweek and Stephanie Linkogle, 91–113. London and New York: Routledge, 2000.

Letherby, Gayle. *Feminist Research in Theory and Practice*. Buckingham and Philadelphia: Open University Press, 2003.

Letherby, Gayle. 'Theorised Subjectivity.' In *Objectivity and Subjectivity in Social Research*, edited by Gayle Letherby, John Scott, and Malcolm Williams, 79–101. London: Sage Publications Ltd, 2012.

Letherby, Gayle. 'Thirty Years and Counting: An-other Auto/biographical Story.' *Auto/Biography Review* 3, no. 1 (August 2022), 13–31, https://doi.org/10.56740/abrev.v3i1.7

Lodge, David. *Nice Work*. London: Secker & Warburg, 1988.

Lukes, Steven. *Power: A Radical View*. Second Edition. London: Red Globe Press, 2005.

Lynch, Michael. *Scotland: A New History*. London: Pimlico, 1992.

MacIntyre, Alasdair. 'Is Patriotism a Virtue?' In *Debates in Contemporary Political Philosophy. An Anthology*, edited by Derek Matravers, and Jonathon Pike, 286–300. London and New York: Routledge in association with the Open University, 2003.

MacIntyre, Alasdair. *After Virtue: A Study in Moral Theory*. Third Edition. London and New York: Bloomsbury Academic, 2007.

May, Simon. *Nietzsche's Ethics and his 'War on Morality.'* Oxford: Clarendon Press, 1999.

McPherran, Mark L. 'Socratic Theology and Piety.' In *The Bloomsbury Handbook of Socrates*, edited by Russell E. Jones, Ravi Sharma, and Nicholas D. Smith, 299–322. London and New York: Bloomsbury Academic, 2024.

Mead, George Herbert. *Mind, Self, & Society from the Standpoint of a Social Behaviourist*, edited and with an Introduction by Charles W. Morris. London: The University of Chicago Press, Ltd. 1967 [1934].

Miller, David. 'In Defence of Nationality.' In *Debates in Contemporary Political Philosophy: An Anthology*, edited by Derek Matravers and Jonathon Pike, 301–318. London and New York: Routledge in association with the Open University, 2003.

Miller, Henry. *Stand Still Like the Hummingbird*. New York: New Directions, 1962.

Minnich, Elizabeth. *The Evil of Banality: On the Life and Death Importance of Thinking*. London: Rowman & Littlefield, 2017.

Mohr, Melissa. *Holy Sh*t: A Brief History of Swearing*. New York: Oxford University Press, 2013.

Morgan, David. 'Sociological Imaginations and Imagining Sociologies: Bodies, Auto/Biographies and Other Mysteries.' *Sociology* 32, no. 4 (1998), 647–663, https://doi.org/10.1177/0038038598032004002

Nagel, Thomas. 'What Is It Like to Be a Bat.' *The Philosophical Review* 83, no. 4 (1974), 435–450. https://doi.org/10.2307/2183914

Nietzsche, Freidrich. *Beyond Good and Evil: Prelude to a Philosophy of the Future*. Translated Reginald J. Hollingdale. London: Penguin Books, 2003 [1886].

Nietzsche, Freidrich. *The will to Power: Selections from the Notebooks of the 1880s*. Translated R. Kevin Hill, and Michael A. Scarpitti. London: Penguin Books, 2017 [1901/6].

Nussbaum, Martha C. *The Fragility of Goodness: Luck and Ethics in Greek Tragedy and Philosophy*. Updated Edition. New York: Cambridge University Press, 2001.

Nussbaum, Martha C. 'Patriotism and Cosmopolitanism.' In *The Global Justice Reader*, edited by Thom Brooks, 306–314. Oxford: Blackwell Publishing, Ltd., 2008.

Nygaard, Lynn P. and Kristin Solli. *Strategies for Writing a Thesis by Publication in the Social Sciences and Humanities*. London and New York: Routledge, 2021.

Plato. 'Apology 31d.' in Plato, *Five Dialogues: Euthyphro, Apology, Crito, Meno, Phaedo*. Second Edition. Translated by Georges M.A. Grube. Indianapolis and Cambridge: Hackett Publishing Company, Inc., 2002.

Poulos, Christopher N. *Accidental Autoethnography: An Inquiry Into Family Secrecy*. New York and London: Routledge, 2019.

Poulos, Christopher N. 'A Liminal Awakening.' In *Writing Philosophical Autoethnography*, edited by Alec Grant, 150–166. New York and London: Routledge, 2024.

Readings, Bill. *The University in Ruins*. Cambridge, MA: Harvard University Press, 1996.

Reginster, Bernard. 'The Will to Power and the Ethics of Creativity.' In *Nietzche and Morality*, edited by Brian Leiter, and Neil Sinhababu, 32–56. New York: Oxford University Press. 2007.

Reissman, Catherine K. *Narrative Methods for the Human Sciences*. New York: Sage Publications, Inc, 2008.

Richardson, Laurel. *Fields of Play: Constructing an Academic Life*. New Brunswick, NJ: Rutgers University Press, 1997.

Richardson, Laurel. 'Getting Personal: Writing Stories.' *Qualitative Studies in Education* 14, no. 1 (2001), 33–38, https://doi.org/10.1080/09518390010007647

Risager, Karen and Fred Dervin. 'Introduction.' In *Researching Identity and Interculturality*, edited by Fred Dervin and Karen Risager, 1–25. London and New York: Routledge, 2015.

Roache, Rebecca. *For F*cks Sake: Why Swearing is Shocking, Rude and Fun*. New York: Oxford University Press, 2024.

Rolfe, Gary. *The University in Dissent: Scholarship in the Corporate University*. London and New York: Routledge, 2013.

Ross, David. *Scotland: History of a Nation*. NEW EDITION. Broxburn: Lomond Books Ltd, 2017.

Sarbin, Theodor R. (editor). *Narrative Psychology: The Storied Nature of Human Conduct*. Westport, CT: Praeger Publishers, 1986.

Sartre, Jean-Paul. *Being and Nothingness*. London and New York: Routledge, 2003 [1943].

Schechtman, Marya. *The Constitution of Selves*. Ithaca and London: Cornell University Press, 1996.

Scheffler, Samuel. *Boundaries and Allegiances: Problems of Justice and Responsibility in Liberal Thought*. New York: Oxford University Press, 2001.

Smout, Christopher (T.C.). *A History of the Scottish People* 1560–1830. Bungay, Suffolk: Fontana/Collins, 1969.

Sparkes, Andrew C. 'Autoethnography as an Ethically Contested Terrain: Some Thinking Points for Consideration.' *Qualitative Research in Psychology* 21, no. 1 (2024), 107–139, https://doi.org/10.1080/14780887.2023.2293073

Spence, Donald. *Narrative Truth and Historical Truth: Meaning and Interpretation in Psychoanalysis*. New York: W.W. Norton, 1982.

Stanley, Phiona. *A Critical Auto/ethnography of Learning Spanish: Intercultural Competence on the Gringo Trail?* Abingdon and New York: Routledge, 2017.

Stanley, Phiona. 'Autoethnography and Ethnography in English Language Teaching.' In *Second Handbook of English Language Teaching*, edited by Xuesong Gao, 1071–1090. New York: Springer International Handbooks of Education, 2019, https://doi.org/10.1007/978-3-030-02899-2_55

Sunstein, Cass R. *Conformity: The Power of Social Influences*. New York: New York University Press, 2019.

Swedberg, Richard. 'How to Use Max Weber's Ideal Type in Sociological Analysis.' *Journal of Classical Sociology* 18, no. 3 (2018), 181–196, https://doi.org/10.1177/1468795X17743643

Szczepaniak, Colette. 'Mental Health and the Body: An Autoethnography of Neuralgia, Migraine and Insulin Resistance.' In *Autoethnography in Psychology and Mental Health: New Voices*, edited by Alec Grant, and Jerome Carson, X–X. London and New York: Routledge, 2024.

Taylor, Cecil P. *Good*. London: Methuen, 1982.

Thacker, Andrew. 'Lost Cities and Found Lives: The 'Geographical Emotions' of Bryher and Walter Benjamin.' In *Life Writing and Space*, edited by Eveline Kilian and Hope Wolf, 41–56. London and New York: Routledge, 2017.

Tønnessen, Siv. 'The Meaningfulness of Challenging the Controlled Drinking Discourse. An Autoethnographic Study.' *Qualitative Social Work* Online First, 0 no. 0 (2023), https://doi.org/10.1177/14733250231200499

Tønnessen, Siv. 'Spurious Emotional Understanding: What Do "Ordinary" People Know about Entrapment in the Bubbly, Fizzing, 'Hung-before' Feeling?' In *Autoethnography in Psychology and Mental Health: New Voices*, edited by Alec Grant, and Jerome Carson, X–X. London and New York: Routledge, 2024.

Tosh, John. *The Pursuit of History: Aims. Methods and New Directions in the Study of History*. Seventh Edition. London and New York: Routledge, 2022.

Trawny, Peter. *Heidegger and the Myth of a Jewish World Conspiracy*. Chicago: The University of Chicago Press, 2015.

Warburon, Nigel. *Thinking from A to Z.* Third Edition. London and New York: Routledge, 2007.

Whitehead, Alfred North. *Process and Reality.* New York: Free Press, 1979.

Whitman, Walt. 'Song of Myself.' In Walt Whitman, *The Complete Poems of Walt Whitman.* Introduction and notes by Stephen Matterson, 24–69. Ware: Wordsworth Editions, 1995.

Williams, Raymond. 'Culture Is Ordinary.' In *Resources of Hope: Culture, Democracy, Socialism,* edited by Robin Gable, 3–18. London and New York: Verso, 1989 [1958].

Willis, Paul. *Learning to Labour: How Working-class Kids Get Working-class Jobs.* Aldershot, Hants: Gower Publishing 1988 [1977].

Wilson, Emily. *The Death of Socrates.* Cambridge, MA: Harvard University Press, 2007.

Wilson, Emily. *The Death of Socrates: Hero, Villain, Chatterbox, Saint.* London: Profile Books, 2007.

Winterson, Jeanette. *Why Be Happy When You Could be Normal.* London: Vintage, 2012.

Wright Mills, Charles. *The Sociological Imagination.* Fortieth Anniversary Edition. New York: Oxford University Press, Inc., 2000 [1959].

Zeeman, Laetitia Kay Aranda and Alec Grant. 'Queer Challenges to Evidence-based Practice.' *Nursing Inquiry* 21, no. 2 (June 2013), 101–111, https://doi.org/10.1111/nin.12039

Zeeman, Laetitia Kay Aranda and Alec Grant. 'Introduction.' In *Queering Health: Critical Challenges to Normative Health and Healthcare,* edited by Laetitia Zeeman, Kay Aranda, and Alec Grant, 1–22. Ross-on-Wye: PCCS Books, 2014.

Zeeman, Laetitia Kay Aranda and Alec Grant. 'Queer Challenges to Evidence-based Mental Healthcare.' In *Queering Health: Critical Challenges to Normative Health and Healthcare,* edited by Laetitia Zeeman, Kay Aranda, and Alec Grant, 79–99. Ross-on-Wye: PCCS Books, 2014.

Zeeman, Laetitia Kay Aranda and Alec Grant, (editors). *Queering Health: Critical Challenges to Normative Health and Healthcare.* Ross-on-Wye: PCCS Books, 2014.

INDEX

Note: Page numbers followed by "n" denote endnotes.

www.ingramcontent.com/pod-product-compliance
Ingram Content Group UK Ltd.
Pitfield, Milton Keynes, MK11 3LW, UK
UKHW022037260225
455631UK00008B/100